NATO FORCES

NATO FORCES

An Illustrated Reference to their Organization and Insignia

Brian L. Davis

BLANDFORD

Left: Senior officers of various nations at Supreme Headquarters Allied Power Rocquencourt, France on the occasion of the retirement of Général d'Armée Alphonse Juin (France) from the post of Commander-in-Chief Allied Army Forces in Central Europe (see page 19). General Juin stands to the right of General Gruenther, SACEUR (behind microphones). Field Marshal Viscount Montgomery, Deputy Supreme Allied Commander is to General Gruenther's left.

First published in Great Britain
in 1988 by Blandford Press, Artillery House,
Artillery Row, London SW1P 1RT.

Distributed in the USA by Sterling Publishing Co. Inc.,
2 Park Avenue, New York, NY 10016.

Distributed in Australia by
Capricorn Link (Australia) Pty. Ltd., P.O. Box 665,
Lane Cove, New South Wales 2066, Australia.

British Library Cataloguing in Publication Data:
  Davis, Brian L. (Brian Leigh), *1935–*
  Nato forces: an illustrated reference to their
  organization and insignia.
  1. North Atlantic Treaty Organization military forces. Insignia
  I. Title
  355.1'4
  ISBN 0-7137-1737-8

Jacket illustrations: Front left, Decaneas (corporal) of the Greek
Military Police; front right, Platoon sergeant and drill instructor of
the US Army; back left, 1er Maréchal des logis, Belgian Gendarmerie;
back right, Korporaal de 1e klasse (corporal 1st class) of the
Netherlands Military Police. Photographs by the author.

Colour plates painted by Malcolm McGregor.

Designed and edited by DAG Publications Ltd. Designed by David
Gibbons; edited by Michael Boxall; layout by Anthony A. Evans;
typeset by Typesetters (Birmingham) Ltd., camerawork by M&E
Graphics, North Fambridge, Essex; printed and bound in **Portugal**

Contents

Acknowledgements, 8

Introduction, 9

The Development of NATO, 10
Towards an Alliance, 10
The Treaty of Dunkirk, 10
The Treaty of Rio, 10
The Brussels Treaty, 10
The North Atlantic Treaty, 10
The Fourteen Articles of the North Atlantic Treaty, 11

The North Atlantic Alliance Today, 12
The North Atlantic Council, 12
The Defence Planning Committee, 12
The Nuclear Planning Group, 13
The Permanent Representatives and National Delegations, 13
The Secretary General and the International Staff, 13
The Military Committee, 13
The International Military Staff, 14
The NATO Commands, 14

Towards an Integrated Defence Force, 14
The formation of NATO's Integrated Defence Force, 14
Eisenhower, first Supreme Commander Allied Powers Europe, 16
First and temporary Headquarters of SHAPE, 16
The first established Supreme Headquarters Allied Powers Europe, 16
Eisenhower leaves SHAPE, 16
General Matthew B. Ridgway, SACEUR, 16
General Alfred M. Gruenther, third SACEUR, 16
General Norstad succeeds General Gruenther as the fourth SACEUR, 16
General Lemnitzer replaces General Norstad as SACEUR, 16
General Goodpaster, new Supreme Allied Commander Europe, 16
General Haig succeeds General Goodpaster as SACEUR, 19
Attempted assassination of General Haig, outgoing SACEUR, 19
General Bernard Rogers, SACEUR, 19
General John Galvin succeeds General Bernard Rogers as Supreme Allied Commander Europe, 19

The First European Defence Commands and their Commanders, 19
Supreme Headquarters Allied Powers Europe, 19
The Central European Command, 19
The Northern European Command, 20
The Southern European Command, 20
'General Order No. 1', 20
First foreign troops under SHAPE command in Europe, 20
First permanent NATO Headquarters, 20

NATO, The First Five Years, 1949–54: Military Organization, 21
The Military Committee, 21
The Standing Group, 21
The main NATO Commands and their Subsidiary Commands, 21
The European Command, 21
The Atlantic Command, 22
The Channel Committee and the Channel Command, 22
The Canada–United States Regional Planning Group, 22
NATO Military Agencies, 22

Salient Events in NATO's Development, 23
Entry of the German Federal Republic into NATO, 23
The first German divisions under NATO Command, 23
The first operational Luftwaffe squadron, 23
Final West German Panzer Division raised for NATO, 23
The first West German Army unit to train in Great Britain, 23
The first German troops in Denmark since the Second World War, 24
West German Border Protection Police, 24
France withdraws from NATO, 24
NATO facilities in France, 25
French forces in Germany, 25
The Timetable for the French withdrawal from NATO and the removal of NATO installations from France, 25
Withdrawal of French forces from NATO Command, 26
NATO Headquarters moved from Paris to Brussels, 26
The relocation of Supreme Headquarters Allied Powers Europe, 26
The new SHAPE complex, 26
Removal of Headquarters Allied Forces Central Europe from Fontainebleau to Brunssum, 26

The dissolution of LANDCENT, AIRCENT and NAVCENT, 27
Greece and Turkey: towards membership of NATO, 27
Anti-Greek riots in Turkish cities: a threat to NATO unity, 27
Greece withdraws its troops from NATO manoeuvres, 27
Greece renews its participation in NATO manoeuvres, 27
Events leading up to the withdrawal of Greek armed forces
from NATO, 27
Hostilities, cease-fires and peace talks, 27
Greece withdraws its armed forces from the Alliance, 28
Greece re-integrates into NATO's military command
structure, 28
Continuing protests, continuing boycots, 28
Spain invited to join North Atlantic Treaty Organization, 28
Spain's accession to NATO, 28
The Socialist Workers' Party of Spain attempt to remove
Spain from NATO, 28
The Spanish people vote to stay in NATO, 28

Allied Command Europe, 29
SHAPE – Supreme Headquarters Allied Powers Europe, 29
The mission of Allied Command Europe, 29
Commands subordinate to Allied Command Europe, 29
United States European Command, 29
United States Army Europe, 29
United States Air Forces in Europe, 32
United States Naval Forces Europe, 32
Canadian Forces Europe, 32

Headquarters Allied Forces Northern Europe, 33
AFNORTH, Strategic Area of Command, 33
Subordinate Commands AFNORTH, 33
NATO and the original Commands of the North European
Region, 33
Allied Land Forces Schleswig–Holstein and Jutland, 34
The establishment of Baltic Approaches Command, 34
The present Headquarters Allied Forces Baltic Approaches
(HQ BALTAP), 34
BALTAP Area of Command, 34
Mission of COMBALTAP, 35
Subordinate Commands BALTAP, 35
COMLANDJUT, 35
COMLANDZEALAND, 35
COMNAVBALTAP, 35
COMAIRBALTAP, 35
Headquarters Allied Forces North Norway, 35
The mission of COMNON, 35
Commands subordinate to Allied Forces North Norway, 36
Headquarters Allied Forces South Norway, 36
COMSONOR's mission, 36

Headquarters Allied Forces Central Europe, 36
AFCENT's mission, 36
Commands subordinate to CINCENT, 36
The Northern Army Group – NORTHAG, 36
The NORTHAG area of responsibility, 37
NORTHAG's mission, 37
Central Army Group, 37
CENTAG's area of responsibility, 37

CENTAG's mission, 37
Allied Air Forces Central Europe, 37
Headquarters AAFCE, 37
Allied Air Forces Central Europe, its mission, 38
The 1952 reorganization of the Tactical Air Force, Europe, 38
Second Allied Tactical Air Force, 38
Headquarters TWOATAF and area of responsibility, 38
TWOATAF's mission, 38
The establishment of Fourth Allied Tactical Air Force, 38
Fourth Allied Tactical Air Force, 38
FOURATAF's area of responsibility, 38
FOURATAF's mission, 39

Headquarters Allied Forces Southern Europe, 39
AFSOUTH's area of responsibility, 39
AFSOUTH's mission, 39
Commands subordinate to AFSOUTH, 39
Headquarters Allied Air Forces Southern Europe, 39
AIRSOUTH's area of responsibility, 39
AIRSOUTH's mission, 39
Forces subordinate to AIRSOUTH, 40
Fifth Allied Tactical Air Force, 40
FIVEATAF's area of responsibility, 40
Tasks allotted to FIVEATAF, 40
Sixth Allied Technical Air Force, 40
SIXATAF's area of responsibility and mission, 40
SIXATAF's Additional Tactical Air Force Support, 40
Headquarters Allied Land Forces Southern Europe, 40
LANDSOUTH's area of responsibility, 40
LANDSOUTH's mission, 40
Allied Land Forces South-eastern Europe, 40
Headquarters LANDSOUTHEAST, 41
Mediterranean Command, later known as 'Allied Forces
Mediterranean' (AFMED), 41
Mediterranean Command areas of responsibility, 41
The mission of Mediterranean Command, 41
Headquarters Allied Naval Forces Southern Europe, 41
NAVSOUTH and its structure, 42
NAVSOUTH's areas of responsibility, 42
Gibraltar Mediterranean, 42
North-eastern Mediterranean, 42
The formal inauguration of Maritime Air Forces
Mediterranean, 42
The formation of the Allied Naval On-Call Force,
Mediterranean, 42
Naval On-Call Force Mediterranean, 43
Naval Striking and Support Forces Southern Europe, and its
Headquarters, 43
STRIKFORSOUTH's area of responsibility, 43
STRIKFORSOUTH's mission, 43
Naval Commands subordinate to STRIKFORSOUTH, 43
The Southern European Task Force (SETAF), 43

Creation of the Multi-National Mobile Land Force (MLF), 43
Forces involved in MLF, 44
West German troops to serve with the Mobile Land Force, 44
The Mobile Land Force brought into being, 44
Change of Title: MLF to AMF, 44

Allied Command Europe (ACE) Mobile Force today, 44
Composition of AMF, 44
ACE Mobile Force, its task and deployment areas, 44

Towards UKAIR, a Unified Air Defence System, RAF Fighter Command placed under SACEUR, 45
The four NATO Air Defence Regions, 45
RAF Strike Command and the creation of UKAIR, 45
United Kingdom Air Forces – UKAIR, 45
UKAIR, its responsibility, 45
Resources available to UKAIR, 45
UKAIR's mission, 46

Establishment of North Atlantic Command, 46
North Atlantic Sub-Commands, 46
The Atlantic Command, its extent and Headquarters, 46
The Western Atlantic Sub-Command, 46
Atlantic Command, re-designation of certain Sub-Areas, 47
SACLANT, his responsibilities in peace and war, 47
Commands subordinate to the Supreme Allied Commander Atlantic (SACLANT), 47
The establishment of the Standing Naval Force Atlantic, 47
The vessels of the original Standing Naval Force Atlantic, 47
STANAVFORLANT today, 47
The establishment of SACLANT Anti-Submarine Warfare Research Centre – SASWREC, 47
Inauguration of Iberian Command Atlantic, 48

Establishment of Channel Command, 48
Channel Command, Command changes and new headquarters, 48
Allied Command Channel today, its responsibility and mission, 48
Commands subordinate to the Allied Commander-in-Chief Channel Command (CINCHAN), 49
The Standing Naval Force Channel, 49

Establishment of the NATO Defence College, the NATO School (SHAPE) and the SHAPE Technical Centre, 49
NATO Defence College moves from Paris to Rome, 49
NATO School (SHAPE), 49
SHAPE Technical Centre, 50
The Inter-Allied Confederation of Reserve Officers, 50

NATO Airborne Early Warning And Control System, 51
The United Kingdom's Nimrod contribution to the Airborne Early Warning System, 51
Implementation of the Airborne Early Warning Force, 51
NATO Airborne Early Warning Force, 51
NAEW Force operational units, 51
NAEW Force operational ability, 51
NAEW Force operating bases, 51
The mission of the NAEW Force, 51

Euro-NATO Joint Jet Pilot Training Programme, 52

Proposal to build a NATO missile training range on the island of Crete, 52

Agreement signed for the construction of the NATO missile training range in Crete, 52
Formal inauguration of the NATO Guided Missile Firing Range in Crete, 52

The NATO Flag, 53

Badges and Insignia of NATO and National Units Assigned to NATO, 53
(Plates 1–64)

Appendix 1. Acronymns and Abbreviations, 202

Appendix 2. The NATO Military Structure: Formations and Locations, 204

Index, 205

Acknowledgements

The author and the illustrator acknowledge the help provided by the following individuals and organizations in the preparation of the rank insignia charts and certain aspects of the material used in this book:

Sergeant First Class Michael H. Johnson, US Army (Retd) of Fallbrook, California, USA; Lieutenant-Commander W. Maitland Thornton, OBE, RD*, RNR, of London, UK; Doctor Zanettos Tofallis of London; Robert Vis of Amsterdam, the Netherlands; Professor Donal J. Sexton of Greeneville, Tennessee, USA; Jensen Winters of Rotterdam, the Netherlands; Information Centre Oxted Public Library, Surrey, UK; The Military, Naval and Air Attachés, Belgian Embassy, London; Lieutenant-Colonel A. Thysebaert, Public Relations Officer to the Surgeon General, General Staff of the Belgian Medical Services, Brussels, Belgium; Lieutenant-Colonel Nicholas Claypoole, Chief of the Public Services Section; Public Information Office at SHAPE, Mons, Belgium; HQ Chief of Defence, Denmark; The Defence Attaché, The Royal Danish Embassy, London; Ministère de la Défense, Paris, France; The Defence Attaché's Office, The Embassy of the Federal Republic of Germany, London; The Defence Attaché, The Hellenic Embassy, London; Ministère de la Force Publique, Grand Duchy of Luxembourg; Ministerie van Defensie 's Gravenhage, the Netherlands; The Defence Attaché, The Royal Norwegian Embassy, London; The Office of the Defence Attaché, The Portuguese Embassy, London; Ministero de Defensa, Madrid, Spain; The Defence and Naval Attachés' Offices, The Spanish Embassy, London; The Defence and Military Attaché, the British Embassy, Madrid, Spain; The Military Attaché, the Turkish Embassy, London; The British Atlantic Committee, London, under the Director, Major-General C. J. Popham, CB; The Military, Naval and Air Attaches' Offices, the United States Embassy, London; The Defence Intelligence Agency, Washington, DC, USA. Unless otherwise stated all photographs are from the author's collection.

Above: The SHAPE flag being paraded at the Headquarters, France. The flag is carried by a member of the French Military Police and is escorted by an American MP (right) and a Corporal of the Corps of Royal Military Police (UK) (left).

Introduction

The North Atlantic Treaty Organization has been in existence now for almost 40 years and during that time the nations that make up NATO have grown from the original twelve to the present sixteen. This book represents the first commercial publication to illustrate all the insignia of rank of the armed forces of the NATO member countries as they stand today.* The book also deals at some length with the formation, development (and in a number of instances the disestablishment) and function of the majority of the various NATO Commands and Subordinate Commands.

Considerable effort has been made to ensure that the colour art work is accurate and as up to date as possible. The art work consists of two types of plates: those that show the range of rank insignia as worn by military (and paramilitary) personnel of the various branches of service from each of the NATO member countries; and those that show NATO badges and insignia. The rank insignia plates have been designed to a pattern. Certain items of head-dress have been included where rank is displayed on the head gear. This usually takes the form of peak decoration, design of cap badges and differences in colour detail. Other types of head-dress exist for every NATO country, such as the steel helmet and the now ubiquitous beret, but these, with just a few exceptions, have been excluded as it is not the intention of myself or that of the artist, Malcolm McGregor, to illustrate all the known varieties of military head-dress for their own sake. It was decided to show the style of rank insignia as worn by officers and men when wearing service uniform, working dress,

certain items of protective clothing and, to a limited extent, combat dress. These forms of dress are the most likely ones to be encountered. Rank insignia worn in ceremonial dress, mess dress, evening wear, full or parade uniforms and the like have been excluded.

The insignia of rank depicted on the colour plates consist of shoulder-boards, collar patches and collar insignia, epaulettes, shoulder-straps and slip-on shoulder insignia, cuff rings, cuff stripes, rank chevrons and sleeve badges. Other methods of displaying rank exist within the various armed forces assigned to NATO, but space prevents their inclusion. It should be noted that all ranks are dealt with in strict descending order, from the most senior officer to the lowest rank. Privates, or their equivalent, do not normally wear a visible indication of their rank, but their rank titles have been given in the caption lists.

The remaining colour plates feature the badges worn by the military personnel of the various NATO Commands and Sub-Commands, both past and present as well as a small selection of the national insignia worn by the forces assigned to NATO Command. In addition to their being captioned these items are inter-linked with the text.

*With the exception of Iceland, a nation that possesses neither an army nor a navy, but under the North Atlantic Treaty has US forces stationed on the island acting as the Iceland Defence Force, the rank insignia of all the armed forces of the remaining fifteen NATO member countries are dealt with, including the armed forces of both France and Spain although neither country participates in NATO's integrated military force.

The Development of NATO

The Treaty of Washington, better known by its more familiar title of the North Atlantic Treaty, was signed at the State Department in Washington, District of Columbia, USA, on 4 April 1949 by the Foreign Ministers of the twelve signatory nations in the presence of President Truman. Mr Paul-Henri Spaak signed first for Belgium, followed by Mr Lester Pearson (Canada), Hr Gustav Rasmussen (Denmark), M Robert Schuman (France), Hr Bjarni Benediktsson (Iceland), Count Carlo Sforza (Italy), M Joseph Bech (Luxembourg), Dr Dirk Stikker (Netherlands), Hr Halvard Lange (Norway), Dr José Caeiro de Mata (Portugal), Mr Ernest Bevin (United Kingdom) and Mr Dean Acheson (United States of America).

The North Atlantic Treaty officially came into force on 24 August 1949 under a proclamation issued on that date by the President of the United States of America.

Towards an Alliance The North Atlantic Treaty was the fourth – and the most far reaching – of the treaties signed since the end of the Second World War, all of which were aimed at the collective defence and security of the Western world against possible aggression.

The Treaty of Dunkirk The first of these was the Treaty of Dunkirk, signed on 4 March 1947 by France and the United Kingdom. It was a mutual defence pact of fifty years' duration which provided for a collective Anglo-French resistance to any future revival of German aggression.

The Treaty of Rio The second treaty was the Treaty of Rio de Janeiro – the inter-American Treaty of Reciprocal Assistance – signed on 2 September 1947 by the United States and twenty Latin-American countries (excluding Nicaragua and Ecuador).

The Rio Treaty is an Inter-American Treaty of Reciprocal Assistance whereby the signatories, the OAS – Organization of American States – agreed that an attack on any nation of the American continent would constitute aggression against all.

The Treaty established a collective defensive alliance within the framework of the United Nations Charter, but it makes no reference to the use of armed force in response to aggression; rather it provides for joint action to deal with emergencies.

The Brussels Treaty The third treaty – the Brussels Treaty, or to give it its full title, the Brussels Treaty of Economics, Social and Cultural Collaboration and Collective Self-Defence – was signed in March 1948. Belgium, France, Luxembourg, the Netherlands and the United Kingdom were the signatories and these countries became known as The Western Union.

In many ways the Brussels Treaty represented the first steps towards the North Atlantic Treaty. Unlike the bilateral Dunkirk Treaty it was the first multi-national regional arrangement for the security of Western Europe to be established under the United Nations Charter (but like the Dunkirk Treaty, its operative period was limited to fifty years).

The signing of the Brussels Treaty was the evidence the US Administration needed to convince the American Congress of the determination on the part of the major countries of Europe to organize themselves for collective defence – a prerequisite for US involvement in the future Atlantic Alliance.

The Brussels Treaty powers established a political structure consisting of a Consultative Council of Foreign Ministers and a Permanent Commission and a Military Committee. Each of these played a significant role in the further negotiations leading to the North Atlantic Treaty.

The Military Committee of the Brussels Treaty powers was in fact created in response to an American request for information on European military plans and actual and potential sources of military supplies, to assist in preparing Congress and US public opinion for American participation in the North Atlantic Treaty.

In September 1948 a military body was formed within the framework of the Brussels Treaty, known as the Western Union Defence Organization. Its headquarters was established at Fontainebleau, France, with Field Marshal Montgomery (UK) created Chairman of the newly appointed Commanders-in-Chief of the land, air and naval forces.

Following the signing of the North Atlantic Treaty in April 1949, the Brussels Treaty powers agreed to merge the military structure of the Western Union with that of NATO. The responsibilities of the Western Union Commanders-in-Chief Committee were transferred to General Eisenhower (USA) in April 1951 when he became NATO's first Supreme Allied Commander (see page 16) and the staff and facilities of the land, air and sea commands of the Western Union were placed at his disposal.

Under the Paris Agreements of 1954 the Federal Republic of Germany and Italy acceded to the Brussels Treaty and the Western Union became the Western European Union (WEU).

The North Atlantic Treaty In July 1948 negotiations were held in Washington for a treaty between the United States, Canada and the five Brussels Treaty powers, namely Belgium, France, Luxembourg, the Netherlands and the United Kingdom.

This Washington conference followed discussions held between the two American political parties, the Democrats and the Republicans, on the desirability of a formal alliance with the free nations of Western Europe. The Republicans were not in favour of such an alliance and advocated instead an American guarantee to Europe similar to the Monroe Doctrine. (In his message to the American Congress of 2 December 1823 President James Monroe had declared: 'The American continents, by the free and independent condition which they have assumed and maintained, are henceforth not to be considered as subjects for future colonization by any European powers.' Over the years the interpretation of this Doctrine has grown with successive Presidents and various political and military events until the Havana Conference of 1940 when the assembled republics declared that aggression against any one of them should be considered aggression against them all. This was, and still is, the principle of mutual defence that binds together the member nations of NATO.) The majority of the Republicans, however, preferred a formal treaty. On 11 June 1948 agreement was reached between the two parties, the so-called Vandenberg Resolution (Senate Resolution No. 239), which authorized the government of the United States to open negotiations about an Atlantic Security Pact.

In March 1949 Norway, Denmark, Portugal, Italy and Iceland were invited to participate in these consultations. The original plan to restrict the joint security system to the countries of the Western Union and the North-American continent was considerably enlarged. Initially this extension to the plan met with some resistance both in the USA and in Europe. However, the acquisition of a large number of military bases, harbours and airfields of great importance for the control of the exits to the Baltic Sea (Denmark and Norway), the northern sector of the Atlantic Ocean (Iceland and Greenland) and the Mediterranean (Portugal and Italy) tipped the scales of the argument and determined the initial extent of the Atlantic Union.

In April 1949 the Washington negotiations resulted in the signing of the North Atlantic Treaty.

The Fourteen Articles of the North Atlantic Treaty 'The Parties to this Treaty reaffirm their faith in the purposes and principles of the Charter of the United Nations and their desire to live in peace with all peoples and all Governments. They are determined to safeguard the freedom, common heritage and civilization of their peoples, founded on the principles of democracy, individual liberty and the rule of law. They seek to promote stability and well-being in the North Atlantic area. They are resolved to unite their efforts for collective defence and for the preservation of peace and security. They therefore agree to this North Atlantic Treaty:

Article 1. The Parties undertake, as set forth in the Charter of the United Nations, to settle any international dispute in which they may be involved by peaceful means in such a manner that international peace and security and justice are not endangered, and to refrain in their international relations from the threat or use of force in any manner inconsistent with the purposes of the United Nations.

Article 2. The Parties will contribute towards the further development of peaceful and friendly international relations by strengthening their free institutions, by bringing about a better understanding of the principles upon which these institutions are founded, and by promoting conditions of stability and well-being. They will seek to eliminate conflict in their international economic policies and will encourage economic collaboration between any or all of them.

Article 3. In order more effectively to achieve the objectives of this Treaty, the Parties, separately and jointly, by means of continuous and effective self-help and mutual aid, will maintain and develop their individual and collective capacity to resist armed attack.

Article 4. The Parties will consult together whenever, in the opinion of any of them, the territorial integrity, political independence or security of any of the Parties is threatened.

Article 5. The Parties agree that an armed attack against one or more of them in Europe or North America shall be considered an attack against them all, and consequently they agree that, if such an armed attack occurs, each of them, in exercise of the right of individual or collective self-defence recognized by Article 51 of the Charter of the United Nations,* will assist the Party or Parties so attacked by taking forthwith, individually, and in concert with the other Parties, such action as it deems necessary, including the use of armed force, to restore and maintain the security of the North Atlantic area.

Any such armed attack and all measures taken as a result thereof shall immediately be reported to the Security Council. Such measures shall be terminated when the Security Council has taken the measures necessary to restore and maintain international peace and security.

Article 6.† For the purpose of Article 5, an armed attack on one or more of the Parties is deemed to include an armed attack.

■ on the territory of any of the Parties in Europe or North America, on the Algerian Departments of France,‡ on the territory of Turkey or on the islands under the jurisdiction of any of the Parties in the North Atlantic area north of the Tropic of Cancer;

■ on the forces, vessels, or aircraft of any of the Parties, when in or over these territories or any area in Europe in which occupation forces of any of the Parties were stationed on the date when the Treaty entered into force or the Mediterranean Sea or the North Atlantic area north of the Tropic of Cancer.

Article 7. The Treaty does not affect, and shall not be interpreted as affecting, in any way the rights and obligations under the Charter of the Parties which are members of the United Nations, or the primary responsibility of the Security Council for the maintenance of international peace and security. Each Party declares that none of the international engagements now in force between it and any other of the Parties or any third State is in conflict with the provisions of this Treaty, and undertakes not to enter into any international engagement in conflict with this Treaty.

Article 9. The Parties hereby establish a Council, on which each of them shall be represented to consider matters concerning the implementation of this Treaty. The Council shall be so organized as to be able to meet promptly at any time.

The Council shall set up such subsidiary bodies as may be necessary; in particular it shall establish immediately a defence committee which shall recommend measures for the implementation of Articles 3 and 5.

Article 10. The Parties may, by unanimous agreement, invite any other European State in a position to further the principles of this Treaty and to contribute to the security of the North Atlantic area to accede to this Treaty. Any State so invited may become a party to the Treaty by depositing its instrument of accession with the Government of the United States of America. The Government of the United States of America will inform each of the Parties of the deposit of each such instrument of accession.

Article 11. This Treaty shall be ratified and its provisions carried out by the Parties in accordance with their respective constitutional processes. The instruments of ratification shall be deposited as soon as possible with the Government of the United States of America, which will notify all the other signatories of each deposit. The Treaty shall enter into force between the States which have ratified it as soon as the ratification of the majority of the signatories, including the ratifications of Belgium, Canada, France, Luxembourg, the Netherlands, the United Kingdom and the United States, have been deposited and shall come into effect with respect to other States on the date of the deposit of their ratifications.

Article 12. After the Treaty has been in force for ten years, or at any time thereafter, the Parties shall, if any of them so request, consult together for the purpose of reviewing the Treaty, having regard for the factors then affecting peace and security in the North Atlantic area including the development

of universal as well as regional arrangements under the Charter of the United Nations for the maintenance of international peace and security.

Article 13. After the Treaty has been in force for twenty years, any Party may cease to be a Party one year after its notice of renunciation has been given to the Government of the United States of America, which will inform the Governments of the other Parties of the deposit of each notice of renunciation.

Article 14. This Treaty, of which the English and French texts are equally authentic, shall be deposited in the archives of the Government of the United States of America. Duly certified copies will be transmitted by that Government to the Governments of the other signatories.

*Article 51 of the United Nations Charter to which reference is made in Article 5 of the North Atlantic Treaty.

'Nothing in the Charter shall impair the inherent right of individual or collective self-defence if an armed attack occurs against a member of the United Nations, until the Security Council has taken the measures necessary to maintain international peace and security.

Measures taken by members in the exercise of this right of self-defence shall be immediately reported to the Security Council and shall not in any way affect the authority and responsibility of the Security Council under the Charter to take at any time such action as it deems necessary in order to maintain or restore international peace and security.'

†As amended by Article 2 of the Protocol to the North Atlantic Treaty on the accession of Greece and Turkey (see page 27).

‡On 16 January 1963, the French Representative made a statement to the North Atlantic Council on the effects of the independence of Algeria on certain aspects of the North Atlantic Treaty. The Council noted that insofar as the former Algerian Department of France was concerned the relevant clauses of this Treaty had become inapplicable as from 3 July 1962.

The North Atlantic Alliance Today

NATO is an organization of sovereign nations, each one equal in status. At present there are sixteen member nations: The Kingdom of Belgium, the Dominion of Canada, the Kingdom of Denmark, the Federal Republic of Germany, the French Republic, the Hellenic Republic, the Republic of Iceland, the Italian Republic, the Grand Duchy of Luxembourg, the Kingdom of the Netherlands, the Kingdom of Norway, the Portuguese Republic, the Kingdom of Spain, the Republic of Turkey, the United Kingdom of Great Britain and Northern Ireland and the United States of America. Of these countries only France, Iceland and Spain do not participate in NATO's integrated military structure. Decisions that are taken are the expression of the collective will of the member governments arrived at by common consent.

The North Atlantic Council The highest decision-making body and forum for consultations within the Alliance is the North Atlantic Council. This is composed of representatives of the sixteen member nations. At Ministerial Meetings of the Council, member nations are represented by Ministers of Foreign Affairs. These meetings are held twice a year. The Council also meets on occasion at the level of Heads of State and Government. In permanent session, at the level of Ambassadors (Permanent Representatives), the Council usually meets at least once a week.

The Defence Planning Committee The Defence Planning Committee is composed of representatives of the member nations participating in NATO's integrated military structure. It deals with matters specifically related to defence. Like the

Council, it too meets both in permanent session at the level of Ambassadors and twice a year at Ministerial level. At Ministerial Meetings, member nations are represented by Defence Ministers. The Council and Defence Planning Committee are chaired by the Secretary General of NATO at whatever level they meet. Opening Sessions of Ministerial Meetings of the Council are also presided over by the President, an honorary position held annually by the Foreign Minister of one of the member nations.

The Nuclear Planning Group Nuclear matters are discussed by the Nuclear Planning Group in which fourteen countries now participate. It meets as required at the level of Permanent Representatives and twice a year at the level of Ministers of Defence.

The Permanent Representatives and National Delegations The Permanent Representatives of the member countries are supported by national delegations located at NATO Headquarters. The delegations are composed of advisers and officials who represent their countries on the various committees created by the Council.

The Secretary General and the International Staff To assist its work, the Council has established a number of committees whose main areas of responsibility are indicated in the diagram shown below. These committees are supported by an International Staff, made up of personnel drawn from all member countries, responsible to the Secretary General. The Secretary General himself is responsible for promoting and directing the process of consultation within the Alliance. He may propose items for discussion. He has the authority to use

his good offices at any time in cases of dispute between member countries, and with their consent, to initiate enquiries or mediation, conciliation or arbitration procedures. The Deputy Secretary General assists the Secretary General in his functions and deputizes for him in his absence.

The International Staff comprises the Office of the Secretary General, five divisions, the Office of Management and the Office of the Financial Controller. Each of the Divisions is headed by an Assistant Secretary General, who is normally the Chairman of the main committee dealing with his responsibilities, through their structure of Directorates and Services. The Divisions support the work of the committees in numerous fields.

The Military Committee The Military Committee is the highest military authority in the Alliance. It is composed of the Chiefs of Staff of all member nations except France, Iceland and Spain. France is represented by the Chief of the French Military Mission to the Military Committee. Iceland has no military forces, but can be represented by a civilian, and Spain sends an Observer. The Chiefs of Staff meet at least twice a year or whenever it is deemed necessary. However, to enable the Military Committee to function on a continuous basis with effective powers of decision, each Chief of Staff appoints a Permanent Military Representative.

The Military Committee is responsible for making recommendations to the Council and Defence Planning Committee on those measures considered necessary for the common defence of the NATO area, and for supplying guidance on military matters to the major NATO Commanders. It is also

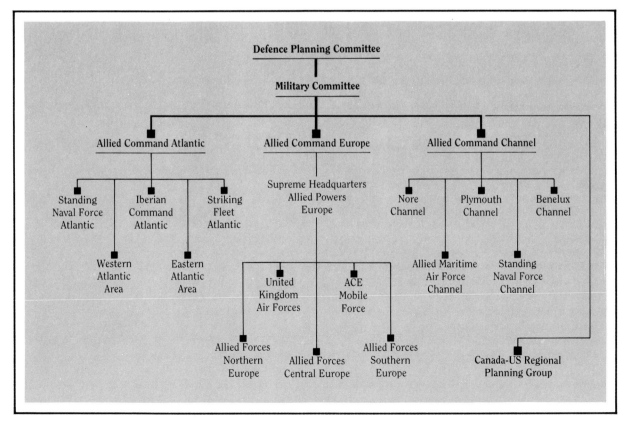

responsible for a number of NATO military agencies and for the NATO Defence College in Rome.

The Presidency of the Military Committee rotates annually among the nations in order of the English alphabet. The Chairman of the Military Committee is elected by the Chiefs of Staff normally for a period of three years. He directs the day-to-day business of the Committee and acts as its spokesman. The Chairman is assisted by the Deputy Chairman who is also specifically responsible for the co-ordination of nuclear matters, arms control and MBFR (Vienna negotiations on Mutual and Balanced Force Reductions in Central Europe) matters, and by the Director of the International Military Staff. The Military Committee is represented by its Chairman at meetings of the North Atlantic Council.

The International Military Staff The Military Committee is assisted by an integrated International Military Staff (IMS) headed by a Director of three star rank selected from one of the member nations. The Director is assisted by six Assistant Directors and the Secretary of the IMS, who are of general officer rank. The Assistant Directors head the Divisions for Intelligence; Plans and Policy; Operations; Logistics and Resources; Command, Control and Communication Systems; and Armaments, Standardization and Inter-operability. As the executive agency of the Military Committee, the IMS is charged with ensuring that the policies and decisions of the Military Committee are implemented as directed. In addition, the IMS prepares plans, initiates studies and recommends policy on matters of a military nature.

The NATO Commands The strategic area covered by the North Atlantic Treaty is divided among three Commands:
■ Allied Command Europe (see also page 29);
■ Allied Command Atlantic (see also page 46); and
■ Allied Command Channel (see also page 48).

These Commands are under the authority of the three Major NATO Commanders (MNCs): the Supreme Allied Commander Europe (SACEUR), the Supreme Allied Commander Atlantic (SACLANT) and the Allied Commander-in-Chief Channel (CINCHAN). Plans for the defence of the North American area are developed by the Canadian-US Regional Planning Group which makes recommendations to the Military Committee. It meets alternately in the United States (Washington) and Canada (Ottawa).

The authority exercised by the Commands varies in accordance with geographical and political factors and with peace and wartime conditions. Generally, the forces of member countries remain under national command in peacetime; however, some are placed under operational command or control of NATO, some are already assigned to NATO Commands and others are earmarked for these Commands. The Major NATO Commanders are responsible for the development of defence plans for their respective areas, for the determination of force requirements and for the development and exercise of the forces under their Command. The organization of the Commands is flexible enough and the liaison between them close enough to allow for mutual support and the rapid movement of the necessary land, sea and air forces to meet any situation likely to confront the Alliance.

Towards an Integrated Defence Force

In September 1950 the North Atlantic Council agreed upon the establishment at the earliest possible date of an integrated military force under a centralized command. This force was required to be adequate to deter aggression and to ensure the defence of western Europe. The concept of the integrated force approved by the Council was based upon the following principles:
■ The force was to be organized under the North Atlantic Treaty Organization and was to be subject to political and strategic guidance exercised by the appropriate agencies of that organization.
■ The force was to be under a Supreme Commander, who was to have sufficient delegated authority to ensure that national units allocated to his command were organized and trained into an effective, integrated force in time of

peace as well as in the event of war.
■ The Supreme Commander was to be supported by an international staff representing all nations contributing to the force.
■ Pending the appointment of a Supreme Commander (see page 16) a Chief of Staff was to be appointed who was to have the responsibility for training and organization of this integrated force.
■ The Standing Group of the Military Committee of the North Atlantic Treaty Organization was made responsible for training and organization.

The formation of NATO's Integrated Defence Force The Foreign Ministers and the Defence Ministers of the twelve NATO countries, comprising respectively the North Atlantic Council and the Defence Committee, met in Brussels on

18–19 December 1950 and, after a joint meeting, issued a communiqué on the latter date. The communiqué was worded as follows:

'The North Atlantic Council, acting on the recommendations of the Defence Committee, completed the arrangements initiated in September last (1950) for the establishment in Europe of an integrated force under centralized control and command. This force is to be composed of contingents contributed by the participating Governments.

The Council unanimously decided to ask the President of the United States of America to make available General of the Army Dwight D. Eisenhower to serve as Supreme Commander.

Following receipt this morning of a message from the President that he had made General Eisenhower available, the Council appointed him. He will assume his command and establish his headquarters in Europe early in the New Year (1951). He will have the authority to train the national units assigned to his command and to organize them into an effective integrated defence force. He will be supported by an international staff, drawn from the nations contributing to the force.

The Council, desiring to simplify the structure of the North Atlantic Treaty Organization in order to make it more effective, asked the Council Deputies to initiate appropriate action. In this connexion the Defence Committee, meeting separately on 18 December 1950, had already taken action to establish a Defence Production Board with greater powers than those of the Military Production and Supply Board, which it supersedes. The new Board is charged with expanding and accelerating production and with furthering the mutual use of the industrial capacities of the member nations.

The Council also reached unanimous agreement regarding the part which Germany might assume in the common

Right: General of the Army Dwight D. Eisenhower, former wartime Supreme Commander Allied Expeditionary Force and first Supreme Allied Commander Europe (18 December 1950–30 May 1952).

defence. German participation would strengthen the defence of Europe without altering in any way the purely defensive character of the North Atlantic Treaty Organization. The Council invited the Governments of France, the United Kingdom and the United States to explore this matter with the German Federal Republic.

The decisions taken and the measures contemplated have the sole purpose of maintaining and consolidating peace. The North Atlantic nations are determined to pursue this policy until peace is secure.'

Eisenhower, first Supreme Commander Allied Powers Europe General of the Army Dwight David Eisenhower (USA), the former wartime Supreme Commander Allied Expeditionary Force, had retired from the US Army in January 1948, leaving the office of Chief of Staff to accept in June of the same year, civilian employment with an appointment as President of Columbia University, New York. In late 1950 President Truman asked him to return to active military duty in order to assume the command of SHAPE – Supreme Headquarters Allied Powers Europe. General Eisenhower took up his new military appointment at the end of December 1950 and held his first press conference in his new capacity as Supreme Commander at the Pentagon in Washington on 4 January 1951 on the eve of his departure for Europe.

First and temporary Headquarters of SHAPE On 26 December 1950 General Eisenhower chose provisionally to establish his European headquarters at the Hotel Astoria, in the Avenue des Champs-Elysées, Paris. During the Second World War this building had housed German military administrative offices and since 1945 had been used by the US Army in Europe.

The first established Supreme Headquarters Allied Powers Europe On 19 February 1951 it was officially announced in Paris by General Eisenhower's staff that the French Government had made available an area of 60 acres of land at Rocquencourt, about midway between Versailles and St-Germain-en-Laye and fifteen miles west from the centre of Paris, for the permanent site of SHAPE. The site which is on the edge of the Forest of Marly formed part of the French President's hunting preserve and was formally handed over by President Auriol to the Supreme Commander on 23 July 1951.

Eisenhower leaves SHAPE On 11 April 1952 an announcement issued from the White House, Washington stated that General Eisenhower had asked to be relieved of his post as Supreme Allied Commander Europe (SACEUR) by approximately 1 June 1952 and placed on the inactive list after his return to the USA. The US Secretary of Defence, Mr Robert Lovett, with the approval of President Truman, had agreed to this request. General Eisenhower resigned, for the second time, from the US Army in July 1952 in order to run as a Republican candidate for President. On 20 January 1953 he was inaugurated as the 34th President of the United States of America.

General Matthew B. Ridgway, SACEUR General Eisenhower remained Supreme Allied Commander in Europe until May 1952 when he was succeeded by General Matthew B. Ridgway (USA) who formally took over his new duties from General Eisenhower at SHAPE on 30 May 1952.

General Alfred M. Gruenther, third SACEUR It was announced on 12 May 1953 by President Eisenhower in Washington and by NATO Headquarters in Paris that General Ridgway would be succeeded as SACEUR by General Alfred M. Gruenther (USA). General Gruenther had served as Chief of Staff to both Generals Eisenhower and Ridgway at SHAPE, and on 12 May 1953 when General Ridgway was appointed Chief of Staff of the US Army General Gruenther succeeded as SACEUR.

General Norstad succeeds General Gruenther as the fourth SACEUR At a ceremony held on 20 November 1956 General Lauris Norstad (USA) formally took over the post of Supreme Commander Allied Powers in Europe from General Alfred M. Gruenther. General Gruenther, who left for the United States on the following day, took up the appointment of President of the American Red Cross. On 20 July 1962 the White House announced the resignation of General Norstad as SACEUR and Commander-in-Chief US Forces in Europe. His resignation was to have taken effect from 1 November 1962, but a further announcement on 29 October 1962 from NATO Headquarters stated that the North Atlantic Council had agreed to postpone from 1 November 1962 to 1 January 1963 the termination of General Norstad's post as Supreme Allied Commander Europe and the assumption of the post by General Lemnitzer (USA), since the Cuban missile crisis had made it impossible for General Lemnitzer to meet this schedule.

General Lemnitzer replaces General Norstad as SACEUR On 20 July 1962 President Kennedy announced the appointment of General Lyman L. Lemnitzer, Chairman of the US Joint Chiefs of Staff and Commander-in-Chief US Forces as Supreme Allied Commander Europe. General Lemnitzer officially took over the post from General Norstad on 2 January 1963.

General Goodpaster, new Supreme Allied Commander Europe On 12 March 1969 the Defence Planning Committee unanimously agreed to the proposal made by President Nixon that General Lyman L. Lemnitzer should be released from his assignment as SACEUR to permit his retirement from the US Army, and that General Andrew J. Goodpaster be appointed his successor with effect from 1 July 1969. General Goodpaster had served with General Eisenhower and General Gruenther in the early years of SHAPE, and was later a divisional commander with the US forces in Western Germany. He had served in Washington as Assistant to the Chairman of the US Joint Chiefs of Staff and Director of the Joint Staff and had served as Deputy US Commander in Vietnam.

Top left: General Matthew Bunker Ridgway, former Supreme Commander United Nations Forces in Korea and second Supreme Allied Commander Europe (30 May 1952–12 May 1953).
Top right: General Alfred M. Gruenther, third Supreme Allied Commander Europe (12 May 1953–20 November 1956).
Bottom left: General Lauris Norstad, United States Air Force and fourth Supreme Allied Commander Europe (20 November 1956–2 January 1963).
Bottom right: General Lyman L. Lemnitzer, Chairman of the US Joint Chiefs of Staff and Commander-in-Chief US Forces in Europe and fifth Supreme Allied Commander Europe (2 January 1963–1 July 1966).

Top left: General Andrew J. Goodpaster, former Deputy US Commander Vietnam and sixth and longest-serving Supreme Allied Commander Europe (1 July 1966–15 December 1974).
Top right: General Alexander M. Haig, former US Army Vice-Chief of Staff and former Chief of Staff at the White House, seventh Supreme Allied Commander Europe (15 December 1974–29 June 1979).
Bottom left: General Bernard W. Rogers, US Army Chief of Staff and eighth and second longest-serving Supreme Allied Commander Europe (29 June 1979–26 June 1987).
Bottom right: General John Galvin, former Commander US Army Southern Command and latest Supreme Allied Commander Europe (26 June 1987–).

General Haig succeeds General Goodpaster as SACEUR On 16 September 1974 the Defence Planning Committee agreed to a proposal from President Ford that General Andrew J. Goodpaster should be released from his assignment as SACEUR prior to his retirement from the US Army, and that General Alexander M. Haig be appointed his successor with effect from 15 December 1974. General Haig, a former US Army Vice-Chief of Staff, retired from the service on his appointment by President Nixon as Chief of Staff at the White House in June 1973. However, President Ford announced on 16 September 1974 that he was being recalled to active duty. On 3 January 1979 General Haig announced that he would be resigning from the post of SACEUR and retiring from the US Army on 30 June 1979. Haig said that he had originally wanted to resign as SACEUR in the summer of 1978, but had been persuaded to stay on for another year by President Carter.

Attempted assassination of General Haig, outgoing SACEUR General Alexander Haig, the retiring Supreme Allied Commander Europe, escaped unhurt while on his way to work at Casteau (30 miles south-west of Brussels) on 25 June 1979 when a bomb exploded near his car. An accompanying car was badly damaged, although its three occupants were only slightly injured. Two hitherto unknown revolutionary groups, 'Revenge and Freedom' and the 'June 25, 1979, Julien LaHaut Brigade' (named after a former Belgian Communist Party Leader), claimed responsibility for the attack.

General Bernard Rogers, SACEUR On 28 February 1979 the Defence Planning Committee of NATO agreed to the nomination by President Carter of General Bernard W. Rogers, US Army Chief of Staff since October 1976, as Supreme Allied Commander Europe with effect from 1 July 1979, in succession to General Alexander Haig. Haig handed over to his successor on 29 June 1979. On 15 May 1981 approval was given by Pesident Reagan for a two-year extension for General Bernard Rogers as Commander-in-Chief of US forces in Europe, which meant also that he would continue to serve for a further two years as SACEUR. On 4 February 1985 General Rogers was reappointed to a further two-year term as Supreme Allied Commander Europe.

General John Galvin succeeds General Bernard Rogers as Supreme Allied Commander Europe On 26 February 1987 NATO Defence Planning Council approved the nomination of General John Galvin, hitherto Commander of the US Army Southern Command based in Panama, to succeed General Bernard Rogers as SACEUR from the end of June. On 26 June 1987 General Galvin took up his new appointment, the ninth and latest American General in 37 years to hold this important post.

The First European Defence Commands and their Commanders

An announcement from General Eisenhower's Headquarters on 20 March 1951 stated that the Supreme Commander had 'designated his principal deputies and commanders and outlined the broad command structure on which he will base the defence of western Europe'. The announcement gave the names of the Deputy Supreme Allied Commander and of General Eisenhower's Air Deputy (the Naval Deputy was announced on 2 April 1951), and stated that western Europe would be divided for defence purposes into three geographical areas, Northern, Central and Southern, each under its own Commander. The defence structure set up by General Eisenhower was as follows:

Supreme Headquarters Allied Powers Europe
■ Deputy Supreme Allied Commander: Field Marshal Viscount Montgomery (UK).
■ Deputy Supreme Commander (Air): Air Chief Marshal Sir Hugh Sanders (UK).
■ Deputy Supreme Commander (Naval): Amiral André Georges Lemonnier (France).

The Central European Command
■ Commander-in-Chief Allied Army Forces in Central Europe: Général d'Armée Alphonse Juin (France).

- Commander-in-Chief Allied Air Forces in Central Europe: Lieutenant-General Lauris Norstad (USA).
- Naval Flag Officer, Central Europe: Vice-Amiral Robert Janjard (France).

The Northern European Command

- Commander-in-Chief Northern Europe: Vice-Admiral Sir Patrick Brind (UK).
- Commander of Allied Army Forces in Norway: Lieutenant-General Wilhelm Tangen-Hansteen, C-in-C of the Norwegian Army.
- Commander of Allied Army Forces in Denmark: Lieutenant-General Ebbe Görtz, C-in-C of the Danish Army.
- Commander of Allied Air Forces, Northern Europe: Major-General Robert K. Taylor (USA).

The Southern European Command

The Supreme Commander's announcement stated that the command organization in Southern Europe would be made public subsequently and that the command of Allied Land Forces in that region would be given to an Italian General. As regards the Western Union defence organization at Fontainebleau, General Eisenhower added that, in the interests of streamlining the organization and definitely fixing responsibilities, he would request the Brussels Treaty Powers to transfer to his command some of the responsibilities of the Western Union Commanders-in-Chief Committee, which would have to fit into the framework of the North Atlantic Treaty Organization.

'General Order No. 1' On 2 April 1951 General Eisenhower, from his temporary HQ at the Hotel Astoria in Paris, issued his first 'General Order No. 1' announcing that he had formally taken over command of all the Atlantic Pact forces in Europe, including American, British and French occupation forces in Germany. The Order read as follows:

'Section I – Activation.

(1) Allied Command, Europe, consisting of Supreme Headquarters Allied Powers, Europe, and such additional operational headquarters, organizations, and military forces as may from time to time be subordinated to the Supreme Allied Commander, Europe, is activated at 00.01 hours on this day pursuant to the authority vested in me by the North Atlantic Treaty Organization.

(2) Supreme Headquarters, Allied Powers Europe (SHAPE), is activated as the headquarters of Allied Command, Europe, as of 00.01 hours on this date, with temporary station at Paris, France.

Section II – Assumption of Command.

The undersigned hereby assumes Command of Allied Command Europe   Dwight D. Eisenhower'

First foreign troops under SHAPE command in Europe In December 1950 it was announced that the forces initially to come under General Eisenhower's command in Europe were to be the US Seventh Army garrisoned in Germany; the British Army of the Rhine consisting of the 2nd and 7th Armoured Divisions to be augmented by the 11th Armoured Division plus an Infantry Division; the three French divisions stationed in Germany and Austria; the Belgian, Danish and Norwegian brigades stationed in western Germany; and the American and British garrisons in Austria, Trieste and Berlin. The Italian Defence Minister, Signor Pacciardi, announced in Rome on 5 January 1951 that three Italian divisions would be formed as Italy's 'initial contribution to the Atlantic army', and that they would be placed at General Eisenhower's disposal.

First permanent NATO Headquarters The North Atlantic Treaty Organization had its first provisional headquarters in the temporary structure built for the 1951 session of the United Nations General Assembly in the Trocadero Gardens between the Palais de Chaillot and the Eiffel Tower. NATO occupied these headquarters for eight years, but in November 1952 the North Atlantic Council announced that it had accepted an offer from the French Government to place at NATO's disposal a site at Le Chesnay, between Versailles and the then Supreme Allied Headquarters at Louveciennes. This however proved to be an abortive suggestion as the Paris municipal authorities made available a site on the edge of the Bois de Boulogne.

Work began on the new headquarters in December 1955, the architect in charge being M. Jacques Carlu, who had erected the temporary building at the Palais de Chaillot, assisted by an international team of architects. All the NATO member countries of the time contributed to the new headquarters building. Denmark provided the furniture, Belgium was responsible for the steel used and the aluminium window frames, Italy supplied the marble, the Netherlands installed the electronic equipment, lifts, etc., and West Germany the telephone installations. Turkey produced a mosaic. France, for her part, provided the site at a 'peppercorn' rent. The new NATO building lay athwart the old city walls of Paris, in the shape of a gigantic 'A', with the apex at the Porte Dauphine, one arm following the Boulevard Lannes, the other in the Bois de Boulogne. The headquarters was a seven-storey structure containing 1,000 offices of which some 350 were occupied by the various national delegations. It had large conference and committee rooms, a bank, post office, cinema and roof café, a room allocated for press conferences and an assembly room with a seating capacity of 550 where public sessions of the North Atlantic Council were held.

NATO, The First Five Years, 1949–54: Military Organization

SHAPE was established in the Versailles area in 1951. General Eisenhower had been the first Supreme Commander until May 1952 when he was succeeded by General Ridgway, who in turn was followed by General Gruenther. Field Marshal Viscount Montgomery of Alamein had been Deputy Supreme Commander of NATO from the outset. He had two deputies: a First Air Deputy, originally Air Chief Marshal Sir Hugh Saunders, replaced later by General Lauris Norstad, and a First Naval Deputy, Admiral Lemonnier. Under the North Atlantic Council, which met at the Palais de Chaillot in Paris, came the Military Committee of NATO. This was divided into: a Military Representative Committee and a Standing Group; both had headquarters in Washington, DC.

The Military Committee The Military Committee, the supreme military authority, consisted of one Chief of Staff from each of the member countries. It exercised general supervision over four main NATO military organizations:

- The Supreme Allied Commander, Europe,
- The Supreme Allied Commander, Atlantic,
- The Canadian-US Regional Planning Group, and
- The Channel Committee.

The Military Committee would meet periodically in Washington. The Chairmen of the Military Committee during the first five years since its inception were:

1949–50 General Omar N. Bradley (USA)
1951–2 Lieutenant-Général Etienne Baele (Belgium)
1952 Lieutenant-General Charles Foulkes (Canada)
1953 Admiral E. J. C. Qvistgaard (Denmark)
1954 Générals Paul Ely and Guillaume (France)

The Military Representatives Committee consisted of officers of all NATO countries except Iceland, which had and still has no military forces.

The Standing Group This was the permanent agency for the day-to-day work and it consisted of three senior officers drawn from France, the United Kingdom and the United States. At 1 July 1954 these officers were: Général Valluy (France), General Sir John Whiteley (UK) and General J. Lawton Collins (USA).

The main NATO Commands and their Subsidiary Commands By the end of 1955 there were only two main NATO Commands: Allied Command Europe and Allied Command Atlantic. Each was divided into a number of subsidiary Commands.

The European Command Allied Command Europe comprised in 1955 the following four Commands (their headquarters shown in parentheses), all of which were under the general control and direction of SHAPE.

- *Allied Forces Northern Europe (Oslo).* This was sub-divided into the following Commands: (a) Allied Land Forces, Norway (Oslo); (b) Allied Land Forces, Denmark (Copenhagen); (c) Allied Air Forces, Northern Europe (Sandvik, Norway); and (d) Allied Naval Forces, Northern Europe (Oslo). The Commander-in-Chief Allied Forces Northern Europe (CINCNORTH) was General Sir Robert Mansergh (UK). He had under him an American general commanding Air Forces in Northern Europe, a Norwegian Land Forces Commander, and a Danish Land Force Commander.

- *Allied Forces Central Europe (Fontainebleau)* was sub-divided into the following Commands, all of which also had their headquarters at Fontainebleau: (a) Allied Land Forces, Central Europe (see plate 57); (b) Allied Air Forces, Central Europe and (c) Allied Naval Forces, Central Europe. (See plate 60). The Headquarters of the Allied Air Forces Central European Command had been inaugurated at Fontainbleau, France on 19 July 1952. Its extensive electrical and telecommunications installations had been completed by French military engineers within 90 days. Eight weeks later on 11 September the Headquarters were named Camp Guynemer in memory of Captain Georges Guynemer, a French fighter 'ace' of the First World War who was killed in action over Belgium in 1917 after having shot down 53 German aircraft.

A major reorganization in the NATO Command structure had been announced on 3 July 1953 whereby the Central European Sector was put on the same footing as the Northern and Southern European Sectors each with its own Commander-in-Chief and subordinate land, sea and air commanders.

The Commander-in-Chief Allied Forces Central Europe (CINCENT) was Maréchal Alphonse Juin (France) who had under him an Allied Land Forces Commander – a French officer – directly subordinate to him. Maréchal Juin's Command included the Northern Army Group, which consisted of Belgian, British, Canadian and Netherlands forces, and the Central Army Group, which consisted of French and American forces. Vice-Amiral Jaujard (France) commanded Allied Naval Forces Central Europe, while Air Marshal Sir

Basil Embry controlled two Tactical Air Forces, one of which was earmarked to give support to the Northern Army Group and one to the Central Army Group.

■ *Allied Forces, Southern Europe (Naples)* was subdivided into the following Commands: (a) Allied Land Forces, South-Eastern Europe (Izmir) which comprised the Greek and Turkish forces; (b) Allied Land Forces, Southern Europe (Verona); (c) Allied Air Forces Southern Europe (Naples) and (d) Naval Striking and Support Forces, Southern Europe (Naples) (see plate 59). The Commander-in-Chief Allied Forces Southern Europe (CINCSOUTH) was Admiral Fechteler (USA) who had under his command an Italian General commanding Allied Land Forces, an American General commanding Air Forces, and an American Admiral commanding the US Sixth Fleet in the Mediterranean.

■ *Allied Forces, Mediterranean (Malta)* (see also plate 60) was subdivided into the following Commands: (a) Gibraltar Area (Gibraltar) (see also plate 58); (b) Western Mediterranean Area (Algiers); (c) Central Mediterranean Area (Naples); (d) Eastern Mediterranean Area (Athens); (e) North-Eastern Mediterranean Area (Izmir) and (f) South-Eastern Mediterranean Area (Malta). The Commander-in-Chief Allied Forces Mediterranean (CINCAF-MED) was Admiral Sir Guy Grantham (UK) who had succeeded Admiral Earl Mountbatten (UK). He had under his command six Admirals (two British, one French, one Italian, one Greek and one Turkish) who were responsible for the six areas into which the Mediterranean Command was originally subdivided. In time of war the CINCAFMED was to have been responsible for securing the lines of communication through the Mediterranean Sea.

All four Commanders-in-Chief – Maréchal Juin, General Sir Robert Mansergh, Admiral Fechteler and Admiral Sir Guy Grantham all reported direct to General Gruenther, SACEUR.

The Atlantic Command The Allied Command in the Atlantic was headed by the Supreme Allied Commander Atlantic (SACLANT) who was, in 1955, Admiral Jerauld Wright (USA) with Vice-Admiral J. W. M. Eaton (UK) as Deputy Supreme Commander. Its headquarters were then, as they are today, at Norfolk, Virginia (USA). Under SACLANT were: (a) the C-in-C Western Atlantic Area (headquarters at Norfolk, Va); (b) the Commander, Striking Fleet, Atlantic (Norfolk); and (c) the Naval C-in-C Eastern Atlantic Area and Air C-in-C Eastern Atlantic (both with headquarters at Northwood, UK). The staff of SACLANT was drawn from the navies, armies and air forces of eight nations: Canada, Denmark, France, the Netherlands, Norway, Portugal, the United Kingdom and the United States. The Western Atlantic Area was commanded by a US NAval Commander – who was also SACLANT himself – and was divided into sub-areas based on Norfolk and New York (USA) and Halifax (Canada). The Eastern Atlantic Area was headed by British Naval and Air Commander-in-Chief, and was divided into sub-areas based on Plymouth, Gosport and Pitreavie (UK), and Brest (France). A third area – the Iberian Atlantic Command, covering the south-eastern sector of the Atlantic Command – had been defined but had, in 1955, not been established.

The Atlantic Command extends from the North Pole to the Tropic of Cancer, and from the coastal waters of North America to those of Europe and Africa (excluding, however, the English Channel and the waters around the British Isles). The Atlantic islands – Iceland, Greenland, the Azores, Bermuda and the Faroes were placed for military defence purposes under island Commanders, all but one of whom was a national of the sovereign island Power.

The primary task of SACLANT in time of war, was in 1955 as it is to-day, to provide NATO with security in the Atlantic Ocean by guarding the sea lanes and denying their use to an enemy.

The Channel Committee and the Channel Command Apart from the European and Atlantic Commands of NATO there was in existence in 1955 a Channel Committee and a Channel Command, originally set up in 1952 (see page 48). The Channel Committee consisted of the Chiefs of Naval Staff, or their representatives, of Belgium, France, the Netherlands and the United Kingdom. This Channel Committee was considered essential as it was thought that the Standing Group based in Washington was too far away and would have been too occupied with matters of high strategy to attend to the detailed problems which would be encountered in the small but vital Channel area. Directly under the Channel Committee was the Channel Command headed by a Naval Commander-in-Chief Channel and Southern North Sea (who in 1955 was Admiral Sir George Creasy (UK), who was also C-in-C Portsmouth) and an Air Commander-in-Chief Channel and Southern North Sea (who in 1955 was again Air Marshal Sir John Boothman (UK) and who was also chief of RAF Coastal Command).

In time of war the Channel Command was charged with the following essential tasks:

■ to control the English Channel and the southern North Sea and deny these areas to an enemy;

■ to protect sea communications in these areas;

■ to support operations conducted by SACEUR and SACLANT.

The Canada–United States Regional Planning Group This group (the only survivor of NATO's original five* regional planning groups) was, and still is, directed by the Canadian and US Chiefs of Staff, and is responsible for making plans for the defence of the North-American continent. It has its headquarters in Washington and Ottawa and meets alternatively in the United States and in Canada. Its defence plans were seen by the other NATO nations and approved by the Standing Group, in the same way as were, and are, those of the Supreme Commanders.

NATO Military Agencies Apart from the military structures described above, a number of military agencies existed in 1955, some of which still operate to-day, and all of which worked under the general direction of the Standing Group:

■ *The NATO Defence College* (see also page 49). When first established this was housed in the Ecole Militaire in Paris. It trained officers of NATO countries in problems of international co-operation affecting the Atlantic Alliance as a whole. The languages of instruction were French and English.

■ *The Military Agency for Standardization.* This agency

aimed at the standardization throughout the member nations of war material and of operational and administrative practice. It was established in London and was directly responsible to the Standing Group.

■ *The Advisory Group for Aeronautical Research and Development (AGARD).* This group was headed by Dr Theodore von Karman (USA) and consisted of one or two scientific representatives from each NATO country.

■ *The Air Training Advisory Group (ATAG).* This was based at Villacoublay airfield near SHAPE, and manned by highly qualified flying instructors of the various NATO countries.

It had also set up a Flying Instructors' School for the Italian Air Force at Foggia.

*The original five planning groups that had been established on 17 September 1949 were: (1) Northern European Group, which consisted of Great Britain, Denmark and Norway; (2) Western European Group, which comprised the Western Union Powers: Great Britain, France, Belgium, the Netherlands and Luxembourg; (3) Southern European-Western Mediterranean group which consisted of Great Britain, France and Italy; (4) North Atlantic Ocean group, which comprised Belgium, Canada, Denmark, France, Iceland, the Netherlands, Norway, Portugal, Great Britain and the United States of America; (5) Canadian-United States group, which was (and still is as the sole surviving planning group of the original five) responsible for defence planning for the Western Hemisphere.

Salient Events in NATO's Development

Entry of the German Federal Republic into NATO The German Federal Republic achieved its sovereignty and independence almost exactly ten years after the unconditional surrender of Nazi Germany to the Allies which took place on 8 May 1945. Among the immediate effects of the attainment of independence were:

■ The right of Western Germany to rearm within the NATO framework, and the lifting of all prohibitions on armaments except those which the Federal Republic had voluntarily undertaken not to manufacture such as atomic, biological and chemical weapons, long-range bombers, warships over 3,000 tons and submarines over 300 tons.

■ The right to build and operate commercial aircraft.

■ The right to enter into diplomatic relations with any country.

■ The removal of all remaining restrictions on West German industry.

■ The lifting of all Allied censorship and security measures.

One of the immediate results of the ending of the occupation regime was that the British, United States and French High Commissioners in Bonn, and the Federal German envoys in London, Paris and Washington assumed the status of Ambassadors.

Arrangements for establishing the integrated European force with German participation had been decided upon at a joint meeting of the NATO Foreign and Defence Ministers as long ago as 19 December 1950 and on 9 May 1955 the German Federal Republic formally entered NATO as its fifteenth member. German military representatives made their official entry to SHAPE, where they were received on 9 May 1955 by General Gruenther (US), the Supreme Allied Commander, and Général Lehr, representing the French Ministry of Defence. The German representatives, who were in civilian

clothes, were led by Major-General Hans Speidel, the former Chief of Staff to the late Field Marshal Erwin Rommel, and an adviser to Dr Adenauer on defence matters. The black over red over gold flag of the German Federal Republic was formally hoisted at SHAPE side by side with the flags of the other fourteen NATO member countries. Arrangements were also made for a certain number of German officers to join the international staff at SHAPE and that a German military delegation, equivalent to the delegations maintained by the other NATO countries, would be installed there.

The first German divisions under NATO Command The first three of the twelve projected West German Army divisions were officially placed under the command of the Supreme Allied Commander on 5 July 1957 at a ceremony held at Marburg in the presence of General Norstad (USA), Général Valluy (France) (C-in-C Allied Forces, Central Europe), Generalleutnant Speidel (FRG) (Commander of Allied Land Forces, Central Europe) and General Heusinger (Inspector-General of the Bundeswehr). The three divisions were of the Panzer-Grenadier (Armoured Infantry) type, equipped with light armour.

The first operational Luftwaffe squadron The first operational unit of the new Luftwaffe, a transport squadron equipped with French aircraft, was made available to NATO on 24 August 1957.

Final West German Panzer Division raised for NATO The twelfth Panzer (Armoured) Division of the Bundeswehr, the last to be raised under the Federal Government's NATO obligation, was handed over to NATO Command at Würzburg on 10 April 1965.

The first West German Army unit to train in Great Britain The first ever West German Army unit to make use of military training grounds in the United Kingdom, the 84th

Panzer-Battalion, began exercises at the tank-firing range at Castlemartin, Pembrokeshire, in September 1961. The Commanding Officer of the 84th Panzer-Battalion, Oberstleutnant Karl-Wilhelm von Kleist, arrived at Castlemartin on 10 August 1961 with seven other German officers on a two-day visit to inspect the camp and range. An advance party of 50 men reached Castlemartin on 25 August and the last contingent of the armoured battalion arrived on 4 September. The battalion's 40 tanks, transport and ammunition were brought to Pembrokeshire by sea.

The first German troops in Denmark since the Second World War A unit of the Bundesheer visit Denmark from 14 to 20 March 1965 and took part, along with Danish and British troops, in NATO exercises in Jutland. The unit – comprising 169 officers and men – was the first German Army force to be permitted on to Danish soil since the Federal Republic's entry into NATO, although Danish and West German naval forces had previously co-operated in manoeuvres in the Baltic. The presence of the German troops gave rise to some hostile demonstrations on 16–17 March in the garrison town of Randers where they were quartered.

West German Border Protection Police Formed in 1951, the Bundesgrenzschutz perform an important duty in the policing of the borders and the defence of the Federal Republic, both on land and on water. Today the Border Protection Police undertake a variety of tasks ranging from their original function to uphold or to restore public safety and order within the Federal frontier regions, through the

supervision of frontier traffic at border crossing-points (1953) to its most recent role, that of a special federal police force with security functions within the interior of the Federal Republic (1973). In the event of armed conflict, the Border Guard commands, the units and the task forces, including the 'Grenzschutzschule' would be assigned to the Federal German armed forces, the members of the Bundesgrenzschutz being classed as combatants but with their function to perform its policing duties, rather than military ones.

The now famous GSG 9, the Federal Border Guard Group 9 Special, staffed by Grenzschutz personnel was established on 26 September 1972 in the wake of the 'Black September' Palestine terrorist attack on the Israeli athletes at the Munich Olympics of that year.

France withdraws from NATO In his first press conference since being re-elected to the Presidency, General de Gaulle announced on 21 February 1966 his Government's intention to withdraw progressively from NATO although not from the Alliance as such. Fourteen days later General de Gaulle wrote to President Lyndon B. Johnson. In his letter he reiterated France's determination that, even after the 1969 withdrawal date, France would be ready to fight on the side of her allies in the event that any one of them should be the object of an unprovoked aggression. France was determined, however, to regain for her whole territory the full exercise of her sovereignty, which he considered to be diminished by the permanent presence of Allied military elements or by the use which was made of her airspace. He therefore served notice

Left: A tri-national military police patrol at the French Supreme Headquarters Allied Powers Europe. In addition to being responsible for the security of the Headquarters their main business was investigating vehicle accidents.

to cease France's participation in the integrated Commands and no longer to place her forces at the disposal of the North Atlantic Treaty Organization.

NATO facilities in France At the time of President de Gaulle's announcement of the impending withdrawal of France from NATO the following Allied installations and facilities existed on French territory and in French airspace:

■ Supreme Headquarters Allied Powers Europe (SHAPE) at Rocquencourt, outside Paris (see page 21) which was staffed with about 600 officers and 2,000 men from the fourteen member-countries.

■ Headquarters Allied Forces Central Europe (AFCENT) under the French Commander-in-Chief, Général Jean Crépin, based at Fontainebleau, with a staff of 2,100 Allied officers and men. (See page 21).

■ The French sector of the early warning radar system, into which France had agreed to be integrated in September 1960 and which was in the processes of being converted to the automatic NATO Air Defence Ground Environment system (NADGE).

■ The French sector of the intricate NATO communications system which included the 'forward scatter' radio chain from Norway to Turkey.

■ The integrated air defence covering part of Eastern France, which the French Government had accepted subject to certain conditions by agreement of September 1960.

■ Allied overflying rights in French airspace, with the exception of aircraft carrying nuclear weapons. Permission for this category of aircraft had never been given. Allied overflying rights had been based on agreements dating back to 1951 with authorization granted by France, virtually automatically, on an annual basis.

■ The principal US bases and facilities in France were:
(a) US European Command Headquarters at Saint-Germain-en-Laye, near Paris (Camp des Loges);
(b) US Army Communications Zone, Europe, at Orléans;
(c) Four main air bases – at Châteauroux (Déols-La-Martinierie), Evreux, Laon and Toul-Rozières – and several standby bases;
(d) Some twenty Army supply depots which held stocks for the US forces based in Germany, three of which, however, were already in the process of being closed down due to US defence economic measures;
(e) The US oil pipeline which ran from Donges, near Saint-Nazaire, to Huttenheim (Bas-Rhin, Alsace) and which had been laid to supply both air and Army units;
(f) Naval access facilities at Villefranche-sur-Mer, Saint-Nazaire, La Rochelle and Bordeaux although Bremerhaven on the north German coast had by that time virtually replaced La Rochelle and Bordeaux as the main supply port for US forces in Germany. Some 30,000 US military and civilian personnel were stationed at these French bases, with some 37,000 dependents with a further 18,000 French staff being employed.

■ The Headquarters of the Royal Canadian Air Force at Metz and the base at Marville, which was both the station for the CF-104 reconnaissance squadrons and also the Atlantic supply terminal for Canadian NATO forces in Germany and Canadian units serving with the United Nations forces in Cyprus and the Gaza strip. Both Canadian bases had a staff of some 3,500 personnel and employed a further 500 French workers.

■ West German training facilities, which had been regulated by annual agreements since October 1960 and overflying rights for Luftwaffe aircraft on missions to Portugal.

French forces in Germany French forces assigned to NATO and other aspects of French participation in the NATO defence structure were:

■ One Army Corps in Germany which comprised two divisions each of three brigades, stationed mainly in Rhineland-Palatinate and Baden-Württemberg, with an Anti-Aircraft regiment of Hawk missiles in Bavaria, all of which totalled some 65,000 men under Général Jacques Massu, who since November 1965 had held the post of French Commander-in-Chief in Germany, and which formed part of the Central Army Group of Général Crépin's NATO AFCENT command. French armaments in Germany included Honest John missiles equipped with nuclear warheads, but under US control. (The French garrison in Berlin, which consisted of some 2,000 troops, did not form part of the NATO forces.)

■ The First Tactical Air Command, with aircraft that were stationed partly in France and partly at the German air bases of Ramstein, Lahr and Bremgarten and included two Air Force Anti-Aircraft Nike-Ajax and Nike-Hercules missile battalions at Stettin, Munsingen and Frederikshavn. These formed part of the Fourth Allied Tactical Air Force (4ATAF) (see also page 38).

■ French membership of the Military Committee and the Standing Group; French personnel at SHAPE, AFCENT and NATO Southern Europe and Mediterranean commands, and membership of the Channel Committee. Following the French withdrawal from the Atlantic Command staff in 1964, French naval personnel had been attached to SACLANT's HQ as 'national' liaison officers.

■ French utilization of reciprocal overflying rights and joint NATO facilities, especially in the air defence sphere which included the radar early warning shield.

The timetable for the French withdrawal from NATO and the removal of NATO installations from France On 29 March 1966 the French Government laid down a formal timetable for its withdrawal from NATO.

■ Withdrawal of French forces in Western Germany from NATO Command on 1 July 1966, but readiness to discuss with the Federal Government arrangements for the French forces to remain in the Federal Republic;

■ Withdrawal of French personnel from Allied commands and staffs on or about 1 July 1966, but readiness to maintain French liaison missions;

■ SHAPE, AFCENT and the NATO Defence College to leave French territory by 1 April 1967, but readiness to discuss other problems bilaterally or multilaterally;

■ Withdrawal requested of most US and Canadian installations by 1 April 1967, but the possibility of longer time-limits for the more complex US items and of discussion with the United States on the pipeline problem;

■ Readiness for talks with the USA and Canada on practical measures arising from past Franco-American agreements, and on agreements on facilities in the event of a conflict involving the Atlantic Alliance.

A Ministerial Council meeting was held in June 1966 when the fourteen member countries, with French acquiescence, agreed to find new locations for Supreme Headquarters Allied Powers Europe, Allied Forces Central Europe and the NATO Defence College; to simplify the command structure of AFCENT; and to replace the Standing Group by an integrated international Military Staff. The future site of the Council was also discussed, but a decision to transfer it from Paris to Brussels was not finally taken until the December (1966) Ministerial meeting of the North Atlantic Council.

Withdrawal of French forces from NATO Command All French forces were withdrawn from NATO Command on 1 July 1966. The previous day the French Government had been informed by the US Ambassador in Paris that, coincident with the French withdrawal, nuclear warheads would no longer be available to the French forces in Western Germany. On 7 September 1966 the NATO Council was informed that as from 1 January 1967, the French Government would cease its financial contribution towards the costs of the Alliance's installations and most of its military budgets. The French were also not prepared to contribute towards the cost of transferring SHAPE from Paris and its relocation in Belgium. The French, however, wished to continue their participation in the, then new, NATO Ground Defence Environment System (NADGE), in SHAPE's technical research centre at The Hague, the anti-submarine warfare centre at La Spezia (Italy) and the management organization of the Hawk missile. They were prepared to continue to share in the costs of these projects.

A week later, on 14 September, the Council was further informed of France's intention to withdraw from NATO's Military Committee at the end of that month and that her representation would be limited to a liaison mission. On 29 September France served notice of her withdrawal from the Council's Annual Review Committee.

NATO Headquarters moved from Paris to Brussels France's insistence that all NATO military establishments be required to leave French soil by 1 April 1967 did not include the 'political' headquarters of NATO, situated as they were in Paris (see page 20). The permanent representatives of the NATO Council decided, however, that the logic of having the military and the political headquarters in close proximity in one capital city was sufficient reason to justify a move. On 26 October 1966 it was announced that the NATO Headquarters would be moved from Paris to Brussels. The Belgian Government offered NATO a permanent site for the new headquarters at Le Heysel, formerly occupied by the French Pavilion during the Brussels International Exhibition of 1958, on the northern outskirts of Brussels. A new temporary headquarters at Evere, north-east of the Belgian capital, was also offered and work on this site started on 20 March 1967.

The new, and supposedly temporary, Headquarters of NATO – built on the 50-acre site of a disused airfield in the Brussels suburb of Evere, three miles from the centre of the city and on the road to the Brussels international airport – were officially inaugurated on 16 October 1967.

NATO's former Paris headquarters were closed down without ceremony on 18 October 1967. These new, temporary, headquarters, which have since become the established permanent headquarters, were built at an estimated cost of 400,000,000 Belgian francs (US $8,000,000 to $8,500,000). They consist of eighteen three-storey buildings linked by corridors and covering more than 30,000 square yards, housing 1,320 offices and capable of accommodating some 2,000 people, including 1,000 members of the International Secretariat, 550 members of the sixteen national delegations, and 390 officials of the Military Committee. There are also seventeen conference rooms, a communications centre that provides direct links through SHAPE's satellite communications system between the national delegations and their Governments, a restaurant seating 2,200 people and a car park for 1,500 vehicles. The total cost of the 1966 transfer was put at 700,000,000 Belgian francs or about US $14,000,000.

The relocation of Supreme Headquarters Allied Powers Europe The Belgian Government, after consultations with its Benelux partners, agreed on 10 June 1966 to the transfer of SHAPE from Rocquencourt, France to Belgium. This decision was ratified by both Houses of the Belgian Parliament on 21–22 June 1966 and the task of finding a suitable site was given to an inter-ministerial committee. On 20 June the Belgian Government proposed to NATO a location in the Chièvres-Casteau area near Mons and about 30 miles from Brussels; this site also offered a fully operational military airfield and the completion of the Mons-Brussels motorway once NATO had confirmed the choice of venue.

After a visit to the proposed site early in August 1966, the Supreme Allied Commander, General Lemnitzer (USA) was reported to have expressed dissatisfaction with the proposal on the grounds of poor communications, and to have indicated his preference for the area between Waterloo and Wavre, nearer to Brussels. On receiving his report the then NATO Secretary-General Signor Brosio (Italy) asked the Belgian Government for a new location, but the latter declined to suggest an alternative site and eventually, on 14 September 1966, the full NATO Council accepted the offer of Casteau. It was estimated that the total cost of the move from Paris was £15m and that of the construction of the new SHAPE more than £5m.

The new SHAPE complex Work on the new SHAPE complex began in October 1966, and on 31 March 1967 the Headquarters was officially opened by General Lemnitzer twelve months and three weeks from the date of the French Government's request for NATO to leave France. Eighteen buildings had been completed, including a communications centre and living accommodation for 1,200 officers and men. The speed of the construction was reported to have been largely due to the efforts of the Belgian inter-ministerial committee and its executive group headed by Count de Kerckhove de Denterghem, a former Ambassador to the Belgian Congo. On 30 March 1967 SHAPE at Rocquencourt formally closed.

Removal of Headquarters Allied Forces Central Europe from Fontainebleau to Brunssum On 11 October 1966 the NATO Council approved the removal of the headquarters of AFCENT from Fontainebleau, France to the Dutch province of Limburg, the Netherlands Government having offered a site in the village of Brunssum, near Maastricht, about 140 miles south-east of The Hague. The move took effect at the beginning of April 1967, when the new AFCENT Headquarters occupied the buildings of the former Hendrik State colliery at Brunssum.

The dissolution of LANDCENT, AIRCENT and NAVCENT Allied Land Forces Central Europe (LANDCENT), together with Allied Air Forces Central Europe (AIRCENT) and Allied Naval Forces Central Europe (NAVCENT) ceased to exist as separate entities on 15 November 1966 when their Headquarters were merged with those of Allied Forces Central Europe (AFCENT) and their personnel were placed under the direct orders of the then new Commander-in-Chief Allied Land Forces Central Europe.

Greece and Turkey: towards membership of NATO On 4 October 1950 it was announced in Washington, Ankara and Athens that both Turkey and Greece had accepted an invitation by the NATO Council to be associated with the planning work of the Alliance with regard to Mediterranean defence.

The following year the Foreign Ministers of the then twelve NATO member countries met in Ottawa, Canada (16–20 September 1951) and at the end of the conference announced, among other resolutions, unanimous agreement for the admission of Greece and Turkey to the North Atlantic Treaty Alliance.

By 15 February 1952 all the NATO countries had informed the US Government of their acceptance of Greece and Turkey as full members of the Alliance. The two countries would become full members of the Organization as soon as their respective Parliaments had ratified the treaty. This action was taken by the Greek Chamber of Deputies and the Turkish Kamutay (Grand National Assembly) on 18 February 1952.

Anti-Greek riots in Turkish cities: a threat to NATO unity Serious anti-Greek riots occurred on 6 September 1955 in Istanbul and Izmir (Smyrna), and to a lesser extent in Ankara, following incidents in Salonika on the previous day in which the windows of the Turkish Consulate in Salonika, and also of a house next to the Consulate in which Kemal Atatürk was born, were smashed by the explosion of a stick of dynamite. Five persons were detained in connexion with the Salonika incident, which caused no casualties and only minor damage. For several hours during the evening of 6 September mobs of Turkish youths roamed the streets of Istanbul smashing and looting Greek-owned shops and houses and setting fire to Greek property, including a number of Greek Orthodox churches. Many Greek shopkeepers and householders, with their families, were driven into the streets or were forced to hoist the Turkish flag above their premises and on the property of Armenian and Jewish citizens.

In Izmir, where the Headquarters of the NATO South-East European Command is located, mobs attacked houses occupied by Greek officers, setting fire to their homes and ill-treating the officers. In Ankara tear-gas was used to disperse several thousand demonstrators who attempted to march on the Greek Embassy.

In Istanbul, where the streets were described as resembling 'a battlefield', the Turkish police made little or no attempt to deal with the rioters, and order was only restored towards midnight, when an infantry division and an armoured brigade entered the city. The Turkish military authorities placed Istanbul under a state of siege, imposed a curfew, and stationed troops with fixed bayonets in front of Greek-owned premises to prevent further looting. Hundreds of Greek-owned shops and other premises were sacked during these riots, particularly in the suburb of Pera, and more than twenty Greek Orthodox churches were destroyed wholly or in part.

Greece withdraws its troops from NATO manoeuvres In view of the anti-Greek riots that had taken place in Istanbul and Izmir on 6 September 1955 the new Greek Government of M. Karamanlis announced on 11 October that the Greek armed forces would not take part in NATO manoeuvres which were to be held during that month in the eastern Mediterranean, and that the Greek battalion serving in Korea would also be recalled as soon as possible. The Greek authorities stated that these measures had been taken as a protest against the 'passive attitude' of NATO after the anti-Greek incidents in Turkey and that Greece's attitude would remain unchanged until the Turkish Government gave moral and material satisfaction.

Greece renews its participation in NATO manoeuvres Six months after the withdrawal of its troops Greek forces resumed participation in NATO exercises during March 1956 when two Greek submarines took part in naval and air manoeuvres in the Tyrrhenian Sea along with British, US, Italian and Turkish units. However, owing to tension with Great Britain over the island of Cyprus and the EOKA campaign, and because the Greek Government considered that Turkey had not yet made satisfactory amends for the anti-Greek riots of September 1956, the Greek crews were instructed not to fraternize with British and Turkish personnel and to boycott the 'social' side of the exercises.

Events leading to the withdrawal of Greek armed forces from NATO On 15 July 1974 a major international crisis erupted at the eastern end of the Mediterranean as a result of the overthrow of Archbishop Makarios, President of Cyprus, by a military *coup* led by Greek officers of the Cypriot National Guard and the resultant assumption of power by Nicos Sampson, an extremist Greek-Cypriot politician and former EOKA terrorist (gunman).

The seizure of power by Nicos Sampson was followed on 20 July by a Turkish invasion of Cyprus, and two days later, in response to a resolution by the United Nations Security Council, by a cease-fire after the Turkish Army had succeeded in capturing Kyrenia, the only port on the north coast of Cyprus, and a triangle of territory between Kyrenia and Nicosia, the capital. This development, coupled with the fall of the military regime in Greece and the restoration of a civilian government in that country, led in turn to the resignation of Nicos Sampson after barely a week in power, and to the swearing-in as President of Cyprus of Mr Glafkos Clerides, Speaker of the House of Representatives and leader of the Greek-Cypriot delegation in the inter-communal negotiations with the Turkish Cypriots.

Hostilities, cease-fires and peace talks The first phase of the peace talks between Greece and Turkey which opened in Geneva on 25 July 1974 following the Cyprus cease-fire of 2 July, ended on 30 July in agreement on a cease-fire line and the establishment of a security zone between the Greek and Turkish forces. However, the breakdown of the second phase of the talks dealing with the constitutional future of Cyprus led on 14 August 1974 to renewed hostilities and a second cease-fire two days later.

Greece withdraws its armed forces from the Alliance A war council held at the Greek general headquarters outside Athens under the chairmanship of Mr Konstantinos Karamanlis – the Greek Prime Minister – decided on 14 August 1974 to withdraw Greek armed forces from NATO. At that time Greece had an army of 120,000 men, a 22,000-strong air force and an 18,000-man navy. A Government statement at the conclusion of the meeting said: 'After the Atlantic Alliance demonstrated its inability to prevent Turkey from creating a state of conflict between two allies, the Prime Minister ordered that the Greek armed forces should be withdrawn from NATO. Greece shall remain a member of the Alliance only in connexion with its political aspects.' The decision was later 'unanimously approved' at an emergency Cabinet meeting. Greece, in accordance with its decision to withdraw from NATO's integrated defence structure, has ceased to be a member of the Defence Planning Committee since September 1974.

Greece re-integrates into NATO's military command structure The return of Greece to NATO's military command structure had been approved by NATO's Defence Planning Committee in permanent session on 20 October 1980 on the basis of a formula worked out by General Bernard Rogers (US), Supreme Allied Commander Europe (SACEUR), in consultation with Greek and Turkish military leaders. Greece had withdrawn from the NATO Command structure in August 1974 in protest against the Turkish invasion of Cyprus. Since 1977 Turkey had blocked Greece's return by insistence on the pre-1974 NATO Command structure which gave Turkey the exclusive air and sea control of the Aegean, while at the same time demanding broader operational rights in the area. Under the Rogers formula, however, both sides agreed that Greece should return in accordance with the pre-1974 structure on the understanding that permanent arrangements in the Aegean would be negotiated later.

Continuing protests, continuing boycots Naval and air exercises by NATO forces in the Aegean area from 1984 to mid-1986 were boycotted by Greece, continuing a policy begun in October 1983 in protest over the Alliance's support for Turkey on the question of the militarization of Lemnos. During these exercises, which involved US, Turkish and other forces, the Greek Government frequently complained of violations of its airspace by Turkish and US fighter aircraft.

At a meeting of NATO Defence Ministers in Brussels on 5 December 1984 Dr Papandreou offered to assign Greek forces on Lemnos to NATO. This was vetoed by Mr Zeki Yavuztürk, the Turkish Defence Minister, whose own defence plan for 1985 submitted to NATO was then vetoed by Dr Papandreou. As a result no Greek or Turkish forces were committed to NATO for 1985, and Greece ceased to participate in any NATO manoeuvres, having previously taken part in exercises outside the Aegean region.

Spain invited to join the North Atlantic Treaty Organization At a ceremonial plenary session of the North Atlantic Council held in Brussels on 10 December 1981, the fifteen NATO Foreign Ministers signed a Protocol of Accession inviting Spain to become the sixteenth member of the Organization. Speaking at the ceremony, the Spanish Foreign Minister, Sr José Pedro Perez-Llorca, said that Spain had regained 'not without effort, a democratic system with public freedoms and respect for human rights'. Its decision to join NATO was inspired by 'the will to support those values and to reaffirm our presence in Europe and in the West'.

Spain had formally applied to join NATO on 2 December and the initiative had been welcomed the same day by the then Secretary-General of NATO, Dr Joseph Luns. According to existing procedures, Spain's accession to NATO, following negotiations on the detailed terms, would be subject to the ratification of the Protocol of Accession by each individual member country, and would take effect on the day the Spanish instrument of accession was deposited with the United States Government. Ratification was forthcoming in January–February 1982 by Canada, Norway, Belgium, Turkey and Iceland and also approved by the Italian and Portuguese Governments prior to its submission to their respective Parliaments.

Spain's accession to NATO Spain became the sixteenth member of NATO on 30 May 1982 after Sr Alonso Alvarez de Toledo, the Spanish chargé d'affaires in Washington, deposited the formal instrument of ratification with Mr Walter Stoessel, the US Deputy Secretary of State. Spain's membership of NATO came only a few months before the Spanish Socialist Workers' Party (PSOE) was elected in October 1982 on a platform which included plans to hold a referendum on withdrawal from NATO.

The Socialist Workers' Party of Spain attempt to remove Spain from NATO In a statement to the Cortes (the Spanish Parliament) on 25 October 1984 the Prime Minister, Sr Felipe Gonzales, announced that a referendum would be held in February 1986 on whether Spain should continue to be a member of NATO. Sr Gonzalez said that he would seek to maintain Spain's present status as a member of the Alliance's political structure without military integration (shades of General de Gaulle), but would also seek an adjustment in the 1982 bilateral treaty on United States bases in Spain to reduce progessively the US military presence.

The Spanish people vote to stay in NATO On 12 March 1986 a referendum was held on the subject of Spain's continued membership of the Atlantic Alliance, although without participation in NATO's integrated military structure, with a maintenance of the ban on the installation, storage or introduction of nuclear arms and with a progressive reduction of the US military presence in Spain. The Socialist Government favoured the continuance of membership, which was supported by 9,054,509 votes and opposed by 6,872,421, with 1,127,673 blank and 191,855 spoilt papers in a 59.4 per cent poll.

Allied Command Europe

The North Atlantic Treaty Organization's military command in Europe is Allied Command Europe (ACE). This is one of three major NATO Commands, the other two being Allied Command Atlantic (ACLANT), responsible for the Atlantic Ocean (see page 46) and Allied Command Channel (ACCHAN) which has the English Channel as its area of responsibility (see page 48). Allied Command Europe covers the area extending from the North Cape, the northern most tip of Norway, to the Mediterranean, and from the Atlantic to the eastern border of Turkey, excluding the United Kingdom and Portugal, the defence of which does not fall under any one Major NATO Command. This area represents nearly two million square kilometres of land and more than 3 million square kilometres of sea. (See map overleaf).

SHAPE – Supreme Headquarters Allied Powers Europe The European area is under the Supreme Allied Commander Europe (SACEUR), whose headquarters, near Mons in Belgium, is known as SHAPE, the Supreme Headquarters Allied Powers Europe. SHAPE is the senior ACE Headquarters. From SHAPE SACEUR directs efforts to unify defence measures, strengthen his military forces and plan for their most effective use in an emergency. At SHAPE and at other ACE Headquarters, integrated staffs drawn from the NATO nations work to broaden and improve the military capability of this defensive Alliance. Throughout the ACE area, land, sea and air exercises continually test and develop international teamwork towards achievement of the goals of NATO. Fourteen of the North Atlantic countries maintain a National Military Representative (NMR) at SHAPE, providing military liaison with the Allied Chiefs-of-Staff. France has a military liaison mission at SHAPE. SACEUR and his Deputy Supreme Allied Commander are assisted by political and scientific advisers in addition to the usual military staff advisers.

The mission of Allied Command Europe ACE supports the objectives of NATO – peace, security and freedom – by standing as a military deterrent to any would-be aggressor. Should this deterrent ever be challenged, ACE would defend the 320 million peoples of NATO Europe against any aggressor. In peacetime SACEUR's main functions are to prepare and finalize defence plans for the area under his command, and to ensure the combat efficiency of forces assigned to him in the event of war. SACEUR also makes recommendations to the Military Committee on matters likely to improve the organization of his command. Forces assigned to ACE remain under national command, however; communications and air defence are always SACEUR responsibilities – maintaining constant vigilance and the ability for instant response if needed.

In time of war SACEUR would lead forces which NATO nations have committed to achieve the ACE mission. SACEUR would also control all land, sea and air operations in this area. Internal defence and the defence of coastal waters remain the responsibility of the national authorities to carry out such operations as SACEUR considered necessary for the defence of any part of the area under his Command.

Commands subordinate to Allied Command Europe ACE is subdivided into a number of subordinate Commands:

- Allied Forces Northern Europe (AFNORTH) (see page 33).
- Allied Forces Central Europe (AFCENT) (see page 36).
- Allied Forces Southern Europe (AFSOUTH) (see page 39).
- ACE Mobile Force (see page 43).
- United Kingdom Air Forces (UKAIR) (see page 45).

AFNORTH, AFCENT, and AFSOUTH are in turn subdivided into a number of subordinate commands, all of which are dealt with under their respective headings. The ACE Mobile Force is composed of both land and air force units supplied by different member nations. It can be ready for action at very short notice in any threatened area and in particular on the northern and southern flanks of the European Command.

United States European Command The Supreme Allied Commander Europe has, by common consent, always been a US general. This was agreed upon from the beginning of the Alliance and it was further agreed that SACEUR would be responsible for the exercise of control over the United States military commands in Europe. In the early 1950s it was recognized by the United States Joint Chiefs of Staff and the Secretary of Defence that there was a need for a joint command to be set up in Europe that would centralize peacetime control of all United States forces serving in Europe. Accordingly, on 1 August 1952 the Joint Chiefs of Staff established the United States European Command (USEUCOM) with instructions to the Commanders of the United States Army, Navy and Air Force to report directly to the Commander-in-Chief Europe (USCINCEUR). The primary mission of USEUCOM is to provide combat-ready forces to support US commitments to the NATO Alliance, and this includes war planning for both conventional and nuclear wartime operations.

United States Army Europe Headquarters of the United

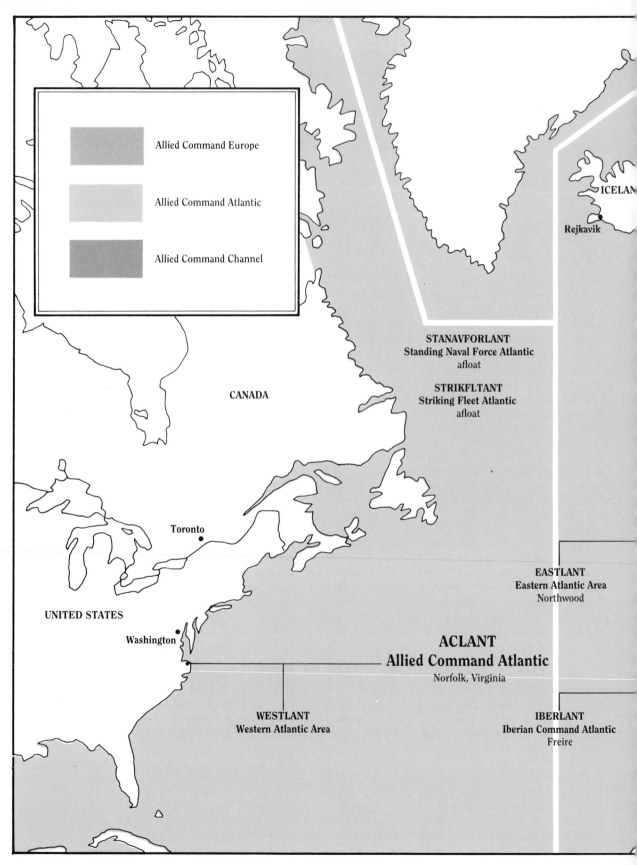

Allied Command Europe

Allied Command Atlantic

Allied Command Channel

ICELAN

Rejkavik

STANAVFORLANT
Standing Naval Force Atlantic
afloat

STRIKFLTANT
Striking Fleet Atlantic
afloat

CANADA

Toronto

EASTLANT
Eastern Atlantic Area
Northwood

UNITED STATES

Washington

ACLANT
Allied Command Atlantic
Norfolk, Virginia

WESTLANT
Western Atlantic Area

IBERLANT
Iberian Command Atlantic
Freire

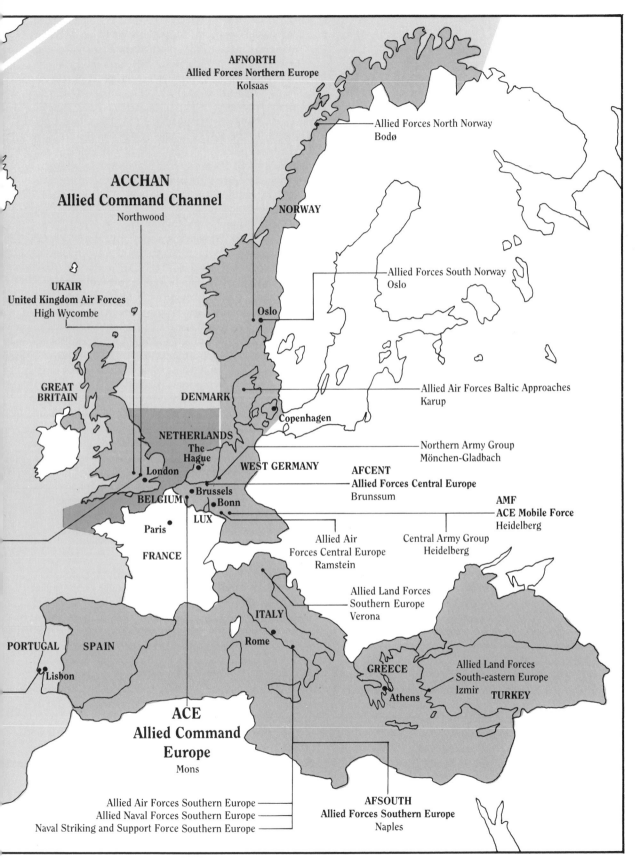

AFNORTH
Allied Forces Northern Europe
Kolsaas

Allied Forces North Norway
Bodø

**ACCHAN
Allied Command Channel**
Northwood

NORWAY

Allied Forces South Norway
Oslo

**UKAIR
United Kingdom Air Forces**
High Wycombe

Oslo

GREAT
BRITAIN

Allied Air Forces Baltic Approaches
Karup

DENMARK

Copenhagen

NETHERLANDS
The
Hague

Northern Army Group
Mönchen-Gladbach

London

WEST GERMANY

**AFCENT
Allied Forces Central Europe**
Brunssum

**Brussels
Bonn

BELGIUM

LUX

**AMF
ACE Mobile Force**
Heidelberg

Paris

Allied Air
Forces Central Europe
Ramstein

Central Army Group
Heidelberg

FRANCE

Allied Land Forces
Southern Europe
Verona

ITALY

Rome

PORTUGAL   SPAIN

GREECE

Allied Land Forces
South-eastern Europe
Izmir

Lisbon

Athens

TURKEY

**ACE
Allied Command
Europe**
Mons

Allied Air Forces Southern Europe
Allied Naval Forces Southern Europe
Naval Striking and Support Force Southern Europe

**AFSOUTH
Allied Forces Southern Europe**
Naples

States Army in Europe (USAREUR), shared with the US Seventh Army, is at Heidelberg (FRG). The Seventh Army is the largest US deployed Field Army, numbering three armoured divisions, two armoured cavalry regiments, four infantry divisions and numerous other supporting units. The chief tactical elements of the US Seventh Army are the V and VII Army Corps with headquarters at Frankfurt-on-Main and Stuttgart respectively. These two Corps are made up of the following units: 1st Armoured Division 'Old Ironsides'; 2nd Armoured Division (FWD) 'Hell on Wheels'; 3rd Armoured Division 'Spearhead'. They have the 2nd and 11th Armoured Cavalry Regiments, 1st Infantry Division (FWD), and 3rd, 4th and 8th Infantry Divisions. The two Corps also deploy the following Brigades: 17th, 41st, 42nd, 56th, 72nd and 210th Field Artillery Brigades; 18th Engineer Brigade, 22nd Signals Brigade and 59th Ordnance Brigade.

Other USAREUR Major Commands are: the US Army Berlin; US Army Southern European Task Force (see page 43); 2nd, 3rd and 21st Support Commands; 32nd Air Defence Command; 7th Medical Command; 1st Personnel Command and 4th Transportation Command. The Commander USAREUR is also the Commander of NATO's Central Army Group (CENTAG) having under his direct control the US Army Element of Central Army Group.

A selection of the Shoulder Sleeve Insignia worn by US personnel of some of the units listed above can be found on plate 64.

United States Air Forces in Europe The origin of the United States Air Forces in Europe (USAFE) can be traced back to the Second World War organization known as the United States Strategic Air Forces in Europe with headquarters initially located at St-Germain-en-Laye, France, moving later to Wiesbaden, Germany.

Activated in 1945 the Command shared in the occupation duties in the American Zones in both Germany and Austria, mainly concerned in disarming the remnants of the defeated Luftwaffe and disposing of vast quantities of surplus US War materials. Completion of these tasks in 1947 resulted in the Command's strength contracting to an administrative force. But in 1948 both men and aircraft from the United States Air Forces in Europe together with the Royal Air Force were heavily engaged in what has come to be known as the Berlin Airlift. The Soviet blockade of Berlin lasted for eleven months.

The formation of the North Atlantic Treaty Organization in August 1949 brought about a major change in the mission of the US Air Forces Command in Europe. A rapid build-up of the Command took place in preparation for its new military role within NATO. Rights were granted for the construction of several air bases in France, and airfield sites in the French Occupation Zone of Germany, west of the River Rhine, were also made available. This situation lasted until 1965 when a major reorganization of the United States Air Forces in Europe was brought about by the withdrawal of France from the Alliance and her request for the removal of all foreign troops from her soil. All USAFE bases were closed down and personnel and aircraft were moved to the Federal Republic of Germany and the United Kingdom.

Today the United States Air Forces in Europe is located at Ramstein (FRG) close to Kaiserlautern. It is commanded by a four star general who is also Commander of Allied Air Forces Central Europe in the NATO chain of command. The USAFE is made up of three numbered Air Forces: 3rd US Air Force, based at RAF Mildenhall, England; 16th US Air Force with headquarters at Torrejon, Spain; 17th US Air Force headquartered at Sembach Air Base, Federal Republic of Germany. There are 21 major operating bases spread out between the United Kingdom and Turkey with more than 650 operational aircraft. Through recent re-alignment and re-configuration of its forces and headquarters operations, United States Air Forces Europe is a streamlined, tightly managed, NATO-committed force possessing a greatly improved combat readiness posture.

United States Naval Forces Europe The US Naval Forces in Europe (USNAVEUR) comprises approximately 39,000 US Navy personnel and 5,000 US Marine Corps troops. Its headquarters are in London, England. The main operational forces are: US Sixth Fleet with about 45 ships, 31,000 personnel and 200 aircraft, organized into major combat groups which regularly patrol the Mediterranean. Combat Group 60 is an attack carrier striking force that consists of two aircraft carriers, two guided missile equipped cruisers together with accompanying destroyers. Combat Groups 61 and 62 are amphibious task forces consisting of amphibious attack transports and cargo ships, minesweepers and a variety of amphibious assault craft. Combat Group 62 is a combat-ready battalion landing team of about 2,000 US Marines. Combat Group 63 is a floating logistical base and service force which provides fuel and supplies to enable the US Sixth Fleet to stay at sea for indefinite periods.

Part of the strategic nuclear force available in the European theatre is the Fleet Ballistic Missile Submarine Force which, under normal peacetime conditions, is on patrol in the Mediterranean. Another integral part of the Sixth Fleet is the Anti-Submarine Warfare Force. Middle East Force, operating in the Indian Ocean, the Red Sea and the Persian Gulf, is also controlled by USNAVEUR.

Canadian Forces Europe Canadian Forces Europe have their headquarters at Lahr (FRG). It is a national entity under national command in peacetime and is directly responsible to the Chief of the Defence Staff in Ottawa, Canada, but it becomes available to the appropriate NATO commanders in time of war. Canadian Forces Europe is composed of two Major Subordinate Commands: Fourth Canadian Mechanized Brigade Group (4 CMBG) and First Canadian Air Group (1 CAG), both with headquarters at Lahr. Approximately two-thirds of the Command is located at Lahr with the rest at Baden-Söllingen.

■ *4 Canadian Mechanized Brigade Group.* This 3,300-strong Brigade Group is made up of the following units: 1st Regiment, Royal Canadian Horse Artillery; Royal Canadian Dragoons; 1st Battalion, Royal 22e Regiment; 4 Canadian Mechanized Brigade Group Headquarters and Signals Squadron; 444th Tactical Helicopter Squadron; 4 Field Ambulance; 4th Service Battalion; 4th CMBG Military Police Platoon and other major units supporting Canadian Forces Europe.

■ *1 Canadian Air Group.* The 800-man Air Group is the air operational unit of Canadian Forces Europe, equipped with CF-104 Starfighters in the fighter-bomber role. 1 CAG is an operational element of the Fourth Allied Tactical Air Force (4ATAF). The Group consists of Nos. 421, 439 and 441 Squadrons, based at Baden-Söllingen Air Base, Germany. The origins of Canada's NATO air commitment dates back to the early 1950s with the formation of the Royal Canadian Air Force's 1st Air Division. From its headquarters at Metz, France the Division commanded twelve Squadrons in four Wings, one each located at Marville and Grostenquin,

France and Zweibrucken and Baden-Söllingen, Germany. Each wing flew the F-86 Sabre, later joined by the CF-100 Super-Sabre all-weather fighter. In 1962 the CF-104 Starfighter arrived on the scene marking the change from air defence to the strike-reconnaissance role. After the move from France in 1967 and the subsequent various reorganizations, the Canadian Forces' Air Element in Europe was changed from 1st Canadian Air Division to 1 Canadian Air Group with its headquarters at Lahr and its operational units at Baden-Söllingen.

Headquarters Allied Forces Northern Europe

Headquarters AFNORTH was established in April 1951, its first location being in London (UK) before being moved to Holmenkollen north of Oslo, Norway. The present headquarters building at Kolsaas (Kolsås), fifteen kilometres west of Oslo, was built especially to house the staff of HQ AFNORTH, including personnel from Canada, Denmark, the Federal Republic of Germany, Norway, the United Kingdom and the United States. The Commander-in-Chief AFNORTH (CINCNORTH) is a United Kingdom four star general.

AFNORTH Strategic Area of Command The area of responsibility of HQ AFNORTH, comprises Norway, Denmark, the Federal Republic of Germany north of the river Elbe and the adjacent sea areas and air space. The strategic importance of northern Europe springs naturally from the geographic position of the areas concerned. For example, Norway is one of the two North Atlantic Treaty Organization nations having a common border with the Soviet Union, and in the south, Schleswig-Holstein is of particular importance to the defence of northern Europe and serves as an important link between the Northern and Central Regions of NATO.

In order to understand the defence problems of this Command, the enormous distances involved should be borne in mind. If it were possible to swing the land mass of Norway round, its southernmost tip would project south of Rome. So if the CINCNORTH were sitting in his headquarters in Oslo and was fighting a battle in Finnmark, the northernmost part of Norway, he would be about the same distance away as if he were in London fighting a battle in southern Italy.

AFNORTH, which stretches across a third of the NATO area in Europe, dominates the sea routes from the Baltic in the south to the Barents Sea in the north. It is also astride the direct air routes from Central Russia to the North-American continent. It provides vital early warning facilities and would,

in time of war, constitute an important base for allied counter-offensive operations.

Subordinate Commands AFNORTH AFNORTH is divided into three tactically separate but interdependent areas:
■ Allied Forces North Norway (DEFCOMNON).
■ Allied Forces South Norway (DEFCOMSONOR).
■ Allied Forces Baltic Approaches (BALTAP).

In peacetime, the Commander Allied Forces North Norway (COMNON) is a national commander with certain Alliance functions in addition to his national duties (see also page 35). Command subordinate to COMNON are Allied Land Forces North Norway (LANDNON), Allied Naval Forces North Norway (NAVNON) and Allied Air Forces North Norway (AIRNON). There is a unified command for South Norway with a tri-service commander (Commander Allied Forces South Norway – COMSONOR) (see also page 36). Subordinate commands of COMSONOR are Allied Land Forces South Norway (LANDSONOR), Allied Naval Forces South Norway (NAVSONOR) and Allied Air Forces South Norway (AIRSONOR). All allied forces in the Baltic area are subordinate to the Commander Allied Forces Baltic Approaches (COMBALTAP) (see page 35).

NATO and the original Commands of the North European Region The military organization of NATO was established in 1951, before West Germany joined the Alliance (see page 23), and it did not, therefore, provide a joint command for the Danish area. Instead the North European Region was organized with a COMLANDDENMARK, a COMLANDNORWAY, a COMNORTH (with the Norwegian and Danish navies earmarked), a COMAIRNORTH (with the Norwegian and Danish air forces earmarked), and with a wartime-designated Task Force Commander North Norway.

West Germany joined NATO in 1955 (see page 23), prompting a review of the Organization. During the subsequent negotiations, it was agreed that the border between the Northern Region and the Central Region should remain on the river Elbe, and that a joint tri-service command was needed for the area covering Denmark and Schleswig-Holstein. NATO instituted this new organization late in 1961 with the full agreement of Denmark and the Federal Republic of Germany.

Allied Land Forces Schleswig-Holstein and Jutland Shortly after the Second World War, Schleswig-Holstein was occupied by British troops. In 1948 a Norwegian brigade was transferred from Harz to Schleswig-Holstein. In 1949 a Danish brigade was moved from north-west Germany into the same area and designated the Danish Command in Germany. The arrival of these troops heralded the establishment of a co-ordinated defence planning group under the Commanding General of Western Land Command at Aarhus, Denmark. Military operations were conceived at this early stage as the concentration and deployment of all forces north of the Kiel Canal with only small reconnaissance units south of the Canal.

In 1953 an Allied Command Organization was created under the title of Allied Land Forces Schleswig-Holstein. It did not, however, have a NATO status at this time.

In 1958, some three years after the establishment of the Federal German Army, all foreign troops were withdrawn and the responsibility for the defence of Schleswig-Holstein was delegated to a German national headquarters. Through bilateral agreement, a number of Danish and British officers were attached as liaison officers to these new headquarters. This move represented the beginning of the co-ordinated planning for the defence of Schleswig-Holstein and Jutland together with combined exercise activity to be held in that area.

The establishment of Baltic Approaches Command Following talks between Danish and West German military representatives held at the Headquarters of Allied Powers, Northern Europe, it was announced in Oslo on 22 November 1961 that agreement had been reached on the establishment of a new, unified NATO Command covering Denmark and Northern Germany. The new command structure had been formally proposed to the Danish and German Federal Governments by General Norstad (SACEUR) in January 1961, but agreement on it was reported to have been delayed by the initial reluctance on the part of the Danes to accept a German commander for any part of their forces as suggested in the Norstad plan.

The agreed proposals, which were submitted to General Norstad for his approval of details, provided:

■ The setting up of a Baltic Approaches Command (BALTAP) which would, however, operate only in the event of war and during NATO exercises.

■ BALTAP, covering Denmark and Schleswig-Holstein together with the surrounding sea area, would be under a Danish commander (COMBALTAP) with a German deputy commander and a Danish chief of staff, and would remain responsible to the Allied Commander-in-Chief Northern Europe.

■ The new command area would comprise the following four sub-commands: (1) An air command under a Danish

Officer; (2) A command for land forces in East Denmark, i.e., the islands of Zealand and Bornholm, under a Danish officer; (3) A command for land forces in Jutland, Funen and Schleswig-Holstein, to be headed alternately by a Danish and a German officer.

The staff of the new Command was arranged so that one-third were Danish personnel, one-third West German personnel, and one-third made up of members from other NATO countries (initially suggested as British, American, Canadian and Norwegian). All individual units in the Command remained under officers of their own nationality.

Following the approval of the agreement by the Danish Parliament, General Tage Andersen was appointed by General Norstad on 8 December 1961 as the first Commander Baltic Approaches (COMBALTAP). General Andersen had been Commander-in-Chief Allied Air Forces, Northern Europe since July 1959 after having been Commander-in-Chief of the Danish Air Force, and was at the time the highest ranking Danish officer serving with NATO. Major-General Peter von der Gröben, the former West German commander of the 6th Panzer-Grenadier Division was appointed as Deputy Commander Baltic Approaches. Appointments to the four subsidiary commands were announced on 19 December 1961. In addition to the two Danish officers – Major-Generals H. J. Pagh and E. Kragh – appointed respectively to the Air Command (COMAIRBALTAP) and the land command in East Denmark (COMLANDZEALAND), a Danish officer, Major-General F. B. Larsen, became commander of the land forces in Jutland, Funen and Schleswig-Holstein (COMLANDJUT), while a German naval officer, Konteradmiral G. Wagner, became commander of the naval forces (COMNAVBALTAP).

The present Headquarters Allied Forces Baltic Approaches (HQ BALTAP) Headquarters BALTAP is one of the most recent Headquarters formed in NATO. It was established on 8 January 1962 in Karup, Jutland (Denmark) and activated on 1 July 1962. HQ BALTAP is one of the Principal Subordinate Commands under the authority of the ACE Major Subordinate Command, AFNORTH, and is under the overall control of the Commander-in-Chief Allied Forces Northern Europe (CINCNORTH) at Kolsås near Oslo, Norway. (See page 33). The Commander Allied Forces Baltic Approaches (COMBALTAP) is Danish, the Deputy Commander (COMBALTAP) is German and the Chief of Staff is Danish. The structure of the Headquarters staff proceeds from the principle of international and inter-service organization. It is composed of one-third Danish, one-third German and the remaining third composed of American, British and Norwegian military personnel. The command language, in which all conferences and communications are conducted, is English.

BALTAP Area of Command The Allied Command Baltic Approaches comprises Denmark and Schleswig-Holstein, including Hamburg, north of the River Elbe and the adjacent sea areas and air space. Guarding the gates of the Baltic, BALTAP reaches from Skagen to the River Elbe, and from the island of Bornholm to the North Sea off the mouth of the Elbe. Jutland and Schleswig-Holstein together form, from a topographical point of view, a single unit. The area is well equipped with road and rail services, and communications are simple. The flat area, of which 75 per cent is cultivated acreage, has only a few natural defence barriers such as the lake district and some marshy areas in Holstein; the Kiel Canal, which is 98 kilometres long and twelve metres deep, the Schlei Estuary, which narrows the land strip to 35 kilometres and some fiords in Jutland. The Danish islands are more complex, divided by the three major straits of the Little Belt, the Great Belt and the Sound, with minimum widths of 0.6 kilometres, fifteen kilometres and four kilometres respectively. The tactical problems involved in the defence of the islands are bound to be rather different from those faced by the Commander in Schleswig-Holstein and Jutland. The command area as a whole is, however, a strategic entity and constitutes a significant flank area for operations in Central Europe.

The mission of COMBALTAP Within the framework of NATO and under the direction of CINCNORTH it is the mission of COMBALTAP to plan for the defence of the territories of Denmark, the northern part of the Federal Republic of Germany and the adjacent waters known as the Baltic Approaches. This planning includes co-ordination of the activities of the subordinate commanders, co-operation with national authorities and adjacent NATO commanders, and conduct of exercises.

In peacetime, COMBALTAP's mission is to carry out planning, co-ordination, and training for the wartime combined operations of the Danish and Germany army, naval and air forces in his area of responsibility. In time of war, COMBALTAP will have operational command of Danish-German corps; Danish and German regular army and territorial forces; all Danish and German naval forces, including the German naval air arm; and all Danish and German air forces in the area. The defence effort will also be supported by the Danish Home Guard, consisting of 77,000 volunteers. Defence of this vital area will also involve the use of external allied reinforcements.

Subordinate Commands BALTAP The Commander BALTAP (COMBALTAP) is a tri-service commander, with an integrated and international staff. COMBALTAP has four subordinate commanders. For geographical reasons the land forces are under two separate commanders:

- Commander Allied Land Forces Schleswig-Holstein and Jutland COMLANDJUT.
- Commander Land Forces Zealand and Bornholm COM-LANDZEALAND.
- Commander Allied Naval Forces Baltic Approaches COM-NAVBALTAP.
- Commander Allied Air Forces Baltic Approaches COMAIR-BALTAP.

COMLANDJUT. COMLANDJUT has his headquarters in the Eider Barracks, Rendsburg and is responsible for the defence of Schleswig-Holstein, Jutland and Funen. In time of war he has operational command of the German 6th Panzer-Grenadier Division and the Danish Jutland Division (Jyske Divisionskommando), each consisting of three Brigades (1, 2 & 3 Jyske Brigades), plus some corps support units. HQLANDJUT is the only multi-national Corps Headquarters

within NATO with five nations represented at the Headquarters: Canada, Denmark, Germany, UK and USA.

The commander and chief-of-staff appointments of COMLANDJUT alternate between Danish and German officers in such a way that the commander and his chief of staff are always of different nationality.

COMLANDZEALAND. His Headquarters are on Zealand at Ringsted, having been moved from the original location at Copenhagen. He is responsible for the defence of the Danish islands east of the Great Belt, including Bornholm; he has a total of two brigades (1 and 2 Sjaellandske Brigades) plus some corps support units available on Zealand, and one reduced brigade on Bornholm. In addition to these units, there will be available after mobilization in Denmark, a number of local defence battalions, corresponding to the strength of five brigades, and the Home Guard with a total of 77,000 volunteers, men and women. In Schleswig-Holstein, national Territorial Defence Forces exist. Two special engineer battalions and some other units are also at his disposal; the establishing of the Danish Home Defence Forces (Heimatschutztruppe) started in April 1966. The Command Staff of COMLANDZEALAND and the Commander of LANDZEALAND (COMLANDZEALAND) will always be Danish.

COMNAVBALTAP. Has had his Headquarters at Karup since December 1976. With a few exceptions all operational Danish and German naval forces, including the German naval air arm, will, in time of war, come under his operational command. COMNAVBALTAP and his Chief of Staff will change nationalities in the same way as COMLANDJUT.

COMAIRBALTAP. Has his Headquarters at Karaup Air Base, north Denmark, and in time of war has operational command of the Danish Air Force and German Air Force (Luftwaffe) units, stationed at Schleswig-Holstein. These air forces comprise fighter-bomber, fighter, and tactical reconnaissance squadrons. COMAIRBALTAP and his Chiefs-of-Staff will change nationalities in the same way as COMLANDJUT.

Headquarters Allied Forces North Norway Headquarters Allied Forces North Norway is located at Reitan, near Bodoe, well north of the Arctic Circle. This is a joint tri-service headquarters manned by all-Norwegian personnel. The present organization was formally established on 1 September 1971, a new office building at Reitan being put into use on 1 March 1974.

The mission of COMNON In peacetime, the Commander Allied Forces North Norway (COMNON) is a national commander directly responsible to the Chief of Defence Norway (CHOD Norway). In the Allied chain of command, COMNON is a Principal Subordinate Commander to the Commander-in-Chief Allied Forces Northern Europe (CINCNORTH). The transfer to Allied command is to be decided by the Norwegian Government when the situation arises. Operational command of the air defence units, however, is exercised by CINCNORTH even in peacetime. The mission of Allied Forces North Norway is to ensure the defence of this critical flank area of Allied Command Europe's Northern Region. To carry out this mission, the Norwegian forces have available the full panoply of modern weapons. In addition, the use of external reinforcements will also be a vital part of NATO strategy in this area.

Commands subordinate to Allied Forces North Norway Directly under COMNON are the three service commanders:

- Commander Allied Land Forces North Norway (COMLANDNON);
- Commander Allied Naval Forces North Norway (COMNAVNON);
- Commander Allied Air Forces North Norway (COMAIRNON).

Operating under each of the three service commanders is a small staff element and an operations centre.

Headquarters Allied Forces South Norway Headquarters Allied Forces South Norway is located in the Norwegian capital of Oslo. In the structure of Allied Command Europe (ACE), this is a Principal Subordinate Command (PSC) under the Commander-in-Chief Allied Forces Northern Europe (CINCNORTH). In peacetime, this joint tri-service head-quarters operates under the national commander of Chief of Defence Norway (CHOD Norway) and is staffed by Norwegian military personnel only. The Commander Allied Forces South Norway (COMSONOR) is a Norwegian lieutenant-general or vice-admiral. Immediately subordinate to him are three single-service commanders with their staff elements and operational centres.

COMSONOR's mission The mission of the Commander Allied Forces South Norway is threefold:

- To defend the command area;
- To reinforce Allied Forces North Norway;
- To receive and employ external reinforcements.

In peacetime, the total command strength is restricted to standing units that total some 5,500 personnel. If mobilization is declared the army element will expand from approximately 1,400 to 11,000 troops; the navy from 1,300 to approximately 13,000; and the air force to about 18,500. In addition, the Norwegian Home Guard totals about 60,000 personnel.

Headquarters Allied Forces Central Europe

AFCENT is one of the four Major Subordinate Commands under the direct control of the Supreme Allied Commander Europe (SACEUR).

Headquarters AFCENT was first established at Fontainebleau, France, in 1951 (see page 21) and then moved to Brunssum in the Netherlands in April 1967 when France withdrew from the integrated military structure of the NATO Alliance (see page 26).

Commander-in-Chief AFCENT (CINCENT) is responsible for the defence of the Central Region of Allied Command Europe, which extends from the North Sea and the river Elbe to the borders of Austria and Switzerland (see map on page 31). CINCENT controls approximately 50 per cent of the total military forces under SHAPE.

AFCENT's mission The essential mission of AFCENT is to deter aggression against the Central Region and, should deterrence fail, to be prepared to defend the area on a line as far to the east as possible, using all available resources.

To be able to carry out these missions, peacetime activities include preparing emergency plans for joint strategy and tactics, training troops in international and Allied organizations, and ensuring the availability of logistics, administrative, and communications support. Credible deterrence and an effective fighting force, if necessary, demand no less.

Military forces from seven nations (Belgium, Canada, the Federal Republic of Germany, Luxembourg, the Netherlands, the United Kingdom and the United States) are assigned to AFCENT. With the exception of certain air defence and quick-reaction forces, these forces are under national command in peacetime, but are placed under CINCENT command for various exercises and when so directed by higher authority.

Commands subordinate to CINCENT Supporting CINCENT are three Principle Subordinate Commands:

(1) HQ Northern Army Group (NORTHAG) based at Mönchen-Gladbach, Federal Republic of Germany.

(2) HQ Central Army Group (CENTAG) at Heidelberg, West Germany (see page 37).

(3) HQ Allied Air Forces Central Europe (AAFCE) at Ramstein Air Base FRG (see page 38).

AAFCE has operational control, in turn, of two Allied Tactical Air Forces (AFAFs) – the Second ATAF and the Fourth ATAF (see page 38).

The Northern Army Group – NORTHAG NORTHAG was formed in 1952 and initially consisted of a Belgian, British and a Netherlands Army Corps, with a German Army Corps being added in 1957. The original NORTHAG Headquarters was established at Bad Oeynhausen (FRG) in November 1952 but moved to its present location in 1954.

Headquarters of the Northern Army Group is today located at Rheindahlen, Mönchen-Gladbach (FRG) and co-located with the Headquarters Second Allied Tactical Air Force (HQ TWOATAF) and two British national headquarters, Headquarters British Army of the Rhine (HQ BAOR) and Head-quarters Royal Air Force Germany (HQ RAFG).

This completely integrated, international headquarters is staffed by the four NATO nations who provide the four national Corps – Belgium, the United Kingdom, the Federal Republic of Germany and the Netherlands. These Corps remain under national command in peacetime coming under NATO command when the situation demands. The United States also provides a military element at the headquarters.

NORTHAG is one of the Principal Subordinate Commands under the Allied Command Europe (ACE) Major Subordinate Command, AFCENT. The Commander Northern European Army Group (COMNORTHAG) is a British general of four-star rank, who in peacetime is also Commander-in-Chief of the British Army of the Rhine.

The NORTHAG area of responsibility This area stretches approximately from Hamburg to Kassel (FRG), and from the Inner German Border to the Dutch and Belgian borders.

NORTHAG's mission NORTHAG's basic mission is to deter aggression against this vital area and to prepare together in peace to fight together in war to defend its part of NATO territory, should deterrence fail.

NORTHAG is a powerful and well-armed force of 200,000 men in peacetime, increasing to half a million in time of war. To carry out its mission each of the Corps is equipped with all the elements required to conduct battle in its area of responsibility. These include armoured, infantry, artillery, engineer, communications and logistic units.

Intensive peacetime training and regular exercises are conducted to ensure that NORTHAG's deterrent strength remains credible. The West German Leopard tank is NORTHAG's main battle tank, except for the 1st British Corps, which has the Chieftain. In general, the US series of artillery pieces M109 (155mm) howitzer, M107 (175mm), M110 (230mm) and Lance surface-to-surface missiles can be found with all Corps. The main air defence system is Gepard, employed by the German, Dutch and Belgian Corps. The British Corps is equipped with Rapier missiles.

Central Army Group Originally established in 1952 as part of United States Army Europe (USAEUR) based at Heidelberg, Central Army Group or CENTAG as it is referred to, has undergone a number of evolutionary changes over the years. In 1953 a full-time CENTAG Planning Group was formed within the USAEUR staff, which contained both French and US officers with German officers joining the Group in 1956. In December 1959 the CENTAG Planning Group became a provisional headquarters and in September 1960 the NATO Council of Ministers approved its reconstitution as a NATO Command (effective from 1 October 1960). This reorganization was in accordance with the recognized NATO principle of integrating headquarters at the Army Group and Tactical Air Force level. 1966 saw the withdrawal of the French troops from CENTAG, but in 1970 Canadian forces were committed to the Group and the Headquarters reverted to its tri-national status.

A year after being upgraded to a NATO Command the Central Army Group Headquarters were moved to a permanent home at Hammond Barracks near Mannheim in 1961. At its present Heidelberg headquarters, set up in December 1980, CENTAG is co-located with FOURATAF, the Seventh US Army and the Headquarters United States Army Europe.

Its present structure dates from 1970. The assigned CENTAG forces now include two German Corps, two United States Corps and a Canadian Mechanized Brigade Group. Headquarters CENTAG is located in Heidelberg (FRG). CENTAG is one of the three Principal Subordinate Commands (PSCs) in Allied Forces Central Europe. Commander CENTAG (COMCENTAG) is a US four-star general. His staff includes officers and troops from the three nations whose forces are assigned to CENTAG. The Commander CENTAG is responsible to the Commander, Allied Forces Central Europe for the supervision of the training of forces concerned for their assigned tasks.

CENTAG's area of responsibility CENTAG is responsible for the ground defence of an area that includes the middle and southern mass of the Federal Republic of Germany, south of a line running east-west just north of the capital, Bonn. In peacetime, Headquarters CENTAG plans for the defence of this area, oversees the training of its assigned forces, and conducts exercises to test and improve the readiness of the CENTAG units and command structures.

CENTAG's mission The basic mission of CENTAG is to deter any possible Warsaw Pact aggression against this key sector of the Allied Command Europe (ACE) Central Region. Should deterrence fail, COMCENTAG will assume command of the West German and US Army Corps and the Canadian Mechanized Brigade, which in peacetime, remains under national command. The CENTAG forces would then include more than 300,000 soldiers, in four infantry divisions, five armoured divisions, one mountain division, one airborne division and one mechanized brigade group. CENTAG weapons include Leopard and M1 Abrams tanks; M109, M107 and M110 artillery pieces; Lance surface-to-surface missiles; and Gepard and Hawk surface-to-air missiles.

Allied Air Forces Central Europe Allied Air Forces Central Europe – AAFCE – was established on 28 June 1974 in order to improve the effective employment of air resources in the Allied Command Europe (ACE) Central Region. At the spring Ministerial Meeting of the North Atlantic Council held in Ottawa, Canada on 18–19 June 1974 and attended by the Foreign Ministers of the then fifteen member countries, recommendations were approved by the NATO military authorities on integrated command structure to ensure the more effective use and joint operation of Allied Air Forces in the Central Region. They agreed that the new headquarters of Allied Air Forces Central Europe should be established initially at Ramstein (FRG) and that its permanent location should be co-located with the existing AFCENT Headquarters at Brunssum (Netherlands) (see page 26). This command is one of the Principal Subordinate Commands under ACE's Major Subordinate Command, AFCENT.

Headquarters AAFCE The multi-national headquarters, located at Ramstein Air Base in the Federal Republic of Germany, is staffed by personnel from six NATO nations, Belgium, Canada, West Germany, the Netherlands, the United Kingdom and the United States.

Allied Air Forces Central Europe, its mission Exercising operational command over the Second and Fourth Allied Tactical Air Forces (TWOATAF and FOURATAF), Commander Allied Air Forces Central Europe (COMAAFCE) has the mission of directing the integrated employment of Central Region air resources in accordance with the directives of the Commander-in-Chief Allied Forces Central Europe (CINCENT). In other terms, COMAAFCE is responsible for deterring air aggression, countering it if it occurs, and maintaining the integrity and security of his area of responsibility, which geographically corresponds with the AFCENT area. The Commander of AAFCE is also the Commander-in-Chief United States Air Forces Europe. HQ AAFCE peacetime functions include establishing common air doctrines; assessing the threat; determining policies and plans; standardizing procedures, tactics and training; and carrying out exercises, special training programmes and flying meets. Resources available include some 1,500 tactical aircraft and both an offensive and defensive missile force capability. An advanced-design radar system performs warning and control functions, to meet the quick-reaction requirements of defence today.

The 'command-forces' – comprising the integrated air defence system – are placed under COMAAFCE's authority in peacetime, while the 'assigned forces' will come under his command as soon as the appropriate political decision is made.

The 1952 reorganization of the Tactical Air Force, Europe A reorganization of the Tactical Air Force hitherto under the command of General Norstad, Commander-in-Chief Allied Air Forces, Central Europe, was announced on 20 April 1952 under which two Allied Tactical Air Forces were formed with immediate effect:

■ The 2nd Allied Tactical Air Force under the command of Air Marshal Sir Robert Roster (UK), with temporary headquarters at Bad Eilsen, Lower Saxony (FRG);

■ The 4th Allied Tactical Air Force under the command of Major-General Dean C. Struther (USA) with its headquarters at Landsberg, Bavaria (FRG).

It was stated that 2AFAF would include the British Royal Air Force 2nd Tactical Air Force, the Netherlands Tactical Air Command and a Belgian wing of three squadrons. The 4ATAF would include the US 12th Air Force, the French 1st Air Division and the Royal Canadian Air Force squadrons in Europe. Both Tactical Air Forces would remain responsible to General Norstad.

Second Allied Tactical Air Force The Second Allied Tactical Air Force (TWOATAF) is part of the NATO forces in the Central Region and is subordinate to Headquarters, Allied Forces Central Europe (AFCENT). The Commander TWOATAF is an Air Marshal of the Royal Air Force who in peacetime is also Commander-in-Chief Royal Air Force Germany (RAFG).

Headquarters TWOATAF and area of responsibility The TWOATAF headquarters is located at Rheindahlen near Mönchen-Gladbach, in the Federal Republic of Germany. Its area of responsibility covers Germany from the German-Danish border in the north down to a Bonn-Kassel line in the south, and part of the North Sea, Belgium and the Netherlands. In order to meet the unit's various tasks the

original three air forces of Belgium, the Netherlands and the United Kingdom have been added to. The United States committed squadrons to TWOATAF in 1954 and Luftwaffe squadrons of the Federal Republic of Germany followed in 1958. In 1978 the United States increased their contribution to the Allied Air Command by the addition of squadrons stationed in the United Kingdom.

TWOATAF's mission One of TWOATAF's most important tasks is 'round-the-clock' surveillance of assigned air space with a highly trained alert force of aircraft and missile squadrons able to respond at short notice. Because his defence responsibilities cover both peace and war, the TWOATAF commander has operational control in peacetime of integrated NATO Air Defence Forces. These elements include those land and naval air defence forces within the TWOATAF area which are normally assigned to NATO. In support of air defence fighters and missiles during peacetime, there is assigned the NATO Air Defence Ground Environment System (NADGE) consisting of fixed and mobile early warning radars. The low level reporting system (LLRS) completes the surveillance of TWOATAF's air space. Additionally, TWOATAF is responsible for preparing and co-ordinating plans and training crews to conduct offensive operations. Modern weapons systems are at the disposal of TWOATAF aircraft and missile personnel to accomplish air defence and offensive operations.

The establishment of Fourth Allied Tactical Air Force 'General Order Number 1' dated 2 April 1952 and issued by the former NATO Command AIRCENT established the Fourth Allied Tactical Air Force. It ordered the establishment of FOURATAF Headquarters at Landsberg/Lech, FRG and placed under its command the facilities and flying units of the 12th United States Air Force, the 1st French Tactical Air Corps and the 1st Royal Canadian Air Force Air Division. A year later the headquarters was re-located at Trier (FRG) only to be moved again during December 1980 to its present location at Heidelberg where it is now co-located with Central Army Group (CENTAG). To-day the national operational units which make up FOURATAF are the 17th United States Air Force, the 3rd United States Air Force and the 32nd US Army Air Defence Command.

Fourth Allied Tactical Air Force Headquarters, Fourth Allied Tactical Air Force (FOURATAF) at Heidelberg (FRG) is a component of Allied Air Forces Central Europe. FOURATAF is a tri-national force, composed of American, Canadian and West German air forces. The three nations appoint air force personnel of all ranks to man the headquarters staff and contribute parts of their air forces to the organization. These forces come under operational control of Headquarters FOURATAF in the event of an emergency.

FOURATAF's area of responsibility The FOURATAF area of responsibility comprises a surface of 90,000 square kilometres and a population of approximately 29 million people. In the east, its borders touch those of the Inner German Border and Czechoslovakia; in the south, it borders on Austria and Switzerland; in the west FOURATAF's area bounds the territory of France and includes Luxemburg and part of Belgium. The northern border is marked by the southern border of Headquarters TWOATAF. FOURATAF shares its area of responsibility with CENTAG – NATO's Central Army Group – also located at Heidelberg, Federal Republic of Germany. For these ground forces the formations of FOURATAF provide the air shield needed. In fact, FOURATAF's mission is 'to employ its forces in conjunction with those of CENTAG, to maintain the integrity and security of the FOURATAF and CENTAG area, and to provide support as directed to TWOATAF and FIVEATAF'.

FOURATAF's mission FOURATAF's basic mission is to help secure the NATO air space of Central Europe, achieve and maintain air superiority, destroy enemy forces, and provide air support to Army units in its region. The unit also has to obtain tactical information facilitating future engagement of targets and determine the effectiveness of offensive operations.

Headquarters Allied Forces Southern Europe

AFSOUTH was originally established in June 1951, with headquarters on a US naval warship in the Bay of Naples. AFSOUTH Headquarters, established by a NATO-Italian agreement of 29 August 1952, are now located in the Bagnoli district of Naples, Italy. The Southern Region is the largest of Allied Command Europe's (ACE's) four military regions, covering an area of approximately four million square kilometres (1½ million square miles). AFSOUTH is the ACE Major Subordinate Command with the responsibility for defending this region. The three regional countries of Italy, Greece and Turkey, along with the United Kingdom and the United States of America, are the five nations represented on the AFSOUTH staff.

AFSOUTH's area of responsibility AFSOUTH's area of responsibility covers Italy, Greece, Turkey, the Black Sea, and the entire Mediterranean Sea, including the Tyrrhenian, Adriatic, Ionian and Aegean Seas.

AFSOUTH's mission The wartime mission of the AFSOUTH organization is to defend Italy, Greece and Turkey, and the sea lines of communication throughout the Mediterranean and Black Seas. Preparation for this mission is accomplished during peacetime with the organization and training of assigned and designated units into an effective integrated military force. The command structure is maintained as an efficient nucleus for expansion in wartime. During peacetime, approximately 5,000 servicemen and women of the Southern Region countries are assigned full-time to AFSOUTH, mainly in the various NATO military command headquarters in the region. In addition to these headquarters staff members, national personnel are permanently assigned to the Southern Region air defence organization.

Commands subordinate to AFSOUTH Operating under the Commander-in-Chief AFSOUTH (CINCSOUTH) who is a four-star United States admiral, are five Primary Subordinate Commands (PSCs).

■ Allied Air Forces Southern Europe (AIRSOUTH) with headquarters at Naples, Italy.
■ Allied Land Forces Southern Europe (LANDSOUTH), with headquarters at Verona, Italy (see page 40).
■ Allied Land Forces South-eastern Europe (LANDSOUTH-EAST), headquarters at Izmir, Turkey (see page 41).
■ Allied Naval Forces Southern Europe (NAVSOUTH), headquarters on Nisida Island in the Bay of Naples, Italy (see page 41).
■ Naval Striking and Support Forces Southern Europe (STRIKFORSOUTH), with headquarters aboard the USS *Puget Sound* (AD-38), whose home port is at Gaeta, Italy (see page 43).

Headquarters Allied Air Forces Southern Europe AIRSOUTH was established in August 1951 and underwent a number of evolutions until reaching its present structure after the Cyprus conflict of 1974 when Turkish troops invaded the Turkish areas of northern Cyprus. AIRSOUTH, headquartered at the Allied Forces Southern Europe (AFSOUTH) Post in the Bagnoli district of Naples, is one of the five Principal Subordinate Commands in the Allied Command Europe's Southern Region. Commander AIRSOUTH (COMAIRSOUTH) is a three-star United States Air Force general with a multi-national staff at his headquarters comprising personnel from Greece, Italy, Turkey, the United Kingdom and the United States.

AIRSOUTH's area of responsibility AIRSOUTH has an area of responsibility in the air space over the Southern Region which covers the mainland areas and island possessions of Italy, Greece and Turkey, including Sardinia, Sicily, Crete, etc. In all, AIRSOUTH defends a 3,600 kilometre (2,000 mile) border stretching from the Italian Alps to eastern Turkey.

AIRSOUTH's mission To prepare for its wartime mission of conducting the air defence of the Southern Region, the peacetime activities of AIRSOUTH include standardizing training and operating procedures, co-ordinating the exchange of information and use of facilities between the various countries and solving the ever-present problems of personnel, equipment, tactics and techniques. The equipment available to the operational forces under COMAIRSOUTH control include F1 Mirages, F-4 Phantoms, F-5 Freedom Fighters, Fiat G91s, A-7 Corsairs and Tornado Multi-role Combat Aircraft (MRCAs), plus NIKE Hercules and HAWK surface-to-air missiles.

Forces subordinate to AIRSOUTH Allied Air Forces Southern Europe also comprises the Fifth Allied Tactical Air Force (FIVEATAF) based at Vicenza, Italy (see below) and the Sixth Allied Tactical Air Force (SIXATAF) at Izmir, Turkey (see below). Both of these Tactical Air Forces exercise unified control of existing Allied air forces in their respective countries.

Fifth Allied Tactical Air Force The NATO Council approved the creation of a Fifth Allied Tactical Air Force (FIVEATAF) which, it announced, would come into operation on 1 January 1956 with headquarters at Vicenza, Italy, where it is based today. The original FIVEATAF included air force personnel from Italy, France, Greece, Turkey and the United States. France and Greece no longer participate in FIVEATAF, and today the integrated staff includes personnel from the Federal Republic of Germany, Italy, Turkey and the United States. France has assigned a French Air Force liaison officer to Headquarters FIVEATAF. The bulk of the forces assigned to FIVEATAF is represented by Italian and US Air Force units which include offensive, defensive, and reconnaissance fighter squadrons, surface-to-air missiles and an air defence ground environment.

FIVEATAF's area of responsibility In May 1962, when the National Air Defence systems were integrated into the overall NATO Air Defence organization, the Italian air defence forces, facilities and ground environment were placed under NATO operational control. Consequently, the FIVEATAF commander was assigned operational control of these forces and given responsibility for air defence of the entire Italian territory including Sicily and Sardinia, its air space and adjacent waters.

Tasks allotted to FIVEATAF FIVEATAF's area of responsibility includes the Italian peninsula, its islands and adjacent waters. Its primary mission, in times of tension, is to conduct activities to counter possible aggression through offensive and defensive operations within its area of responsibility. Headquarters FIVEATAF's main peacetime task is to direct and control air defence assets, develop plans for possible wartime use of forces available, participate in major NATO exercises, and conduct tactical evaluations on the level of combat readiness by its subordinate assigned air units.

Sixth Allied Tactical Air Force A new NATO Allied Tactical Air Force, staffed by United States, Greek and Turkish components and known as the Sixth Allied Tactical Air Force (SIXATAF) was established on 14 October 1953 with its headquarters at Sirinyer Garrison, south of Izmir (Smyrna), Turkey. The new group, which was under the command of Major-General Robert E. Eaton (US Air Force), was the first international tactical air force to be set up in southern Europe. The international staff of SIXATAF Headquarters today includes personnel from Italy, Turkey, the United Kingdom and the United States.

SIXATAF's area of responsibility and mission SIXATAF's geographical area of responsibility is one of the largest of any Allied tactical air force command in NATO. It has the peacetime mission of providing full-time air defence of Turkey. In addition to its air defence role, the headquarters serves as a planning and advisory agency, and conducts tactical evaluations of assigned units on a regular basis to ensure that a high state of readiness is maintained. SIXATAF's wartime mission is to counter aggression by conducting air operations in defence of Turkey. Maintaining its air defence role, SIXATAF would also provide tactical air support to NATO naval and land forces.

SIXATAF's Additional Tactical Air Force Support In the event of war in the south-eastern NATO region, the SIXATAF commander would assume operational control, following national approval, of two Turkish tactical air forces (TAF). These are: First TAF with headquarters at Eskisehir, east of Istanbul, and Second TAF, located at Diyarbakir in south-eastern Turkey.

Both TAFs include several types of aircraft squadrons equipped and trained to conduct counter-air, close air support, air interdiction, reconnaissance and air defence operations.

Headquarters Allied Land Forces Southern Europe Headquarters LANDSOUTH is located in Verona, in the historic Palazzo Carli. LANDSOUTH is one of the five Principal Subordinate Commands under Allied Forces Southern Europe (AFSOUTH). The LANDSOUTH organization consists of personnel from six NATO nations: Italy, Federal Republic of Germany, Greece, Turkey, Portugal and the United States. Commander LANDSOUTH (COMLANDSOUTH) is an Italian four-star army general.

LANDSOUTH's area of responsibility The area of responsibility allocated to Allied Land Forces Southern Europe consists of the western portion of Allied Command Europe's Southern Region, i.e., the Veneto-Friuli Plain.

LANDSOUTH's mission LANDSOUTH's wartime mission is to defend its area of responsibility as far forward as possible, to prevent the enemy from having access to the Po Plain, Italy's main industrial area. It must also prevent the Southern Region from being physically separated from the Central Region. To accomplish these goals, COMLANDSOUTH will employ mechanized and major armoured units, alpine brigades, surface-to-surface and surface-to-air missile units, combat support and logistic support units, as well as a number of United States forces incorporated in a special unit called the 'Southern European Task Force' (SETAF) which was established in 1955 (see page 43). The above-mentioned units deploy modern vehicles and weapons, such as the West German Leopard tank, the TOW anti-tank missile, the Lance surface-to-surface missile, and the Hawk air defence missile.

Allied Land Forces South-eastern Europe Immediately following the Second World War the Soviets embarked on a concerted policy of extending their influence and control into the eastern Mediterranean and the Middle East. Although Soviet techniques have varied since that time, domination of the area is clearly a primary goal of their current strategy.

Turkey and Greece, but in particular Turkey, are critically important to the NATO Alliance. They lie astride the natural and historic routes of passage from Europe to the Middle East, and guard the European approaches to the eastern Mediterranean. The Dardanelles and the Bosphorus serve as a gateway which could be slammed shut to block the Soviet Black Sea Fleet from joining its naval elements already in the Mediterranean. Turkey holds a key strategic position for NATO and its Southern Region, providing a window to both the Soviet Union and the oil-rich countries of the Middle East. In the east Turkey shares a common border with the Soviet Union. It is some 600 kilometres (370 miles) in length and is one of the two places where NATO borders directly on the Soviet Union, the other being the Finmark area (see page 34). In addition there are 1,300 miles of Black Sea coast facing the USSR.

Greece, in the west, has a common border with Albania for a distance of 249 kilometres (155 miles) and with Bulgaria for 708 kilometres (440 miles). Turkey also borders on to Bulgaria for 225 kilometres (140 miles).

Headquarters LANDSOUTHEAST The creation of a new land-based command had been announced on 16 July 1952 by General Matthew B. Ridgway shortly after taking on his new duties as Supreme Allied Commander Europe. The new command, Allied Land Forces South-eastern Europe, would be within the Allied Forces Southern Europe Command then under the overall command of Admiral Carney (CINCSOUTH) United States Navy, whose headquarters were in Naples, Italy. The new Land Force was to be commanded by an American officer – at the time of the July 1952 announcement he had not been named – who was to have operational control of Turkish and Greek ground forces assigned to NATO, with separate Greek and Turkish Army commands operating under his authority. The location of the LANDSOUTHEAST headquarters also remained undecided.

Two months later, on 8 September 1952, LANDSOUTH-EAST was established in Izmir (Smyrna), Turkey under the command of Lieutenant-General Willard G. Wyman (US Army). General Wyman was appointed to head LANDSOUTH-EAST on 28 July 1952. He had previously commanded the US Ninth Corps in Korea.

The command was originally staffed by Hellenic, Turkish, British, Italian and American personnel, but of recent years the Greek forces no longer participate at Command Headquarters.

The Mediterranean Command, later known as 'Allied Forces Mediterranean' (AFMED) The North Atlantic Council, which met in Paris on 15–18 December 1952, approved various NATO command arrangements for the Mediterranean Sea as formulated by the Military Committee. The principal change was the establishment of a Commander-in-Chief Mediterranean. By agreement, C-in-C Med was initially a British Royal Naval officer, confirmed subsequently as Earl Mountbatten of Burma, who had been Commander-in-Chief of the British Mediterranean Fleet since May 1952. In his NATO role his staff included officers from all nations concerned and C-in-C Med was made directly subordinate and responsible to the Supreme Allied Commander Europe.

Mediterranean Command areas of responsibility The Mediterranean was sub-divided into a number of areas for the exercise of those functions which were of local or national nature. The several area commanders were responsible to C-in-C Med for all allied tasks, but remained under their own national authorities for those functions which were national in character. These areas included the important French and Italian areas in the western and central Mediterranean. National coastal areas were deemed a national responsibility.

The mission of Mediterranean Command Commander-in-Chief Mediterranean in time of war was responsible for the security of all sea communications, the protection of shipping and convoys, the co-ordination of logistic support, and the support of adjacent commands. Other important responsibilities were the co-ordination of mine warfare and of submarine and anti-submarine operations. For all these purposes his command included air as well as naval forces. The heavy carriers, amphibious and support forces of the United States Sixth Fleet remained under the command of the Commander-in-Chief South. Sometimes referred to as the 'Striking Force', the Sixth Fleet was primarily a force organized for the support of land campaigns in southern Europe.

Headquarters Allied Naval Forces Southern Europe Today, what is known as Allied Naval Forces Southern Europe (NAVSOUTH), was originally entitled Allied Forces Mediterranean (AFMED). Based in Malta, the Commander-in-Chief Allied Forces Mediterranean (CINCAFMED) had been directly responsible to the Supreme Allied Commander Europe (SACEUR) at SHAPE. On 24 May 1967 it was announced that a new NATO appointment of Commander, Allied Naval Forces Southern Europe (COMNAVSOUTH) would be made effective not later than 5 June 1967 and would be directly responsible to the Commander-in-Chief Allied Forces Southern Europe (CINCSOUTH). This new post was filled by Italian Admiral Luciano Sotgiu. NAVSOUTH was formally inaugurated on 5 June 1967.

General elections held in Malta during the three-day period 12–14 June 1971 resulted in a victory for the Labour Party of Malta led by Mr Dominic (Dom) Mintoff, which by obtaining a one-seat majority in the new House of Representatives ended nine years of rule by the Nationalist Government and brought the Labour Party back into power after thirteen years. During his election campaign Mr Mintoff had called for the early re-negotiation of the ten-year defence and air agreement which the Maltese Government had with Britain. He also pledged himself to keep the island free of American, Soviet or Italian bases and indicated that a Maltese Labour Government might pursue a more neutralist policy, and he had also pressed for closer relations with the revolutionary regime in Libya.

A series of dramatic developments after Mr Mintoff's electoral victory included the termination of the island's defence agreement with Great Britain, the replacement of a British by a Maltese Governor-General, the replacement of almost all Maltese diplomats abroad, a ban – for the time being – on visits of US warships to Malta, talks with Colonel Qadhafi's regime, and a visit to Valletta by the Soviet Ambassador in London, Mr Mikhail Smirnovsky for talks with Mr Mintoff and other Maltese Ministers. On 13 August 1971 NATO Head-quarters in Brussels announced that the new Government of Malta had informed the North Atlantic Council 'that it desires to alter the existing relationship between Malta and NATO'; that NATO had replied that it was 'ready to respect the wishes of the Government of Malta'; and that NATO's Defence Planning Committee had accordingly given instructions 'to start the preparations for the transfer of NATO's activities elsewhere'. A further NATO statement on 20 August 1971 said that the Defence Planning Committee 'following its decision of 13 August . . . has directed that – in accordance with long-term planning aims agreed upon in NATO in 1965 – the activities of the Headquarters of Allied Naval Forces Southern Europe, be relocated in Naples'.

Today NAVSOUTH has its headquarters on the Island of Nisida, in the Bay of Naples. COMNAVSOUTH is still an Italian admiral. His international staff includes personnel from Greece, Italy, Turkey, the United Kingdom and the United States.

NAVSOUTH and its structure NAVSOUTH is one of the Principal Subordinate Commands (PSCs) under the Allied Command Europe Major Subordinate Command AFSOUTH. NAVSOUTH's structure divides the Mediterranean and Black Seas into the following geographical areas, each under the naval commander exercising operational authority over the area:

- Gibraltar-Mediterranean,
- Central Mediterranean,
- Eastern Mediterranean, and
- North-eastern Mediterranean.

Two other oceans areas, West Mediterranean and South-east Mediterranean, are under the direct command of Commander NAVSOUTH (COMNAVSOUTH). There are also three 'functional commands' subordinate to NAVSOUTH: Maritime Air Forces Mediterranean (MARAIRMED) inaugu-rated 21 November 1968, Allied Submarine Forces Mediter-ranean (SUBMED) and Naval On-Call Force Mediterranean (NAVOCFORMED), activated 22 April 1970. NAVSOUTH works closely with STRIKFORSOUTH, CINCSOUTH's other naval PSC (see page 43).

NAVSOUTH's areas of responsibility The areas of respon-sibility allotted to Allied Naval Forces Southern Europe, as indicated above, include all of the Mediterranean Sea from the Straits of Gibraltar to the Coast of Syria, together with the Adriatic, Ionian, Tyrrhenian and Aegean Seas, plus the Sea of Marmara and the Black Sea, outside the Soviet Union's terri-torial waters. In this vast ocean area, NAVSOUTH is entrusted with the conduct of sea control operations and the support of resupply and reinforcement in the Southern Region. During peacetime, NAVSOUTH has no forces under its control except during exercises, when Allied warships and maritime aircraft are made available to the Command, and during the activation of a multi-national Naval On-Call Force Mediterranean. In addition, NAVSOUTH co-ordinates, on a 24-hour daily basis, surveillance of Soviet Bloc maritime forces from the surveil-lance co-ordination centre in its peacetime headquarters.

Gibraltar Mediterranean Gibraltar Mediterranean Command was instituted on 1 September 1954 as a sub-area under the

AFMED whose headquarters were then in Malta. Despite the move from Malta to Naples and the change in name from Allied Forces Mediterranean (AFMED) to Allied Naval Forces Southern Europe (NAVSOUTH), the Command name Gibraltar Mediterranean has remained constant. Commander Gibraltar Mediterranean is now responsible to Commander Allied Naval Forces Southern Europe (COMNAVSOUTH) with Headquarters in Naples. The Commander Naval Forces South is in turn responsible to the Commander-in-Chief Allied Forces Southern Europe (CINCSOUTH) who takes his orders from SACEUR. Commander Gibraltar Mediterranean has no subordinate commands.

North-eastern Mediterranean COMEDNOREAST was estab-lished as an Area Command in March 1953 at the same time as the Headquarters Allied Forces Mediterranean was establish-ed in Malta. At that time, AFMED was a Major Subordinate Command directly responsible to SACEUR and on the same level as CINCSOUTH. In June 1967, AFMED was changed to a Naval Principal Subordinate Command under CINCSOUTH and re-named Commander Naval Forces Southern Europe. The North-east Mediterranean Area remained an Area Com-mand, but now under COMNAVSOUTH with responsibility for the area that includes the eastern Mediterranean, the eastern part of the Aegean Sea, the Sea of Marmara, the Turkish Straits and the Black Sea.

The formal inauguration of Maritime Air Forces Mediter-ranean The build-up of Soviet naval units operating in the Mediterranean Sea since the Arab-Israeli war of June 1967 was the cause of considerable concern to NATO, the result of which was the creation of a new NATO Command, subordinate to Allied Naval Forces Southern Europe and entitled Maritime Air Forces Mediterranean (MARAIRMED). MARAIRMED was formally inaugurated in Naples on 21 November 1968. An official statement from SHAPE had announced on 15 October 1968 that the decision to establish the Command had been taken by the Defence Planning Committee during the Minis-terial Council Meeting held at Reykjavik, Iceland in June of that year, and that its task would be to improve air surveil-lance of surface ships and submarines in the Mediterranean area. Under Rear-Admiral Edward C. Outlaw (US Navy) the command would exercise operational control over maritime aircraft assigned by the United States, the United Kingdom and Italy, in the event of war or 'from the time such authority is given by the national authorities'.

The formation of the Allied Naval On-Call Force, Mediter-ranean A Ministerial meeting of the NATO Defence Planning Committee took place in Brussels on 16 January 1969 which resulted in the following communiqué being issued:

'As one of the measures envisaged at the Ministerial meeting held at Reykjavik in June 1968 to safeguard the security interests of NATO members in the Mediterranean area, Ministers approved the concept of an Allied naval force capable of being assembled on call. The force will be designed to demonstrate Allied solidarity and to carry out surveillance in the Mediterranean. It would be called together periodically for exercises and visits.'

According to Press reports of the time, the purpose of the projected Allied Naval On-Call Force – NAVOCFORMED – was to increase surveillance of the Soviet Fleet and to demonstrate NATO solidarity in the area. Initially the Force was to consist of three or four destroyer-type ships, the nucleus of which being provided by Great Britain, Italy and the United States, with Greece, Turkey and other NATO countries contributing additional ships on an *ad hoc* basis. The Force operated on a national basis except when called together for joint exercises or when there was an emergency. The existence of the Force did not increase the number of NATO ships operating in the Mediterranean as those which took part were drawn from the national fleets already in the area.

Naval On-Call Force Mediterranean NATO's Naval On-Call Force Mediterranean (NAVOCFORMED) was established in 1969 and activated in April 1970. Destroyer/frigate-type ships of member nations operating in the Mediterranean participate at periodic intervals in exercises and port visits. The force is not permanently in being and between exercises the ships remain under national command.

Naval Striking and Support Forces Southern Europe, and its Headquarters On 19 March 1953 a new NATO naval command was set up known as 'Naval Striking and Support Forces, Southern Europe'. The Commander of the US Sixth Fleet, Vice-Admiral J. H. Cassady was appointed to command this new force with his headquarters at Naples, Italy. Today STRIKFORSOUTH is one of the five Principal Subordinate Commands (PSCs) within Allied Forces Southern Europe (AFSOUTH). Therefore, Commander STRIKFOR-SOUTH (COMSTRIKFORSOUTH) is directly subordinate to the Commander-in-Chief Allied Forces Southern Europe (CINCSOUTH).

COMSTRIKFORSOUTH is the US three-star admiral who also commands the US Sixth Fleet. Therefore, COMSTRIK-FORSOUTH is normally embarked in the Sixth Fleet flagship, the USS *Puget Sound* (AD-38), whose home port is Gaeta, Italy. The STRIKFORSOUTH staff, comprised of approximately 50 US and Allied officers and enlisted personnel, and the Deputy Commander (DEPCOMSTRIKFORSOUTH) are located at the AFSOUTH Post in the Bagnoli district of Naples, Italy.

STRIKFORSOUTH's area of responsibility The area of responsibility allotted to STRIKFORSOUTH parallels that of Allied Naval Forces Southern Europe (NAVSOUTH), that is all of the Mediterranean Sea, from the Straits of Gibraltar to the coast of Syria, including the Adriatic, Ionian and Aegean Seas, plus the Sea of Marmara and the Black Sea outside the USSR's territorial waters.

STRIKFORSOUTH's mission The basic mission of STRIK-FORSOUTH is to contribute, together with other Allied Command Europe Forces, to the deterrence of all forms of aggression against the NATO nations in the Mediterranean area, and to carry out exercises and other planning and training activities in preparation for effective joint operations in war, in case this deterrence should fail. When so decided by higher authority STRIKFORSOUTH will include all of the surface combatant units of the US Sixth Fleet, their associated aircraft, the US Landing Forces located in the Mediterranean, and other assigned elements.

Naval Commands subordinate to STRIKFORSOUTH Subordinate naval commands in STRIKFORSOUTH are:

- Task Force 502 (Carrier Striking Forces);
- Task Force 503 (Amphibious Forces); and
- Task Force 504 (Landing Forces).

The Southern European Task Force (SETAF) The Southern European Task Force – SETAF – was officially inaugurated on 25 October 1955. The original force comprised the former US occupation troops in Austria, numbering about 5,500 men, and had its headquarters at Vicenza in northern Italy. The Force exists today with its headquarters still at Vicenza, and American military personnel assigned to the Force are under the control of the US Army in Europe. SETAF's command structure is such that during peacetime as well as in time of war it is a Major Subordinate Command of the United States Army Europe. Upon a certain pre-designated alert condition prior to actual war, SETAF would provide designated support to both US and NATO commands in the NATO Southern European Region (LANDSOUTH). FIVEATAF has also been assigned to co-operate with SETAF. During 1972–3 two US artillery groups and an airborne battalion were added to SETAF. SETAF was assigned the mission of readying and deploying this strengthened Force for employment by Allied Command Europe (ACE).

Creation of the Multi-National Mobile Land Force (MLF)

On 2 March 1960 it was announced by General Norstad, Supreme Commander Allied Powers Europe, that it was proposed to establish a multi-national Allied task force to be called the Mobile Land Force (MLF) which was to be equipped with both conventional and atomic weapons. It was stated that 'tacit' agreement had previously been given by France, the

United Kingdom and the United States to the integration of a battalion from each of these countries into this 'fire brigade' force, which it was hoped would be in existence within a year.

Forces involved in MLF SACEUR explained that the MLF, which would have its own aircraft, would initially consist of 2,500–3,000 men under a single commander who, he hoped, would not be an American. It was intended to expand the force at a later date to Brigade Group or Divisional strength, with the addition of units from other NATO countries. The constituent units would be brought together from time to time for joint training, but for most of the time they would remain with their own national formations. General Norstad added that the force would perhaps have more political than military value since it would give an 'Atlantic colouration' to an intervention in any area to which the MLF might be sent to operate.

West German troops to serve with the Mobile Land Force On 10 December 1960 it was subsequently announced in Bonn that General Norstad had formally requested the Federal German Government to supply a contingent for this force. On 17 December 1960 Herr Strauss (FRG) stated in Paris that his government was prepared to take part and expected to provide a reinforced battalion of paratroops – about 1,200 men.

The Mobile Land Force brought into being On 20 June 1961 General Norstad stated that the multi-national 'fire brigade' force, the Mobile Land Force, whose forthcoming establishment he had disclosed in March 1960, was 'in being' and comprised five reinforced infantry battalions, each of different nationality.

Change of title: MLF to AMF On its formation in 1960, the Force was called the Mobile Land Force (MLF) and was based at Mannheim-Seckenheim (FRG). In 1963 this title was changed to the one that is used to-day, ACE Mobile Force (AMF). The Force now comprises two components: land units, entitled ACE Mobile Force (Land); and air components, known as ACE Mobile Force (Air), abbreviated respectively as AMF(L) and AMF(A).

Allied Command Europe (ACE) Mobile Force today The ACE Mobile Force, commonly referred to as AMF, is a small multi-national, conventional force composed of elements of land and air forces. Eight North Atlantic Treaty Organization nations provide these ground and air forces: Belgium, Canada, the Federal Republic of Germany, Italy, Luxemburg, the Netherlands, the United Kingdom and the United States of America. Luxemburg contributes only to the AMF's land forces; the Netherlands only to the air component.

Composition of AMF The Land Component comprises infantry, artillery, helicopters, armoured reconnaissance, combat and administrative support from Belgium, Canada, the Fed-

eral Republic of Germany, Italy, Luxemburg, the United Kingdom and the United States, the last two countries providing air-portable battalion groups for the AMF (the UK Mobile Force, an expeditionary brigade of some 13,000 men and the American 'Marine Amphibious Force' with a strength of 40,000 men and 'planes to match). Most units are based in their own countries and deploy to join the force during exercises and operations, the exception being the units provided by the United States which are drawn from the US Forces in Europe.

The Land Component has a permanent headquarters located since 15 December 1980 at Heidelberg (FRG) and is staffed by officers and non-commissioned officers from the countries that contribute to the force. The Allied Commander AMF is directly responsible to SACEUR.

The Air Component comprises squadrons from Belgium, Canada, the Federal Republic of Germany, Italy, the Netherlands, the United Kingdom and the United States brought together when required. It has no permanent headquarters or commander, but is under the operational command of the Allied Tactical Air Force or regional NATO Air Commander of the area to which it is deployed.

ACE Mobile Force, its task and deployment areas The AMF is mostly concerned with the vital flanks of NATO, that is those areas where member nations have common frontiers with the Soviet Union or her satellite countries and/or where NATO forces are weakly represented. These areas are northern Norway, along the 200-kilometre border with the Soviet Union; Denmark and the Baltic Sea, especially the Approaches areas; northern Italy especially along the border with non-aligned but Communist Yugoslavia; Greece and the Dardanelles, in particular Thrace along the border with Bulgaria and the north-western part of Asian Turkey and finally Turkey itself with its 400 kilometre border with the Georgian People's Republic in the Caucasus.

Although the primary mission of the AMF is to deter aggression by demonstrating NATO's unity of purpose, if deterrence fails the force is fully equipped and trained to fight alongside the local forces in defence of the areas concerned. Rapid deployment is one of the key factors in the success of this force and it is, therefore, a major consideration in the initial planning for any exercises or operation. Supreme Headquarters Allied Powers Europe is responsible for the planning and co-ordination of all airlifts. Throughout the year, study periods, reconnaissance and full-scale exercises are carried out by the AMF. Their location, scope, setting and time of year are varied as much as possible so that the flexibility and combat effectiveness of this unique force can be constantly improved.

Towards UKAIR, a Unified Air Defence System, RAF Fighter Command placed under SACEUR

On 21 December 1960 it was announced in the House of Commons that Royal Air Force Fighter Command was to be placed under the orders of the Supreme Allied Commander Europe. This move was in accordance with a scheme for unified air defence approved by the NATO Council on 28 September 1960 following agreement in principle at the Defence Ministers' meeting held during March 1960. Even in 1960 the speed and range of aircraft was considered to be such that NATO Europe was in need of a unified air defence system, and under the scheme devised by NATO the United Kingdom was to form one of four NATO Air Defence Regions, with RAF Fighter Command coming under SACEUR's command.

The United Kingdom Ministry of Defence amplified on the House of Commons' statement by explaining that General Norstad, SACEUR, would not be able to deploy Fighter Command aircraft without the British Government's approval and that the Government would be free to deploy its aircraft as it thought fit, although the United Kingdom would be obliged to inform SACEUR of any such deployment. There was no change in the operational role of Fighter Command and the British Government was free to alter the size and composition of the Command subject to consulting SACEUR, since any such changes might affect his operational plans.

The four NATO Air Defence Regions In addition to the United Kingdom Air Defence Region three other NATO Regions were formed:

- Northern Europe – Scandinavia,
- Southern Europe – Italy, Greece and Turkey,
- Central Europe – including Western Germany, the Low Countries and part of France, but excluding the greater part of Metropolitan France, an area which remained the responsibility of the French Air Defence Command as agreed by the NATO Council on 28 September 1960.

RAF Fighter Command officially passed under General Norstad's orders as from 1 May 1961.

RAF Strike Command and the creation of UKAIR In April 1968 a series of amalgamations were begun within the Royal Air Force whereby the various RAF Commands, Fighter, Bomber, Coastal, Transport, etc., were merged into a single unified Strike Command, with Headquarters at High Wycombe, Buckinghamshire. Eight years later, on 10 April 1975, Air Chief Marshal Sir Denis Smallwood, Air Officer Commander-in-Chief RAF Strike Command assumed the additional post of Commander-in-Chief UK Air Forces (CINC-

UKAIR). Under the new command, the first to be created in Britain since NATO's formation, the full range of Strike Command's resources comprising, at that time, of about 800 aircraft and more than half the manpower of the RAF was made available to NATO and placed in a direct chain of command to SACEUR.

United Kingdom Air Forces – UKAIR UKAIR is a Major Subordinate Command (MSC) under the Supreme Allied Commander Europe. It was formed in 1975 with its headquarters at High Wycombe, Buckinghamshire (UK), the former wartime RAF Bomber Command Headquarters, approximately 50 kilometres (30 miles) north-west of London. As a regional command within Allied Command Europe (ACE), it is unique in that it is essentially a single-service, being solely Royal Air Force, single-nation MSC and has no Principal Subordinate Command.

UKAIR, its responsibility Since adoption of the NATO concept of Flexible Response, the United Kingdom has become a major base for offensive, defensive, and reinforcement operations, and the security of this base has, therefore, assumed increasing importance. The United Kingdom is the rear base for SACEUR in Europe and the forward base for maritime operations in the Atlantic and British waters. The Commander-in-Chief United Kingdom Air Forces (CINC-UKAIR) is responsible to SACEUR for the air defence of Britain and for protecting the United Kingdom Air Defence Region (UKADR) against air attack.

Resources available to UKAIR For its front-line forces, the Command draws on most of the home-based operational air resources of the United Kingdom. It is a genuinely multi-role Command, spanning all the functions of air power – strike/attack, air defence, reconnaissance and air transport. These front-line resources are provided to SACEUR by three subordinate Royal Air Force formations:

- No. 1 Group, based at RAF Upavon, Wiltshire (UK) which assumed the mantle of the old RAF Bomber Command, namely that of strike and attack – nuclear strike, conventional attack, strategic reconnaissance and in-flight refuelling plus the British Army support helicopter force.
- No. 11 Group, using the former RAF Fighter Command Headquarters at Bentley Priory, Middlesex (UK) and responsible for providing the air defence of the United Kingdom.
- No. 18 Group with Headquarters at Northwood, Middlesex

(UK), responsible for offensive support, tactical reconnaissance, strategic airlift and tactical fixed-wing and rotary air mobility.

UKAIR's mission Stretching some 1,800 kilometres (1,200 miles) from north to south, the Region sits astride the main air and sea reinforcement routes from North America and the United Kingdom to mainland Europe. To carry out this mission CINCUKAIR employs Phantom and Tornado fighters, Victor, DC10 and Lockheed Tri-Star air-to-air refuelling tankers, Shackleton Airborne Early Warning (AEW) aircraft (see also page 51) expected to be replaced by the first squadron of Boeing E-3 AEW aircraft in 1991, Bloodhound and Rapier surface-to-air missiles and the extensive UK ground radar control and reporting system. CINCUKAIR is also required by SACEUR to provide combat-ready air forces for employment within Allied Command Europe and to participate, on order, in SACEUR's nuclear programmes. To meet these responsibilities, CINCUKAIR provides Vulcan and Buccaneer squadrons (presently supplemented by and eventually to be replaced by the Tornado) in the strike/attack role.

Establishment of North Atlantic Command

On 30 January 1952 the North Atlantic Deputies' Council, on behalf of the North Atlantic Council, issued a statement announcing:

- That Admiral Lynde D. McCormick, Commander-in-Chief US Atlantic Fleet had been appointed Supreme Allied Commander, Atlantic (SACLANT).
- That the naval, air and land forces making up this Command in time of war would be contributed by the several North Atlantic Treaty Powers.
- That it had been agreed that the Deputy Supreme Commander, Atlantic should be a British naval officer.
- That the Command would exercise through an integrated international staff drawn from the countries contributing to the North Atlantic Ocean Command.
- That the latter Command, and General Eisenhower's Command in Europe were 'mutually supporting Commands whose activities will be co-ordinated by the Standing Group'.

Simultaneously, the British Admiralty announced:

- Vice-Admiral Sir William Andrews, Commander-in-Chief, American and West Indies Station, would be Deputy Supreme Commander, Atlantic, retaining his present command of the American and West Indies Station.
- The Commander-in-Chief Eastern Atlantic, under NATO, would be the Commander-in-Chief Home Fleet (at that time, Admiral Sir George Creasy) who would have his headquarters ashore in time of war.
- The Commander-in-Chief Home Station (not a NATO appointment) would be the Commander-in-Chief Portsmouth (which in 1952 was Admiral Sir Arthur Power).

North Atlantic Sub-Commands Supreme Allied Commander Atlantic, Admiral McCormick (USN) added to the statement regarding the establishment of North Atlantic Command by revealing that his overall Command would be divided into two sub-commands, one for the Western Atlantic under himself, and the other for the Eastern Atlantic under a British Commander-in-Chief. He expected that a specific number of ships would be committed for war service and for training by all the North Atlantic countries except Iceland; and that, of the total naval forces in the Atlantic Command, about 60 per cent would be American and 30 per cent British, the remaining 10 per cent being contributed by Canada, France, Norway, Denmark, the Netherlands, Belgium and Portugal.

The Atlantic Command, its extent and Headquarters The Atlantic Command, from its inception, has extended from the North Pole to the Tropic of Cancer and from North-American shores to the coastal waters of western Europe and Africa, and includes Iceland and the Azores, but with the exception of the English Channel and the waters around the British Isles. Admiral McCormick, the first SACLANT, and all successive Supreme Allied Commanders, Atlantic have dual command headquarters, both as Supreme Allied Commander Atlantic and Commander-in-Chief US Atlantic Fleet at Norfolk, Virginia (USA), while Vice-Admiral Andrews, as Commander-in-Chief America and West Indies Station, had his headquarters at Bermuda. (Headquarters of the Deputy Supreme Allied Commander Atlantic is now at Norfolk, Virginia).

The Western Atlantic Sub-Command Allied Command Western Atlantic Area is a sub-command subordinate to Allied Command Atlantic. The sub-command is headed by the Commander-in-Chief who is directly responsible to the Supreme Allied Commander Atlantic for the performance of his mission and the tasks assigned to him. CINCWESTLANT commands a military body with an identified NATO mission which is both international in character and has an international personnel establishment authorized by the Military Committee of NATO. To assist the Commander-in-Chief in his responsibility, an international staff is provided, comprised of personnel from the United States, the United Kingdom and Canada.

Atlantic Command, re-designation of certain Sub-Areas On 21 July 1952 the British Admiralty announced that:

- The naval sub-area under the Supreme Allied Commander, Atlantic previously designated the North-East Atlantic Sub-Area, would in future be known as the Central Sub-Area.
- That the sub-area previously known as the Northern European Sub-Area would become the Northern Sub-Area.
- That the areas of these Commands lying within the United Kingdom Home Station Command would in future be known as the Western Approaches and the Northern Approaches respectively.
- That the corresponding air commands would similarly be designated the Central and Northern Sub-Areas respectively.

SACLANT, his responsibilities in peace and war The Supreme Allied Commander Atlantic (SACLANT) has peacetime responsibility for preparing defence plans, conducting joint training exercises, establishing training standards and supplying the NATO authorities with information on his strategic requirements. SACLANT's primary task in time of war is to provide for the security of the Atlantic area by guarding the sea lanes and denying their use to an enemy in order to safeguard them for the reinforcement and resupply of NATO Europe with men and *matériel*.

Commands subordinate to the Supreme Allied Commander Atlantic (SACLANT)

- The Western Atlantic Command, which comprises:
(a) A Submarine Force Western Atlantic Area.
(b) An Ocean Sub-Area.
(c) A Canadian Atlantic Sub-Area.
(d) The Bermuda, Azores and Greenland Island Commands.
- The Eastern Atlantic Command which comprises:
(a) Maritime Air Eastern Atlantic Area.
(b) Northern Sub-Area.
(c) Maritime Air Northern Sub-Area.
(d) Central Sub-Area.
(e) Maritime Air Central Sub-Area.
(f) Submarine Force Eastern Atlantic Area.
(g) The Island Commanders of Iceland and the Faroes.
- The Striking Fleet Atlantic Command comprises:
(a) A Carrier Strike Force.
(b) Carrier Strike Groups One and Two.
- The Submarine Allied Command Atlantic.
- The Iberian Atlantic Command (see page 48). This command includes the Island Command of Madeira.
- The Standing Naval Force Atlantic – afloat.

The establishment of the Standing Naval Force Atlantic The Foreign and Defence Ministers attending the winter Ministerial meeting of the North Atlantic Council held at the new, but temporary, headquarters in Brussels on 13–14 December 1967 decided to transform the 'Matchmaker' Naval Training Squadron into a Standing Naval Force Atlantic consisting of destroyer-type ships. This force, continuously operational, was formed to enhance the existing co-operation

between the naval forces of the NATO member countries. STANAVFORLANT was formally established on 13 January 1968 at Portland (UK).

The vessels of the original Standing Naval Force Atlantic Under the command of Captain G. C. Mitchell, Royal Navy, the force initially comprised the British anti-submarine frigate *Brighton* (2,200 tons); the US escort destroyer *Holder* (2,425 tons); the Dutch anti-submarine destroyer *Holland* (2,215 tons); and the Norwegian frigate *Narvik* (1,450 tons). Although under the overall command of Admiral E. P. Holmes, SACLANT, the Force, when in European waters, was responsible to Admiral Sir John Bush, Allied Commander-in-Chief Channel and Commander-in-Chief, Eastern Atlantic.

STANAVFORLANT today The Standing Naval Force Atlantic today continues to be made up of ships from NATO countries, and is under the direct command of SACLANT. Operational control of STANAVFORLANT is assigned by SACLANT to the Commander-in-Chief of the area in which it is operating. This force is the world's first permanent international naval squadron formed in peacetime and assigned to SACLANT on a continuous basis. In addition, for training purposes and in the event of war, forces earmarked by the nations involved are assigned to SACLANT. Although these forces are predominantly naval, they also include ground forces and land-based air forces. STANAVFORLANT takes part in numerous exercises, manoeuvres and port visits in European and North-American waters, thus providing a tangible reminder of the unity and solidarity of the Alliance. It is constantly deployed throughout the 12 million square miles of the North Atlantic.

The establishment of SACLANT Anti-Submarine Warfare Research Centre – SASWREC A NATO establishment for oceanographic research – the SACLANT Anti-Submarine Warfare Research Centre – was formally inaugurated at La Spezia, Italy on 2 May 1959. Although its purpose was to carry out research in the field of anti-submarine warfare, the centre concentrated primarily on basic oceanographic research rather than actual development of anti-submarine weapons. In many respects the work of the centre complemented that carried out by the US Navy and such US Government agencies as the National Science Foundation. The Centre – directly responsible to the Supreme Commander Atlantic – was staffed by nineteen senior scientists under the direction of Dr E. T. Booth (USA), and organized in three basic divisions: oceanography, applied research and operational research and analysis.

A Scientific Advisory Council comprising members from the nine participating countries of Canada, Denmark, France, the Federal Republic of Germany, Italy, the Netherlands, Norway, the United Kingdom and the United States, made recommendations for the Centre's work, advised on programmes and examined progress; the NATO Secretariat was represented on this Council by the NATO Science Adviser. The project was financed by a US grant of two and a half million US dollars under a mutual weapons development programme. Since the creation of the Centre in May 1959 operations had been financially backed only by the United States and administered by a non-profit making Italian organization (SIRIMAR), owned and managed by Pennsylvania State University under contract with the US Department of Defence.

In January 1963 it was announced that the SACLANT Anti-Submarine Warfare Research Centre was to be completely re-organized so as to receive full NATO support as an international military organization. With the change-over to full NATO support, the scientific and business operations then being conducted by SIRIMAR would be terminated; the Centre continuing to advise and assist NATO commanders and nations in the anti-submarine research field, its policy direction remaining in the hands of the Supreme Allied Commander, Atlantic.

Inauguration of Iberian Command Atlantic The new Iberian Command Atlantic (IBERLANT), established to protect Allied shipping in the western approaches to the Mediterranean, was inaugurated on 22 February 1967 under the command of Rear-Admiral Edwin S. Miller, US Navy, with a staff of American, British, Dutch and Portuguese naval officers.

Attached to Allied Command Atlantic and directly responsible to SACLANT, IBERLANT initially occupied headquarters near Lisbon (Portugal) while permanent buildings were in the course of construction at Fort Gomes Freire, on the Lisbon-Estoril coast road. The new Command, the first NATO institution to be based in Portugal, filled the gap in communications left by the withdrawal from NATO command of the French Mediterranean Fleet in March 1959 and of other French naval units in January 1964. IBERLANT covers an area of approximately 600,000 square miles of ocean from the Tropic of Cancer to Portugal's northern border and extending some 800 kilometres (500 miles) westward into the Atlantic. Through this area pass the majority of the sea lanes to and from South Africa, South America, the Mediterranean via the Straits of Gibraltar and north-west Europe. Along these lanes are carried the oil supplies essential for the economy of western Europe. Iberian Command Atlantic therefore controls an area vital to the safeguard of NATO and its member countries.

Establishment of Channel Command

On 21 February 1952 it was announced from NATO Headquarters, London, that an Allied naval and air command had been set up for the English Channel and the southern part of the North Sea, under the name of Channel Command. Admiral Sir Arthur Power, Commander-in-Chief Portsmouth and Commander-in-Chief Home Station (designate) was appointed the first Commander-in-Chief Channel Command (CINCHAN). Air Marshal A. G. Stevens, Air Officer Commander-in-Chief Royal Air Force Coastal Command and Commander-in-Chief Air, Eastern Atlantic (designate) was appointed Allied Air Commander-in-Chief Channel Command. The Chiefs of Naval Staff of the adjacent countries (the United Kingdom, France, the Netherlands and Belgium) formed a Channel Committee, for the purpose of acting as a local agency of the Standing Group of the NATO Military Committee, charged with the task of solving immediate mutual problems.

A joint statement issued by the British Admiralty and the Air Ministry amplified the NATO announcement. Representatives of the naval staffs of the four powers were in permanent session in London, under the chairmanship of the First Sea Lord or his representative. Admiral Power, in conjunction with Air Marshal Stevens, was the co-ordinating authority for all naval and maritime air operations within the Channel Command area and the duties of the two officers were defined:

- To exercise maritime control of the area.
- To protect the sea lines of communications.
- To afford naval and maritime air support to operations conducted by SACEUR and SACLANT as necessary.

Channel Command, Command changes and new headquarters In January 1966 the Commander-in-Chief Eastern Atlantic, who was also at that time British Commander-in-Chief Home Fleet, assumed the additional NATO post of Commander-in-Chief Channel (CINCHAN), which hitherto had been an independent NATO Command traditionally held by the Commander-in-Chief Portsmouth. The staff of Channel Command moved from their Portsmouth headquarters to the headquarters of Eastern Atlantic Command at Northwood, Middlesex (UK) in August 1966.

Allied Command Channel today, its responsibility and mission The Allied Command Channel (ACCHAN) covers the English Channel and the southern areas of the North Sea. The Command Area is sub-divided into five Subordinate Commands – see below. The English Channel is almost completely surrounded by NATO land masses and it is not a good waterway for offensive operations by fast deep-running submarines. Air attack on the United Kingdom and the Channel ports by all but the Backfire-type Soviet aircraft would necessitate flying over NATO or neutral air space. Warsaw Pact surface naval forces are not likely to operate in waters surrounded by hostile nations. The major threat to Channel Command is therefore mine warfare. ACCHAN's mission is to control and protect merchant shipping in the area, co-operating with SACEUR in the air defence of the Channel. In emergency the forces earmarked to the Command are predominantly naval, but include maritime air forces. The Allied Commander-in-Chief Channel (CINCHAN) has a Maritime Air Adviser who is also Commander Allied Maritime Air Adviser, and Commander Allied Maritime Air Force Channel.

Commands subordinate to the Allied Commander-in-Chief Channel Command (CINCHAN)

- The Nore Channel Command.
- The Plymouth Channel Command.
- The Benelux Channel Command.
- The Allied Maritime Air Force Channel Command.
- The Standing Naval Force Channel (Mine Counter-Measure) – afloat.

The Standing Naval Force Channel A Standing Naval Force Channel (STANAVFORCHAN), approved by the Defence Planning Committee, was commissioned on 11 May 1973. Operational command of the force, which initially consisted of mine counter-measure ships from the navies of Belgium, The Netherlands and the United Kingdom and with other interested countries participating on a temporary basis, was vested in the Commander-in-Chief Channel Command.

The English Channel is one of the world's busiest shipping areas and the NATO member countries depend on the con-tinuous free access to its sea lanes for their foreign trade and commerce. In the event of war or an emergency, the Channel Command would be an important factor in keeping open the lifeline for the reinforcement of western Europe. A major threat to Allied Command Channel is mine warfare. Sea mines can be planted prior to the opening of hostilities and actuated by a pre-set signal. Mines sown in the shallow, confined waters of the English Channel would be highly effective. Vulnerability to sea mines reinforces the vital importance of the mine counter-measure ships of the Standing Naval Force Channel.

STANAVFORCHAN today is a permanently established multi-national mine counter-measure (MCM) force readily available to NATO and under the command of CINCHAN. STANAVFORCHAN has four basic objectives: to improve effective multi-national team work; to demonstrate the unity and common purpose of the Alliance; to be capable of acting as an Immediate Reaction Force and lastly, to provide the elements for the formation of a more powerful NATO naval force if required. In addition to vessels from Belgium, the Netherlands and the United Kingdom, mine counter-measure ships of the West German Bundesmarine are now a feature of the Force which frequently takes part in NATO, national, bi-national and multi-national exercises, manoeuvres and port visits as an individual force. Operations are, however, not only conducted in the Channel but in other areas as well.

Establishment of the NATO Defence College, the NATO School (SHAPE) and the SHAPE Technical Centre

On 3 July 1951 it was announced that the North Atlantic Council of Deputies had unanimously approved a recommendation by General Eisenhower for the establishment of a NATO Defence College to be situated in the Paris area. It was planned to open the College in the autumn of 1951. Its first Commandant was Vice-Admiral André Lemonnier of the French Navy who remained Deputy Naval Supreme Commander under General Eisenhower. Students at the Defence College were drawn from army, navy and air force officers of the NATO countries as well as from civilians attached to NATO organizations. Officer candidates had to be of the rank of lieutenant-colonel or the equivalent. Courses were planned to last for six months and the languages of instruction were French and English. It was anticipated that the first class would comprise 50 students when the College opened in the autumn of 1951.

NATO Defence College moves from Paris to Rome Fifteen years after it was opened the NATO Defence College was ordered to leave French territory (see page 25). The French Government's decision to withdraw from NATO meant that the College, together with other French-based NATO establishments were compelled to leave France by 1 April 1967. In September 1966 the Italian Government accepted the NATO Council's invitation to provide a new home for the NATO Defence College on the outskirts of Rome. The College's last course at the Ecole Militaire in Paris ended on 22 July 1966 and its first in the Palazzo Fondiaria was officially inaugurated on 18 January 1967, in the presence of President Saragat, Signor Moro, the Italian Prime Minister, leading members of the Italian Government and prominent NATO representatives including General Lemnitzer (USA) and Signor Brosio (Italy).

The NATO School (SHAPE) In January 1953, the then Supreme Allied Commander Europe, General Matthew B. Ridgway, decided that it was appropriate to introduce nuclear battlefield planning into NATO manoeuvres and exercises. He instigated the establishment of two courses of instruction, one a broad orientation course of a few days' duration for senior NATO Commanders, and a second, being a more detailed, two-week course for NATO Staff Officers. Both these programmes of instruction were designed to prepare key officers for their NATO appointments, providing them with an understanding of the plans, policies and procedures of Allied Command Europe related to the employment of advanced weapons systems.

The courses of instruction were conducted at the Special Weapons Branch of the US Army School based at Oberammergau (FRG). This organization was later designated as the NATO Weapons Systems Department and in 1966 was placed under the operational control of SACEUR. The Department's curriculum was enlarged to include additional courses dealing with the tactical aspects of nuclear weapons employment, chemical and biological defence operations and air-delivered conventional weapons. All six courses are still presented today and are constantly being upgraded to reflect the latest developments within NATO and Allied Command Europe.

In 1966 requests were submitted to all NATO member countries soliciting their support in developing a multi-national NATO facility. The expansion was highly successful and today the NATO School enjoys tri-service representation from nine member nations.

In 1973 the Department was re-designated as the NATO Weapons System School and was assigned to US European Command as a separate entity but still under the full operational control of SACEUR. In 1975 the name of the School underwent a further change when it was again re-designated, this time to its present designation as The NATO School (SHAPE) (NSS). Since its inception, more than 28,000 officers, non-commissioned officers and civilians from all the international and national military commands within NATO and from many NATO agencies have attended courses at the School.

SHAPE Technical Centre Only five years after the North Atlantic Alliance came into being, concern was being expressed about the relative weakness of the Alliance's air defences. In 1954 the idea was conceived for the establishment of an 'Operational Research Group', an independent body with no international bias to study in detail the problems of, and possible solutions to, NATO's air defences. The projected

results being that the air defences should be organized internationally according to a general plan, but with each NATO member country implementing the defence of its own areas.

The Operational Research Group has since developed into a scientific and technical centre responsible for the analysis of and solutions to the many and varied technical and scientific problems which affect Allied Command Europe. The implementation of NATO's Air Defence Ground Environment system (NADGE) and the Integrated Communications Network are just two of the major works undertaken on the recommendation of the Technical Centre.

The Centre, set up in The Hague (Netherlands), formally opened in February 1955 as SHAPE Air Defence Technical Centre under US funding arrangements and with Dutch administration. In 1960 the funding became international. In 1963 the scope of the Centre was broadened to encompass all air defence matters pertaining to ACE and the name of the Centre was changed to its present title of SHAPE Technical Centre.

STC's appointed mission is to provide scientific and technical assistance to SHAPE. In fulfillment of this mission it undertakes research, studies, investigation, development projects and operational tests. It also gives scientific and technical assistance on request to individual NATO nations if its primary work programme permits. The Technical Centre is controlled by a Board of Governors composed of scientists and engineers from NATO member countries. It has a staff of 350 of which about 100 are scientists. The Centre has access to defence and research information supplied by the scientists and engineers which is then evaluated and put to the use of the Alliance as a whole.

The Inter-Allied Confederation of Reserve Officers The Inter-Allied Confederation of Reserve Officers (CIOR) was established as early as November 1948 in Brussels by the grouping together of the Reserve Officers Associations of Belgium, France and the Netherlands. Since 1948 other associations from other Alliance countries have joined the Confederation so that today, with the exception of Iceland, Portugal and Turkey, all the NATO countries are represented in the CIOR. The current membership is approximately 300,000 with a potential of more than one million reserve officers.

NATO Airborne Early Warning And Control System

In 1976, at both the spring and winter ministerial meetings of the North Atlantic Council (held in Oslo, Norway on 20–21 May and Brussels, Belgium on 9–10 December respectively), the importance was reaffirmed for the urgent need to set up a NATO Airborne Early Warning Force. The system under discussion, known then as Airborne Warning And Control System (AWACS), was intended to comprise 27 converted Boeing 707 aircraft, each with a rotating radar dish on top, capable of 'peering' 200 miles into Eastern Bloc territory from a cruising altitude of 40,000 feet and giving early warning of impending low-level attack. The estimated cost in 1976 of buying the 27 aircraft from the United States was put at $2,400m.

The United Kingdom's Nimrod contribution to the Airborne Early Warning System On 31 March 1977 an announcement was made in the House of Commons of the British Government's decision to adopt the Nimrod airborne early warning system, comprising the RAF's Fleet of eleven Hawker Siddeley Nimrod aircraft, at that time being used for long-range maritime patrol, fitted with the then newly developed (but not perfected) radar system by Marconi-Elliott Avionics. The Nimrod's were technically assigned to NAEW Force from May 1982.

Implementation of the Airborne Early Warning Force The winter ministerial meeting of the North Atlantic Council held in Brussels on 7–8 December 1978 recommended that the proposed NATO airborne early warning and control management organization be established immediately in order to implement the programme. AWACS costing $1,800m would consist of 16 to 18 modified Boeing 707 aircraft renamed E3A, operating from a main base at Geilenkirchen (FRG) – the former RAF base handed back to Germany in 1968 – from early in 1982. Loaded with radar and computers, the aircraft would be able to monitor military activities up to 300 to 400 miles inside East Germany, Poland, Czechoslovakia and Hungary.

NATO Airborne Early Warning Force The NAEW was officially created in January 1980. The NAEW Force Command (the Force's Headquarters) was granted full status as a major NATO Headquarters by the Defence Planning Committee on 17 October 1980. Commander NAEW Force is currently a US Air Force major-general, his deputy being a Royal Air Force air commodore. The command is co-located with Supreme Headquarters Allied Powers Europe at Casteau, Belgium. From SHAPE Supreme Allied Commander Europe (SACEUR) shares with Supreme Allied Commander Atlantic (SACLANT) and Commander-in-Chief Channel (CINCHAN) operational command over the NATO Airborne Early Warning Force. SACEUR acts as Executive Agent of the Major NATO Commanders in promulgating operational command directives and in the day-to-day exercise of administrative control of this force.

NAEW Force operational units The operational units of the NAEW Force comprise eighteen Boeing E-3A Sentry aircraft. Insurmountable difficulties with the radar system installed in the Hawker Siddeley Nimrod aircraft resulted in the failure of Britain to contribute eleven of her aircraft to the NAEW Force. The E-3As are manned by mixed crews from twelve of NATO's sixteen member countries (Belgium, Canada, Denmark, Federal Republic of Germany, Greece, Italy, the Netherlands, Norway, Portugal, Turkey, the United Kingdom and the United States). The crews are 17-strong, of whom 13 are systems operators. The E-3A component is the only multi-national integrated operational force in the Atlantic Alliance.

NAEW Force operational ability The Airborne Early Warning (AEW) radars employed in the E-3As have the ability to detect and track enemy aircraft operating at low altitudes over all types of terrain, and to identify and give direction to friendly aircraft operating in the same area. In addition, a 'maritime mode' allows detection of enemy shipping and monitoring of its movements. The mobility of the NAEW Force allows aircraft to be deployed rapidly to wherever needed. This mobility, coupled with the aircraft's ability to direct fighter aircraft for its own defence, makes AEW radar far less vulnerable to attack than ground-based radars.

NAEW Force operating bases The Force's aircraft have a main operating base and a number of forward operating bases and locations. The three E-3A Sentry squadrons each of six aircraft and ten crews are stationed at Geilenkirchen (FRG), formally assigned to NATO on 28 June 1982. The forward operating bases (FOBs) and locations are in Konya, Turkey; Previza, Greece; Orland, Norway; Trapani, Italy; and the United Kingdom. The E-3A component was activated in June 1982.

The mission of the NAEW Force The mission of the NATO Airborne Early Warning Force is essentially air surveillance of NATO territory in Europe. Flying just behind the border between NATO and the Warsaw Pact, the Force's aircraft fitted with a rotodome are able to 'see' deep into the potential enemy's territory, providing communications support for various air operations. The airborne radar systems are inter-operable with friendly land and naval forces, and there is a communications capability with both ground-based commanders and naval units at sea.

Euro-NATO Joint Jet Pilot Training Programme

At a winter ministerial meeting of the North Atlantic Council attended by the Foreign Ministers of the fifteen NATO member countries, which took place in Brussels on 11–12 December 1980, a memorandum of understanding was signed by the ministers of twelve of the NATO countries, establishing a co-operative cost-sharing training programme in the United States for the training of jet pilots and instructors to begin in October 1981. The programme was designed to improve the effectiveness and readiness of the NATO air forces through the benefits of enhanced inter-operability, standardized tactics and techniques, and economies of large-scale training.

The memorandum – signed by the Defence Ministers of Canada, the United States, and all the European NATO countries except France, Iceland and Luxembourg – provided for a co-operative pilot training programme to be known as EURO-NATO Joint Jet Pilot Training, ENJJPT. Under the programme, which began in October 1981 at Sheppard US Air Force Base in Texas (USA), each course would train 320 student pilots and 110 student instructor pilots, the programme costs and instructor pilot personnel requirements being proportionately shared and provided by the participating countries.

Proposal to Build a NATO Missile Training Range on the Island of Crete

On 10 April 1960 it was announced in Athens that the NATO Standing Group had approved a proposal to construct a NATO training base for short-range guided missiles on the Mediterranean island of Crete. The base was to be available to all NATO countries for training in the deployment of missiles of a range not to exceed 240 kilometres (150 miles). The base was to have both Greek and American instructors and its administration and operational control was to be entirely in Greek hands. Alternative sites on Greek territory suitable for short-range missile firing had been examined and the one chosen on Crete would include stations for space exploration and tracking satellites.

Agreement signed for the construction of the NATO Missile Training Range in Crete An agreement was signed by Greece and seven of the NATO member countries – Belgium, Denmark, France, Federal Republic of Germany, the Netherlands, Norway and the United States. Turkey refused to sign as she had wanted the training centre to be installed on Turkish territory. The agreement, which dates from 11 June 1964, provided for joint use and the division of the construction costs, initially put at £18m, of the new missile training range which was scheduled to be completed in 1965.

Formal inauguration of the NATO Guided Missile Firing Range in Crete The guided-missile firing range built on the Akrotiri peninsula in north-eastern Crete for NATO use was formally inaugurated on 17 May 1968. Costing in the region of £20m, an increase of £2m from the original estimate, one-third of which was contributed by the USA, the range is used to train NATO troops from the USA, West Germany, Italy, Denmark, Norway, the Netherlands, Turkey and Greece, in firing Nike and Hawk surface-to-air missiles.

The NATO Flag

On 28 October 1953 the North Atlantic Treaty Organization announced that it had adopted navy-blue and white as its official colours and at the same time had adopted a NATO flag. The flag has a field of navy-blue charged with the NATO symbol, a blue-and-white, four-pointed star known as the 'compass rose' set within a narrow white circle. The blue portions of the blue-and-white counter-charged arms have fine white fibrillations tapering towards the points of the star. The ends of the arms to the star overlay the white circle in four places, and there are four narrow white lines extending from the points of the star towards the edges of the flag.

The symbolism of the design of the flag is explained as: the navy-blue field represents the waters of the North Atlantic; the white circle stands for unity and the compass rose represents the common direction towards peace shared by all the member nations of the Alliance. It is these colours and this emblem that are often to be found incorporated into the design of a number of NATO badges.

Badges and Insignia of NATO and National Units Assigned to NATO

Badges and insignia worn by members of NATO military formations can be divided into two categories:

■ Those items worn by military personnel on the staff of, or attached to, NATO establishments.

■ Those items worn by troops from the armed forces of NATO member countries assigned to NATO Command.

Not every known badge or insignia has been illustrated in this work. The insignia that is associated with NATO Commands or Establishments includes both past and present items. The badges of the national units assigned to NATO Command are, in the main, current issues. Far more badges exist than are shown here and those that are illustrated should be regarded only as representative and not as a definitive list.

I would like to think that 'insignia' refers to those items that are worn sewn to a uniform, while 'badges' are those items, usually made of metal, that are worn either as pocket fobs or pin-on items. This definition, however, is my own and may not appeal to all fellow-collectors.

Badges and insignia are produced in either cloth or metal. Cloth items have more of a variety of manufacture than is the case with metal badges. Cloth insignia can be produced with a design embroidered on to a felt background, or on linen, or in the case of US shoulder-sleeve insignia (SSIs) fully embroidered. Signs printed on fabric, usually linen, tend to be of the type in use during the early, formative period of NATO. They were a relatively inexpensive method of producing cloth insignia in bulk. Nowadays these printed signs have been superseded by machine-woven items, normally produced as a continuous strip or band of cloth with the design worked in coloured cotton or silk threads. Designs manufactured in coloured plastics, being heat-mounted on to a cloth backing, are a comparatively recent innovation. Metal badges usually have inlaid designs of coloured enamels, and with just a few exceptions, most NATO badges are produced as shield-shaped items.

As already mentioned these are worn on the military tunic

either as pocket fobs or as pin-on badges. The pocket fob, which is a French innovation, is worn suspended from a tunic button, usually the button of a breast-pocket flap which is passed through the eye of the pocket-fob strap. The fob itself is manufactured from leather or strong plastic, usually black or tan in colour. The metal insignia is mounted on to the fob by being glued into position, affixed with a long pin through the backing of the fob or by metal prongs in a similar manner. Pin-on metal badges, as their name implies, have a form of pin-on brooch fastening mounted on the reverse of the badge. These items are worn on the military tunic, pinned directly into the cloth of the garment. This type of badge is very often worn on those military jackets that have no breast pockets and therefore no pocket buttons.

Badges of national units assigned to NATO Almost from its inception the North Atlantic Treaty Organization has had assigned to it military formations drawn from the armed forces of its member countries. In almost every instance where a military unit passes under NATO command its personnel continue to wear the insignia they normally wear as part of the armed forces of their parent member nation. Unlike the national forces assigned to the United Nations peace-keeping units, with their distinctive sky-blue berets,

white beret badges and pale-blue world-globe arm badges, there is no NATO emblem worn as a universal badge by formations assigned to NATO. This is not to be confused with the use of the NATO compass rose emblem incorporated into the design of many individual unit badges and insignia. Nor should it be confused with the wearing of arm bands and brassards bearing the NATO symbol worn temporarily for military exercises.

Insignia worn by NATO personnel on the staff of NATO establishments Borrowing a practice that has been in use with the French military forces, military personnel attached to, or on the staff of, the various NATO Commands and Establishments have taken to wearing metal badges displaying a design peculiar to their command or establishment. These metal badges are normally worn in the form of a pocket fob or pin-on item (see above) and are regarded and collected by collectors as NATO badges, although with a wide range of individual designs. However, in quite a number of instances, the designs found on some of the metal badges are also produced as cloth or plastic insignia worn sewn to certain items of uniform dress, which in the main are usually by army and air force personnel.

PLATE 1. KINGDOM OF BELGIUM: ARMY

The cockade of concentric rings of red (outer), yellow and black are the national colours of the Kingdom of Belgium. These cockades are worn on the uniform peaked cap by all ranks in the Belgian Army.

Rank is shown on the uniform peaked cap by the use of specific insignia, coloured cap bands, gold bars and piping and different types of chin-cords or chin-straps, as explained below.

The Belgian Army employs a system of colours to indicate its various branches of service, types of formations and, in a number of instances, specific ranks. These colours are used on the cloth collar patches as well as the shoulder-strap slip-ons. The collar patches have a main colour together with a secondary colour used as 2mm thick piping along the upper edge of the patch in the shape of a 45-degree angled chevron.

All collar patches display rank insignia, and in a number of cases, branch of service insignia. These patches are worn on the Service Dress by all ranks. In addition to

this, General Officers also wear shoulder-boards displaying their rank stars on the Service Great-coat. Collar patches are worn in matching pairs as are shoulder-boards and shoulder-strap slip-ons.

Head-dress

1 Uniform peaked cap for General Officers of the Belgian Army (ranks 6 to 9). Caps worn by officers of these ranks are distinguished by the carmine red cap band, the 'Foudre' badge – the bundle of lightning bolts, repeated on their collar patches, the twin double gold bars on each side of the cap badge and gold cap cords.

2 Peaked cap for senior officers (ranks 10 to 13). Caps worn by officers of these ranks display single vertical gold bars on each side of the cap badge, here shown for a Line Battalion officer – the Royal Belgian crown, gold cap cords and gold piping to lower edge of the plain khaki cap band.

3 Cap for junior officers, here shown for a Carabinier officer.

4 Cap for warrant officers, here shown for Engineer warrant officer. Note the silver cap cords.

5 Cap for NCOs and men of the Ardennes Light Infantry. Chin-strap is of brown leather. It should be noted that the khaki beret has become the standard everyday form of head-wear throughout the Belgian Army with the exception of Paratroopers who wear maroon-coloured berets, black for crews of tanks and green berets for personnel of the Chasseurs Ardennes.

Rank and Appointment Insignia

All rank and appointment terms used in the Belgian armed forces are shown here both in Flemish and French.

6 Collar patch worn by Luitenant-Generaal/Lieutenant-Général.

7 Greatcoat shoulder-board for Luitenant-Generaal/Lieutenant-Général. Similar shoulder-boards are worn by Generaal-majoor/Général-major (two gold stars) and Brigade-generaal/Général de Brigade (single gold star).

8 Collar patch for Generaal-majoor/

Général-major.

9 Brigade-generaal/Général de brigade.

10 Kolonel/Colonel Infantry of the Line.

11 Luitenant-Kolonel/Lieutenant-Colonel of Royal Army Ordnance Corps.

12 Majoor/Major of Ordnance.

13 Kapitein-Commandant/Capitaine-Commandant of Grenadiers.

14 Kapitein/Capitaine of Artillery.

15 Luitenant/Lieutenant of Carabineers.

16 Onder-Luitenant/Sous-Lieutenant of the Ardenner Guards.

17 Shoulder-strap slip-on (shirt) insignia for Adjudant-Chef/Adjudant-Chef of Military Police.

18 1ste Adjudant/1er Adjudant of Engineers.

19 Adjudant/Adjudant of Lancers.

20 Cuff insignia for 1ste Sergent-Majoor/1er Sergent-Major.

21 1ste Sergeant/1er Sergent.

22 Sergeant/Sergent.

23 Korporaal-Chef/Caporal-Chef.

24 Korporaal/Caporal.

Soldat (no rank insignia worn).

PLATE 1. KINGDOM OF BELGIUM: ARMY

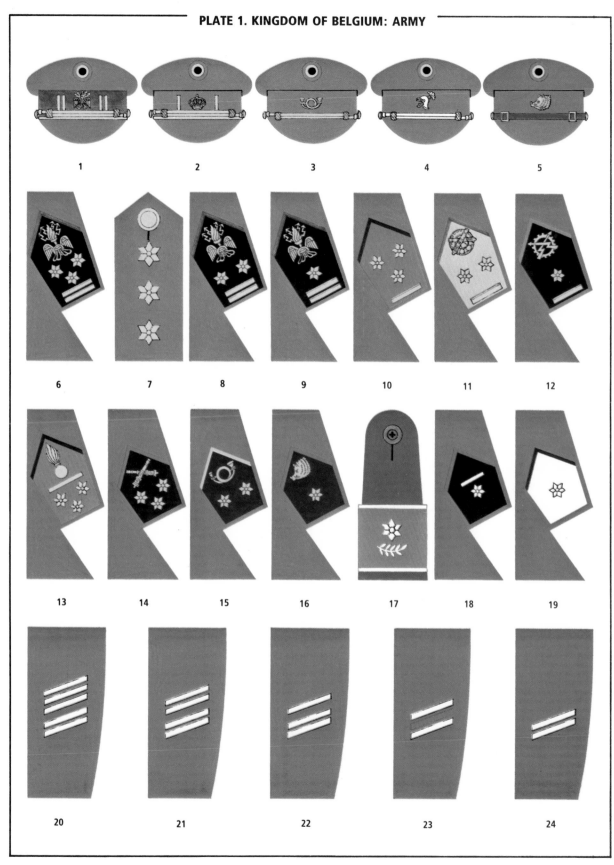

PLATE 2. KINGDOM OF BELGIUM: NAVY

Differences of rank are indicated on Belgian naval head-dress by the use of decoration on the peak and design and colour of the cap badges used. Rank shown on the naval uniform takes the form of sleeve rings, sleeve stripes and, for certain forms of dress, shoulder-strap slip-ons.

Head-dress

1 Uniform peaked cap for wear by naval officers of the ranks of Vice-Admiral, Admiral of Division and Commodore (ranks 7 to 9).
2 Cap as worn by a Captain at Sea and Frigate Captain (ranks 10 and 11).
3 Cap for Captains of Corvettes (rank 12).
4 Cap as worn by remaining officers (ranks 13 to 16).
5 Cap for Petty Officers (ranks 17 and 18).
6 Cap for ratings (ranks 19 to 24).

Rank and Appointment Insignia

7 Cuff rings (sleeve lace) for Vice-admiraal/Vice-amiral.
8 Divisie-admiraal/Amiral de Division.
9 Commodore/Commodore.
10 Kapitein-ter-zee/Capitaine de Vaisseau.
11 Fregat-Kapitein/Capitaine de Frégate.
12 Korvette-kapitein/Capitaine de Corvette.
13 Luitenantter-zee 1ste klas/Lieutenant de Vaisseau de 1ère classe.
14 Luitenantter-zee/Lieutenant de Vaisseau.
15 Vaandrigter-zee/Enseigne de Vaisseau.
16 Vaandrigter-zee 2de klas/Enseigne de vaisseau de 2ème classe.
17 Oppermeester/Maître Principal.
18 Eerste Meester-Chef/1er Maître Chef.
19 Cuff bars for Eerste meester/1ère Maître.
20 Meester/Maître.
21 Tweede Meester/Second Maître.
22 Kwartier-Meester/Quartier-Maître.
23 The insignia for the above rating rank as worn on the white shirt shoulder-strap.
24 Eerste matroos/1er Matelot. Matelot (no rank insignia worn).

Left: Korporaal Vandendries of the Belgian Army Military Police. Note the silver rank bars worn on the lower forearms of the light-weight, tan-coloured summer service uniform and the plain scarlet and white collar patches.

PLATE 2. KINGDOM OF BELGIUM: NAVY

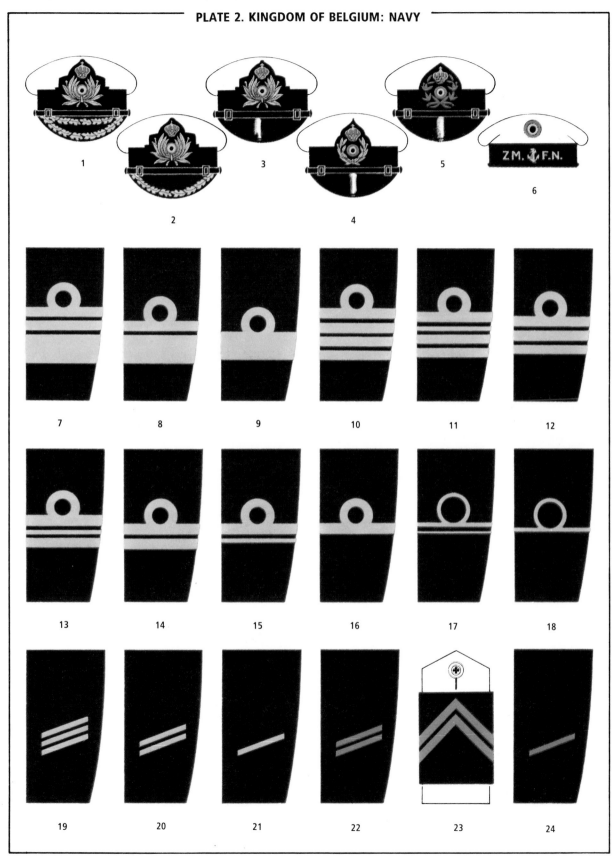

PLATE 3. KINGDOM OF BELGIUM: AIR FORCE

Rank is displayed on the Air Force uniform peaked cap by the means of peak decoration, the difference in cap badge design and colouring and the use of cap cords and chin-straps. The method of indicating rank on the Belgian Air Force's blue-grey uniform is not dissimilar to that used in the Royal Air Force. Sleeve rings and shoulder-boards are used by officers with the addition of distinctive collar insignia for General Officers. Shoulder-strap slip-ons are also used by all ranks, especially on the shirt and working overalls. The modern trend with these slip-ons is to produce them in coloured plastic. They have

the same superficial appearance as the equivalent cloth insignia, but are cheaper to produce. Non-Commissioned Officers display a system of ranks consisting of cuff bars.

Head-dress
1 Uniform peaked cap for General Officers (ranks 9 to 11).
2 Colonels.
3 Lieutenant-Colonels and Majors.
4 Remaining Officers.
5 Warrant Officers.
6 First Sergeants and Sergeants.
7 Peaked cap for remaining ranks.

Rank and Appointment Insignia
8 Collar insignia for Air Force Gen-

eral Officers (ranks 9 to 11). The Belgian Air Force uses the same style of insignia as that used in the Belgian Army (see item 6, plate 1). However the device of the bundle of lightning bolts is not worn as a collar patch, but instead is embroidered directly into the cloth of the collar.
9 Cuff rings as worn on the Service Uniform by a Luitenant-generaal/ Lieutenant-Général.
10 Generaal-majoor/Général-major.
11 Brigade-generaal/Général de brigade.
12 Kolonel/Colonel.
13 Shoulder-board for Luitenant-

kolonel/Lieutenant-Colonel.
14 Cuff rings for a Majoor/Major.
15 Kapitein-Commandant/ Capitaine-Commandant.
16 Kapitein/Capitaine.
17 Luitenant/Lieutenant.
18 Onder-Luitenant/Sous-Lieutenant.
19 Adjudant-Chef/Adjudant-Chef.
20 Adjudant/Adjudant.
21 Cuff bars for 1ste Sergeant-Majoor/1er Sergent-Major.
22 1ste Sergeant/1er Sergent.
23 Sergeant/Sergent.
24 Korporaal-chef/Caporal-Chef.
25 Korporaal/Caporal.
Soldat (no rank insignia worn).

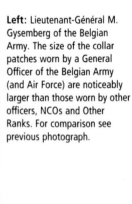

Left: Lieutenant-Général M. Gysemberg of the Belgian Army. The size of the collar patches worn by a General Officer of the Belgian Army (and Air Force) are noticeably larger than those worn by other officers, NCOs and Other Ranks. For comparison see previous photograph.

PLATE 3. KINGDOM OF BELGIUM: AIR FORCE

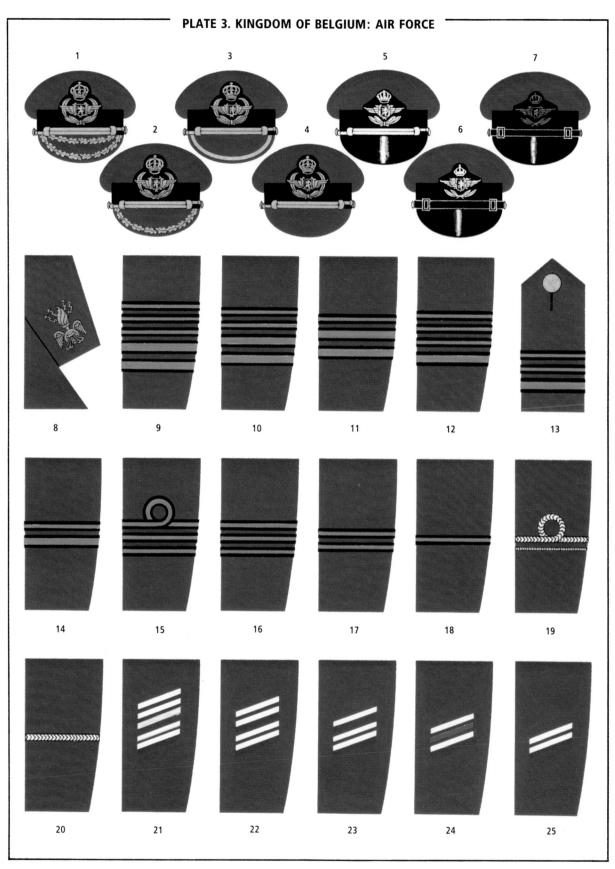

PLATE 4. KINGDOM OF BELGIUM: SERVICE MÉDICAL

Raised in January 1831 on the order of His Majesty King Leopold I of the Belgians, the Belgian Sanitary Service served – as part of the Belgian Army – continuously throughout two world wars until 1974, On 4 May 1974 the Sanitary Service became the Service Médical and was transformed into an independent force. Its khaki uniforms were changed for the present dark-green uniforms and new insignia, as illustrated here, were introduced at the same time.

Today the Service Médical is considered to be the fourth branch of the Belgian armed forces. Its purpose is to render assistance to the Army, Navy and Air Force and to the civilian population in crises such as the Zeebrugge ferry disaster. Its personnel are qualified doctors, dentists, pharmacists, and veterinarians as well as ancillary staff. In keeping with the Belgian Armed Services, the structure of the Service Médical is run on military lines having a General Officer class, senior and junior officers, warrant officers, non-commissioned officers and men. All wear a distinctive green uniform.

Rank is displayed on the uniform head-dress by the use of peak decoration, differences in cap badge colour and patterns of chin-cords and chin-straps. A green beret is worn for everyday use.

Service Médical personnel qualified as parachutists serving with Belgian and Para-Commando units have the distinction of wearing their maroon-coloured beret with the dark, or bottle-green uniform. It is the colour of the Service Médical uniform worn with the maroon beret that has given rise to the para-medics being known as the 'Coca-Cola boys'.

Rank displayed on the uniform is similar to that used in the Belgian Air Force, but with the notable addition of Shoulder-Passants. Shoulder Passants or 'Shoulder-Bars' are worn by all Service Médical/Medische Dienst personnel of the appropriate rank groupings on the green Service uniform. They are worn in pairs and, unlike shoulder-straps, are set across the shoulder following the line of the shoulder seam.

Head-dress

1 Uniform peaked cap for officers of General rank (ranks 8 and 9).
2 Caps for wear by Colonels (rank 10).
3 Lieutenant-Colonels and Majors (ranks 11 and 12).
4 Cap for all (remaining) junior officers.
5 Cap for Chief Adjutant to Sergeant (ranks 19 to 23).
6 Cap for Chief Corporal and below.

Rank and Appointment Insignia

7 Shoulder Passant worn by all General officers and officers down to the rank of Majoor/Major (ranks 8 to 12).
8 Cuff rings for Geneesher Generaal-majoor/Médecin Général-Major.
9 Cuff rings for Geneesheer Brigade-generaal/Médecin Général de brigade (this rank is now thought to be obsolete).
10 Kolonel/Colonel.
11 Luitenant-kolonel/Lieutenant-Colonel.
12 Majoor/Major.
13 Shoulder Passant worn by officer ranks from Commandant to Second Lieutenant (ranks 14 to 17).
14 Cuff rings for Commandant/Commandant.
15 Shirt sleeve shoulder-strap slip-on for Kapitein/Capitaine. (The white shirt worn as part of the formal dress uniform, a beige-coloured shirt for everyday wear and a green shirt as part of the working uniform. Shoulder-strap slip-ons are worn on all three colours of shirts when shirts are worn as shirt-sleeve order).
16 Luitenant/Lieutenant.
17 Onder-Luitenant/Sous-Lieutenant.
18 Shoulder Passant worn by all NCOs from Chief Adjutant and below.
19 Cuff rings for Adjudant-Chef/Adjudant-Chef.
20 Adjudant/Adjudant.
21 Cuff bars for 1ste Sergeant-majoor/1er Sergent-Major.
22 1ste Sergeant/1er Sergent.
23 Sergeant/Sergent.
24 Korporaal-Chef/Caporal-Chef.
25 Korporaal/Caporal.
   Soldat (no rank insignia worn).

PLATE 4. KINGDOM OF BELGIUM: SERVICE MEDICAL

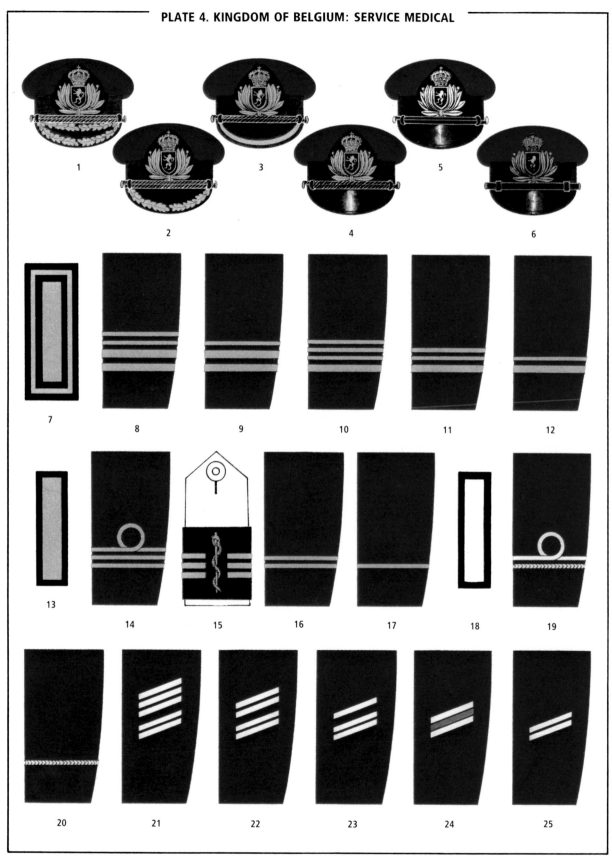

PLATE 5. KINGDOM OF BELGIUM: GENDARMERIE

The Gendarmerie is a paramilitary police force. It is structured along military lines with ranks not dissimilar to those of the Belgian Army. The Service Dress uniform is dark-blue with scarlet collar patches and piping. Rank is indicated on the dark-blue uniform peaked cap by means of cap cords, the colour of the cap badge and the use of gold bars on the cap band. Rank displayed on the uniforms takes the form of collar patches for all officer and warrant officer ranks and shoulder-straps for all lesser ranks.

Head-dress
1 Uniform peak cap worn by General officers (ranks 6 and 7).
2 Cap worn by Senior Officers (ranks 8 to 10).
3 Remaining officers (ranks 11 to 14).
4 Cap worn by Warrant Officers (ranks 15 and 16).
5 Cap worn by remaining NCOs (ranks 17 to 21).

Rank and Appointment Insignia
6 Collar patch for Luitenant-generaal/Lieutenant-Général.
7 Generaal-majoor/Général-Major.
8 Kolonel/Colonel.
9 Luitenant-kolonel/Lieutenant-Colonel.
10 Majoor/Major.
11 Kapitein-Commandant/Capitaine-Commandant.
12 Kapitein/Capitaine.
13 Luitenant/Lieutenant.
14 Onder-Luitenant/Sous-Lieutenant.
15 Adjudant-chef/Adjudant-Chef.
16 Adjudant/Adjudant.
17 Shoulder-strap worn by 1ste Opperwachtmeester/1er Maréchal des logis-chef.
18 Opperwachtmeester/Maréchal des logis-chef.
19 1ste Wachtmeester/1er Maréchal des logis.
20 Wachtmeester/Maréchal des logis.
21 Brigadier/Brigadier.

Left: An Opperwachtmeester of the Belgian Gendarmerie, also referred to as a Maréchal des logis-chef, depending on whether Flemish or French is spoken.

PLATE 5. KINGDOM OF BELGIUM: GENDARMERIE

1   2   3   4   5

6   7   8   9   10   11

12   13   14   15   16

17   18   19   20   21

PLATE 6. DOMINION OF CANADA: CANADIAN ARMED FORCES

On 25 April 1967 the Canadian House of Commons passed the third and final reading of the 'Armed Forces Unification Bill' which abolished the Royal Canadian Navy, the Canadian Army and the Royal Canadian Air Force and replaced them with a single defence service known as the Canadian Armed Forces.

A new uniform to replace the former uniforms of the three services was introduced for wear by all the personnel of the new integrated Defence Force. Dark-green was the colour chosen for the new uniform – this has given rise to the appellation 'Jolly Green Giants' – and except for badges and insignia of rank it is common both in cut and quality of material to officers and other ranks.

The choice of colour green and the quality of the new uniforms was deliberate. It was felt to be in keeping with Canada's classless society and a positive move away from the established European practice which the Canadian authorities claimed perpetuated a system of class differences between different ranks of the various armed services.

However, despite these egalitarian ideals the green uniform has not proved to have been as popular as was expected. New uniforms have therefore been, and are in the process of being, introduced. The Canadian Navy are to wear a dark-blue winter uniform and a white summer uniform. The Canadian Air Force an air force blue uniform and a light-weight khaki-tan summer uniform and the Canadian Army, while retaining the dark-green uniform have also a new light-weight khaki-tan summer uniform. The introduction of these latest uniforms began in September 1986 and the planned completion date is set for 31 January 1989. Half of the Canadian Forces have already received their new winter uniforms this year (April 1987) with their summer uniforms to follow. The remainder will receive their winter uniforms in September 1987 and their summer uniforms in April 1988.

Head-dress as illustrated here for the universal green uniform is of the same dark-green colour and has the same rank decoration on the peaks for officers of all three branches of the Canadian Armed Forces; only the cap badge changes for certain services and branches of the services.

Officers of all services wear cuff rings on the sleeves of the green uniform and rank insignia mounted on the shoulder-straps worn on the shirt.

Head-dress
1 Uniform peaked cap for General Officers of all services (ranks 7 to 10).
2 Cap for Senior Officers, here shown for Senior Naval Officers.
3 Cap for Junior Air Force Officers.
4 Sub-Officers, here shown for the Canadian Royal Artillery.
5 The dark-green beret worn by all ranks and all services. As with the peaked cap only the beret badge changes. Beret badge shown here worn by Security Personnel.

Rank and Appointment Insignia
6 Cuff ring for General Officers of all three services (ranks 7 to 10).
7 Shoulder-board as worn by: General (Army), Admiral (Navy) and General (Air Force).
8 Lieutenant-General (Army), Vice-Admiral (Navy), Lieutenant-General (Air Force).
9 Major-General (Army), Rear-Admiral (Navy), Major-General (Air Force).
10 Brigadier-General (Army), Commodore (Navy), Brigadier-General (Air Force).
11 Cuff rings for a Colonel (Army), Captain (N) (Navy), Colonel (Air Force).
12 Lieutenant-Colonel (Army), Commander (Navy), Lieutenant-Colonel (Air Force).
13 Major (Army), Lieutenant-Commander (Navy), Major (Air Force).
14 Captain (Army), Lieutenant (N) (Navy), Captain (Air Force).
15 Lieutenant (Army), Sub-Lieutenant (Navy), Lieutenant (Air Force).
16 Shoulder-strap slip-on as worn in shirt-sleeve order for Second Lieutenant (Army), Acting Sub-Lieutenant (Navy) and Second Lieutenant (Air Force).
17 Cuff ring for Officer Cadet (Army), Officer Cadet (Navy), Officer Cadet (Air Force).
18 Arm badge worn on forearm by Command Warrant Officer (Army), Command Chief Petty Officer 1 (Navy), Command Warrant Officer (Air Force).
19 Arm badge worn on forearm by Base Warrant Officer (Army), Base Chief Petty Officer 1 (Navy), Base Warrant Officer (Air Force).
20 Chief Warrant Officer (Army), Chief Petty Officer, 1st Class (Navy), Chief Warrant Officer (Air Force).
21 Master Warrant Officer (Army), Chief Petty Officer, 2nd Class (Navy), Master Warrant Officer (Air Force).
22 Warrant Officer (Army), Petty Officer 1st Class (Navy), Warrant Officer (Air Force).
23 Rank chevrons worn on upper arm by Sergeant (Army), Petty Officer 2nd Class (Navy), Sergeant (Air Force).
24 Master Corporal (Army), Master Seaman (Navy), Master Corporal (Air Force).
25 Corporal (Army), Leading Seaman (Navy), Corporal (Air Force).
26 Trained Private (Army), Able Seaman (Navy), Trained Private (Air Force).
Basic Private (Army), Ordinary Seaman (Navy), Basic Private (Air Force), Private Recruit (Army), Seaman (Navy), Private Recruit (Air Force), (no rank insignia worn).

Above: A Major of the Canadian Army Security branch. The insignia of rank is carried on the shoulder-straps of the pale green shirt. The Canadian national badge in the form of the national flag of Canada is worn on both shoulders of the shirt. The item featured here is the smaller of the two sizes that can be worn.

PLATE 6. DOMINION OF CANADA: CANADIAN ARMED FORCES

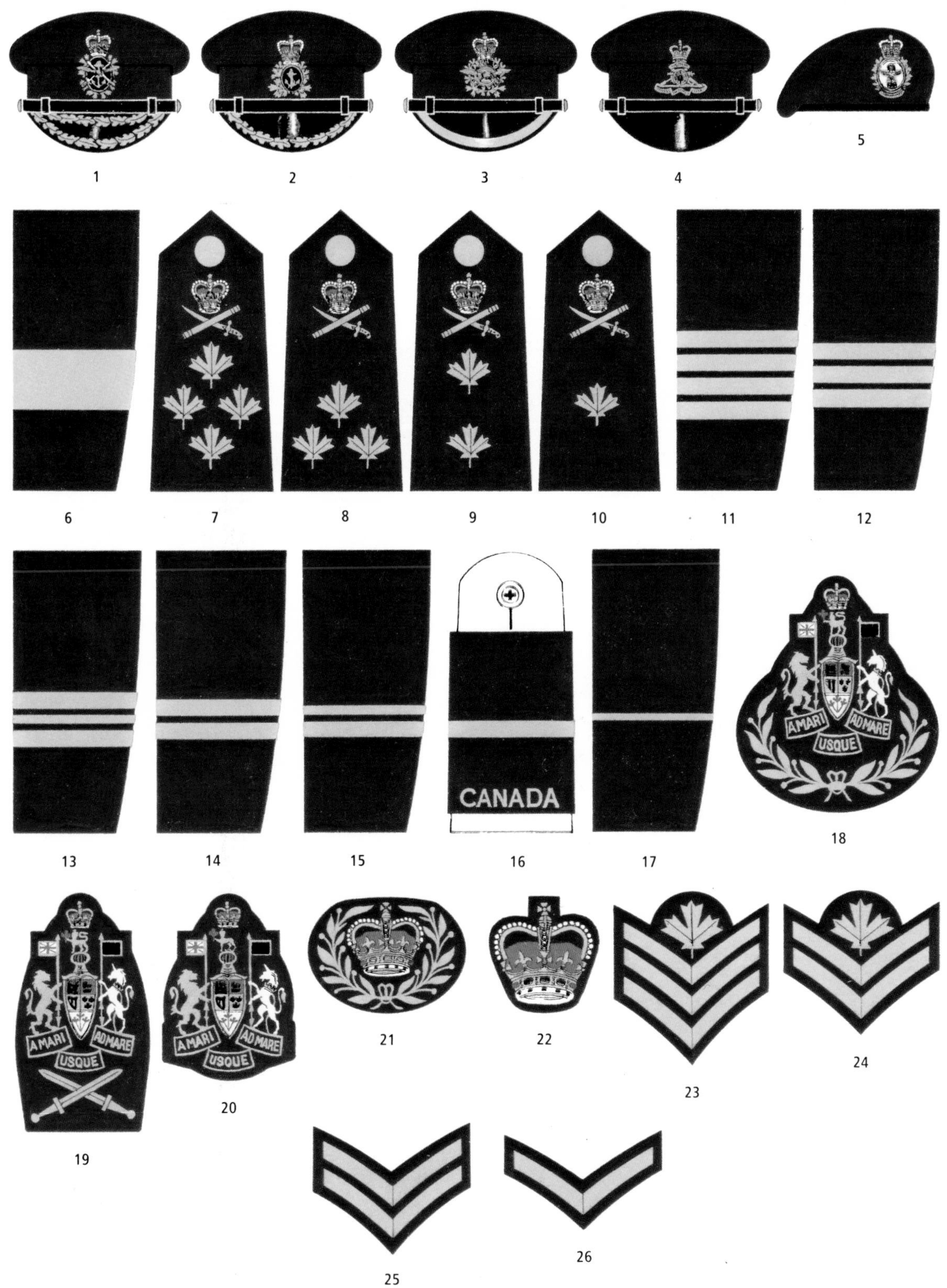

1

2

3

4

5

6

7

8

9

10

11

12

13

14

15

16

17

18

19

20

21

22

23

24

25

26

Above and right: Master Corporal McCoy Scott, Canadian Air Force, a member of the multi-national NATO AWACS maintenance crew.

Above: Sergeant Wionzek, 444 Tactical Helicopter Squadron, Royal Canadian Dragoons (RCAC). The Canadian national flag badge is worn on the right breast of the flying overalls, above the name tab, and the badges of rank are worn on the shoulder-strap above the national title. Squadron badge is shown worn on the left shoulder and the Flight Crewman qualification wings on the left breast.

Right: Insignia of rank for NCOs of the Canadian Armed Forces are worn pinned on the collar of the shirt in the form of miniature rank badges in yellow metal on a dark-green enamelled background. A Master Corporal of the Canadian Army Security Branch is acting as a Colour-bearer.

PLATE 7. KINGDOM OF DENMARK: ARMY

The use of the Uniform Peaked Cap is now restricted to General Officers only. All ranks now wear the dark-blue beret. The peaked cap shown here (item 2) was the pattern worn by officers other than General Officers. Rank displayed on the uniforms of the Royal Danish Army is by the use of shoulder-boards for officers and arm chevrons for NCOs. These rank chevrons in a simpler form are also carried on the shoulder-straps of certain types of uniform dress as slip-ons.

Head-dress
1 Uniform peaked cap for General class officers (ranks 4 to 7).
2 Uniform peaked cap, pattern now obsolete, worn by other Army officers.
3 Beret worn by all ranks below General.

Rank and Appointment Insignia
4 Shoulder-board for General.
5 Generalløjtnant.
6 Generalmajor.

7 Brigadegeneral.
8 Oberst.
9 Oberstløjtnant.
10 Major.
11 Kaptajn.
12 Premierløjtnant.
13 Løjtnant.
14 Sekondløjtnant.
15 Arm chevrons worn by Senior-sergent af 1.grad.
16 Seniorsergent af 2.grad. Shoulder-strap slip-on on shirt or combat jacket.

17 Arm chevrons for Seniorsergent af 2.grad.
18 Oversergent.
19 Sergent.
20 Sergent (Conscript).
21 Korporal.
22 Korporal (conscript).
23 Overkonstabel af 1.grad.
24 Overkonstabel af 2.grad.
25 Konstabel.

Left: Sergent M. Grankvist, a member of the Danish Military Police Detachment from 2 Sjaellandske Brigade. Rank insignia is carried on the shoulder-straps when worn on the shirt. The national title is worn on both shoulders. The 2 Sjaellandske Brigade sign is worn only on the right shoulder of the shirt. The left shoulder carries the Danish Army emblem used by all Military Police troops.

PLATE 7. KINGDOM OF DENMARK: ARMY

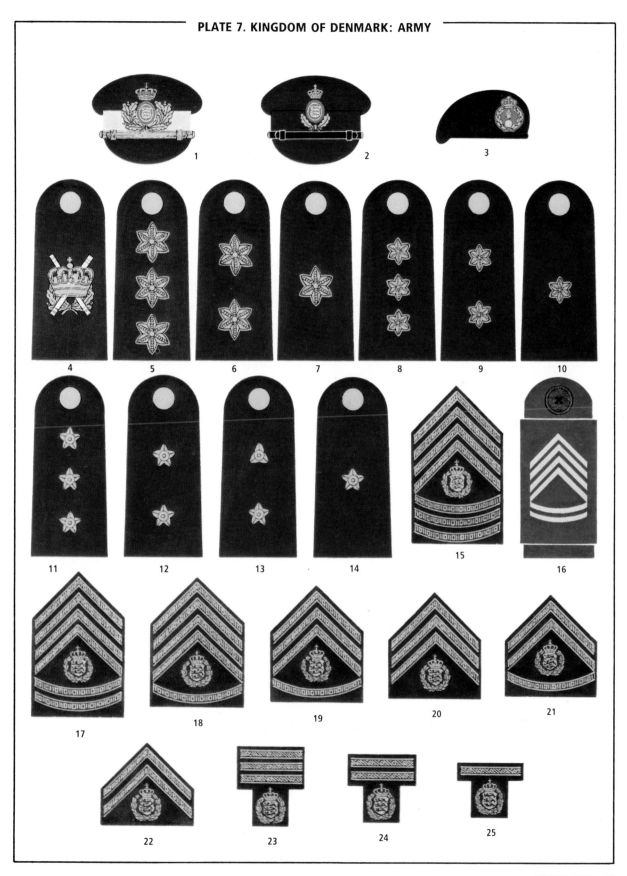

PLATE 8. KINGDOM OF DENMARK: NAVY

Rank displayed on Danish naval head-dress takes the form of peak decoration, differences in design of the cap badge and the use of the sailor's cap by ratings. Cuff rings, shoulder-boards, chevrons and bars make up the insignia of rank and appointment worn on the uniform, the last two patterns worn combined with the wearer's trade badge.

Head-dress

1 Uniform peaked cap with white top worn during summer months 1 May to 31 October by officers of Admiral class (ranks 7 to 9).
2 Uniform peaked cap, winter version worn from 1 November to 30 April by officers ranked as Captain, Commander Senior Grade and Commander (ranks 10 to 12).
3 Cap worn by Lieutenant-Commander, Lieutenant, Lieutenant Junior Grade and Sub-Lieutenant (ranks 13 to 16).
4 Cap worn by Senior Sergeant 1st and 2nd Class, and Petty Officers 1st and 2nd Class (ranks 17 to 20).
5 Cap worn by Petty Officer, 2nd Class Conscript, Leading Seaman and Leading Seaman Conscript (ranks 21 to 23).
6 Cap worn by remaining personnel, Able Seamen and Ordinary Seamen (rank 24 to 28). Note the rosette on the cap band (tally) has been illustrated in this manner in order to show the detail. It would normally lie flat against the cap and when seen from the front would only show a narrow edge. This pattern of rosette is worn by a naval volunteer.

Rank and Appointment Insignia

7 Cuff rings worn by Admiral.
8 Viceadmiral.
9 Shoulder-board for wear by Kontreadmiral. Other shoulder-boards exist for the two previous ranks. Admiral with three silver stars and Viceadmiral with two silver stars.
10 Cuff rings for Kommandør.
11 Kommandørkaptajn.
12 Orlogskaptajn.
13 Kaptajnløjtnant, shown here for the Medical Branch.
14 Premierløjtnant of Coastal Defence.
15 Løjtnant.
16 Sekondløjtnant (Specialist Officer).
17 Arm chevrons worn by Senior-sergent, 1 grad, Gunnery Branch.
18 Arm chevrons worn by Senior-sergent 2.grad (Seaman of Mines).
19 Oversergent, Signals Branch.
20 Sergent, Torpedo Branch.
21 Sergent (Conscript), Machinist.
22 Korporal, Radio Telegraphist.
23 Korporal (Conscript) (Information).
24 Arm bars worn by Overkonstabel, 1 grad. Supply Department.
25 Overkonstabel, 2 grad. Gunner Engineer.
26 Konstable, Carpenter.
27 Konstableelev, Stores.
28 VPL Befaren, Medical Orderly.

Left: Premierløjtnant T. Dansted, helicopter pilot of Danish naval squadron 722. Rank insignia is worn on the shoulder-straps of the olive-drab flying overalls. The Danish Pilots' Wings and the name of the wearer, together with his phonetic call-sign name are worked in yellow threads onto a rectangle of black cloth. The 722 squadron badge is worn on the right chest pocket (see item 10, plate 61). The system for wearing the Danish national titles and emblems on flying overalls is the same for the service tunic and shirt sleeve order.

PLATE 8. KINGDOM OF DENMARK: NAVY

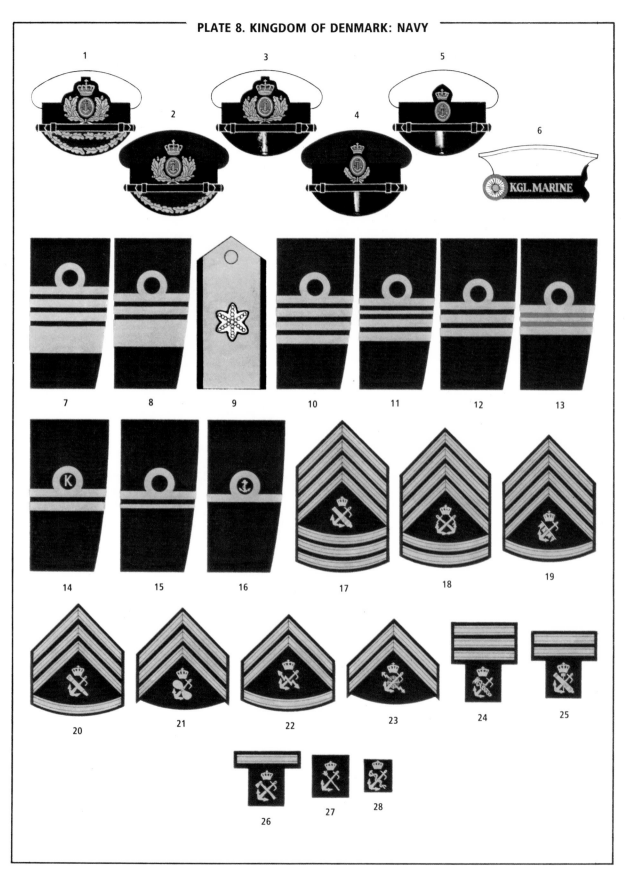

PLATE 9. KINGDOM OF DENMARK: AIR FORCE

Differences of rank are indicated on Royal Danish Air Force head-dress by the use of chin straps and the design of the cap badges. Rank displayed on the Service uniform is by means of cuff rings. Shoulder-strap slip-ons are used on the flying suits and NCOs wear arm chevrons as well as shoulder-strap slip-ons.

Head-dress
1 Uniform peaked cap worn by

General Officers (ranks 4 to 6).
2 Cap worn by all remaining officers, Colonel to Second Lieutenant (ranks 7 to 14).
3 Cap for Senior Sergeants and below.

Rank and Appointment Insignia
4 Cuff rings for General.
5 Generalløjtnant.
6 Generalmajor.
7 Oberst.

8 Oberstløjtnant.
9 Major.
10 Kaptajn.
11 Shoulder-strap rank slip-on also for Kaptajn worn on flying overalls.
12 Cuff rings for Premierløjtnant.
13 Løjtnant.
14 Sekondløjtnant.
15 Arm chevrons for Seniorsergent af 1.grad.
16 Seniorsergent af 2.grad.

17 Oversergent.
18 Sergent.
19 Sergent (Conscript).
20 Korporal.
21 Korporal (Conscript).
22 Overkonstabel af 1.grad.
23 Overkonstabel af 2.grad.
24 Konstabel.

Left: Oversergent B. Nerving of the Danish Military Police. Rank chevrons worn on the dark-green service tunic are in yellow and carried on both upper arms. The national title is displayed on the right shoulder and the same title plus the Dannebrog emblem is worn on the left shoulder. The group of small metal badges backed onto red discs are qualification and skill-at-arms badges.

PLATE 9. KINGDOM OF DENMARK: AIR FORCE

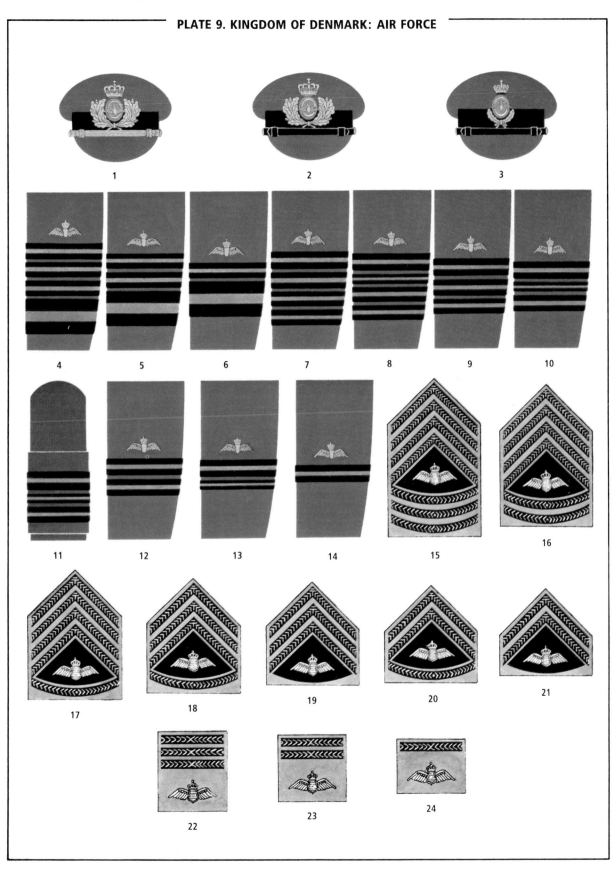

Above: Oversergent J. O. Larsen, Danish Military Police.
Right: A Sergent of the Danish Military Police.

Above: French Naval aircrew member with the rank of Maître. French military personnel frequently wear their insignia of rank attached to the chest of certain uniform garments, the example shown here being the grey leather jerkin.
Right: Captain of 'Troupes Aéroportées d'Infanterie de Marine', a qualified parachutist.

PLATE 10. REPUBLIC OF FRANCE: ARMY

The armed forces of France have a far more elaborate system of displaying rank on their military head-dress than any other European country. Indeed, the more senior ranks of the three armed services as well as the Gendarmerie Nationale have rank insignia displayed on the traditional kepi and peaked cap for each individual rank. The Army kepis and the beret shown here are for Infantry personnel. Rank displayed on the uniform is also varied. Cuff stars, cuff rings, cuff stripes, cuff chevrons and cuff bars abound as do shoulder-boards, shoulder-straps and arm diamonds.

Head-dress
1 Full dress kepi for a General of the Army (rank 7).
2 Service kepi for a General of an Army Corps (rank 8).
3 Dress kepi for General of a Division (rank 9).
4 Kepi for Brigade General (rank 10).
5 Colonel (rank 11).
6 Lieutenant-Colonel (rank 12).
13 Kepi for a Battalion (or Squadron) Chief (rank 17).
14 Captain (rank 18).
15 Lieutenant (rank 19).
16 Kepi worn by Second-Lieutenants, Officer Aspirants and Senior Warrant Officers (ranks 20 to 23).
24 Junior Warrant Officer.
25 Kepi for NCOs.
26 Beret for remaining personnel.

Rank and Appointment Insignia
7 Cuff stars for Général d'Armée.
8 Général de Corps d'Armée.
9 Général de Division.
10 Général de Brigade.
11 Colonel.
12 Lieutenant-Colonel.
17 Breast patch for Chef de Bataillon or Chef d'Escadron.
18 Shoulder-board for Capitaine.
19 Lieutenant.
20 Sous-Lieutenant.
21 Aspirant.
22 Major.
23 Adjudant-Chef.
27 Adjudant.
28 Arm diamond combining regimental number with rank chevrons for Sergent-Chef or Maréchal des Logis-Chef.
29 Sergent or Maréchal des Logis A.D.L.
30 Sergent or Maréchal des Logis P.D.L.
31 Breast patch for Caporal-Chef or Brigadier-Chef.
32 Arm diamond for Brigadier or Caporal.
33 1ère Classe.
Soldat de 2ème Classe (no rank insignia worn).

Left: Sergent of French Infantry.

PLATE 10. REPUBLIC OF FRANCE: ARMY

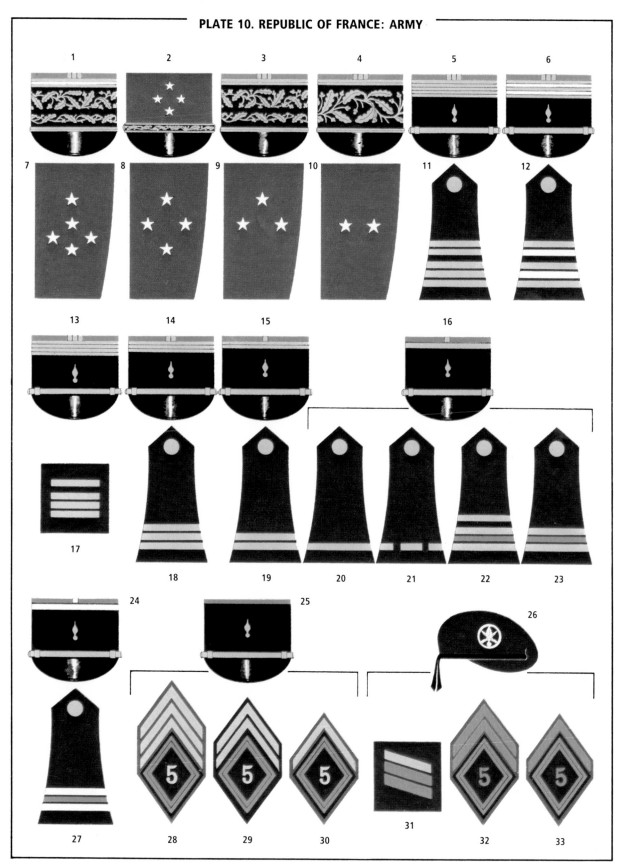

PLATE 11. REPUBLIC OF FRANCE: NAVY

The range of uniform peaked caps worn in the French Navy is, as in the other French forces, extensive. Each naval rank has a separate cap displaying the individual's rank upon it. This rank insignia takes the form of elaborate cap bands, chin-straps and cap badges. Rank is shown on the naval uniform by the use of cuff stars, cuff rings and cuff stripes. The same rank insignia is also worn on shoulder-boards and shoulder-strap slip-ons according to the type of uniform worn.

Head-dress
1 Uniform peaked cap, summer wear, for an Admiral (rank 6).
2 Vice-Admiral in Command of Forces, uniform peaked cap for winter wear (rank 7).
3 Vice-Admiral (rank 8).
4 Rear-Admiral (rank 9).
5 Captain (rank 10).
11 Commander (rank 16).
12 Lieutenant-Commander (rank 17).
13 Lieutenant (rank 18).
14 Ensign 1st Class (rank 19).
15 Ensign 2nd Class (rank 20).
21 Officer Aspirant (rank 24).
22 Peaked cap for summer wear for ranks from Warrant Officer to Chief Petty Officer (ranks 25 to 28).
23 Cap for Second Petty Officer A.D.L. and Second Petty Officer P.D.L. (ADL=au dela de la durée légale; PDL=pendant la durée légale) (ranks 29 and 30).

Rank and Appointment Insignia
6 Cuff stars for Amiral.
7 Vice-Amiral d'Escadre.
8 Vice-Amiral.
9 Contre-Amiral.
10 Cuff rings for Capitaine de Vaisseau.
16 Capitaine de Frégate (Médecine).
17 Capitaine de Corvette.
18 Lieutenant de Vaisseau. Shoulder-boards as worn on white summer uniform.
19 Cuff rings for Enseigne de Vaisseau de 1ère Classe (Commissariat).
20 Enseigne de Vaisseau de 2ème Classe (administration).
24 Aspirant.
25 Major.
26 Maître-Principal.
27 Premier-Maître.
28 Maître. Shoulder-strap slip-on worn on the light-weight tan coloured uniform.
29 Cuff stripes for Second-Maître A.D.L.
30 Second-Maître P.D.L.

Left: Second Maître ADL M. Morradell, French Navy.

PLATE 11. REPUBLIC OF FRANCE: NAVY

PLATE 12 . REPUBLIC OF FRANCE: NAVY AND AIR FORCE

31 Cap for remaining personnel
(ranks 32 to 34).
32 Cuff stripes for Quartier-Maître
de 1ère Classe.
33 Quartier-Maître de 2ème Classe.
Badge worn on left breast of
white rig.
34 Maître-Brevet.
Matelot (no rank insignia worn).

The French Air Force uses an
elaborate system of displaying individual rank on their head-dress in
the form of cap bands, and cap
badges. Rank worn on the uniform
is in the form of cuff stars and cuff
rings with inverted cuff chevrons for
lower ranks. Shoulder-boards are
also worn.

Head-dress
1 Uniform peaked cap for General
Air Army Commander (rank 6).

2 General Air Corps Commander
(rank 7).
3 Lieutenant-General Air Division
(rank 8).
4 Major-General Air Brigade (rank 9).
5 Colonel (rank 10).
11 Lieutenant-Colonel (rank 16).
12 Major (rank 17).
13 Captain (rank 18).
14 Lieutenant (rank 19).
15 Uniform cap for Second-
Lieutenant and Officer Aspirant
(ranks 20 and 21).

Rank and Appointment Insignia
6 Cuff stars for Général d'Armée
Aérienne.
7 Général de Corps Aérien.
8 Général de Division Aérienne.
9 Général de Brigade Aérienne.
10 Cuff rings for a Colonel.
16 Lieutenant-Colonel.
17 Commandant.
18 Capitaine.
19 Lieutenant.
20 Sous-Lieutenant.
21 Aspirant.

Left: Sergent ADL Gibierge of the
French Air Force. The rank insignia
is here worn as a shoulder-strap
slip-on.

PLATE 12. REPUBLIC OF FRANCE: NAVY

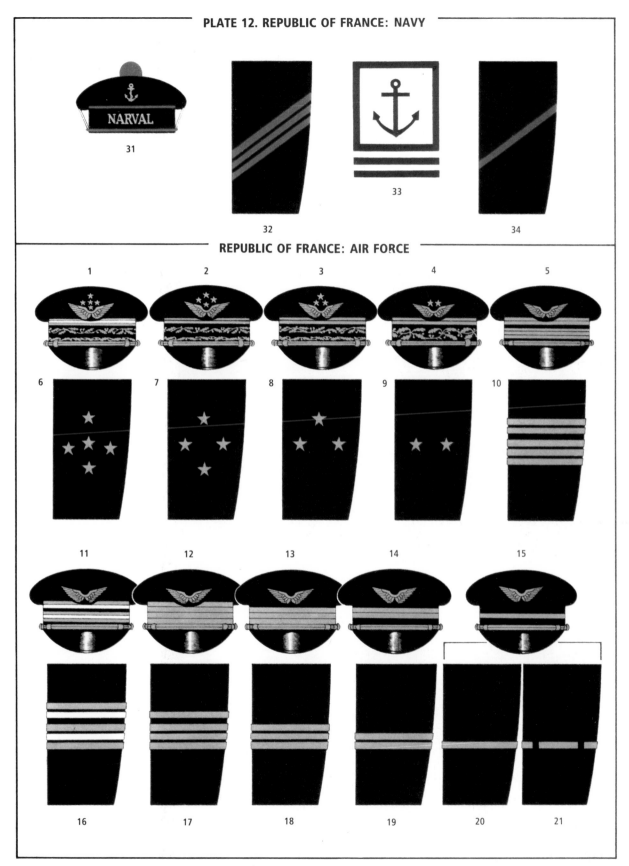

31

32

33

34

REPUBLIC OF FRANCE: AIR FORCE

1   2   3   4   5

6   7   8   9   10

11   12   13   14   15

16   17   18   19   20   21

PLATE 13. REPUBLIC OF FRANCE: AIR FORCE AND GENDARMERIE NATIONALE

22 Chief Warrant Officer (rank 26).
23 Senior Warrant Officer (rank 27).
24 Warrant Officer (rank 28).
25 Peaked cap worn by Sergeant-Major, Sergeants A.D.L. and P.D.L. (ranks 29 to 31).
26 Major.
27 Adjudant-Chef.
28 Adjudant.
29 Sergent-Chef.
30 Sergent A.D.L.
31 Sergent P.D.L.
32 Side cap worn by Corporal-Major (rank 33).
33 Shoulder-board for a Caporal-Chef.

34 Corporal (rank 35).
35 Caporal.
36 Private 1st Class (rank 37).
37 1ère Classe.
Soldat de 2ème Classe (no rank insignia worn).

The Gendarmerie Nationale is an integral part of the Armed Forces of France, but it also co-operates with the civil administration in maintaining public order.

With the exception of the Gendarmerie auxiliaries, there is a kepi displaying individual rank for each rank of the Gendarmerie Nationale.

Differences in rank are indicated by the use of bands of silver or gold lace braiding worn around the top and on the crown of the kepi. Members of the Gendarmerie Nationale use silver braid and Gendarmerie Mobile use gold. Rank displayed on the uniform is carried on the cuff, either as cuff bars or chevrons inverted. Auxiliaries wear shoulder-boards.

Head-dress
1 Kepi for General of an Army Corps (rank 6).
2 General of a Division (rank 7).

3 Brigade General (rank 8).
4 Colonel (rank 9).
5 Lieutenant-Colonel (rank 10).

Rank and Appointment Insignia
6 Cuff stars for Général de Corps d'Armée.
7 Général de Division.
8 Général de Brigade.
9 Cuff bars for a Colonel.
10 Lieutenant-Colonel.

Left: General Gruenther, SACEUR presenting General Juin (left) with a certificate on the occasion of the French General's retirement as Commander-in-Chief Allied Army Forces in Central Europe, September 1956.

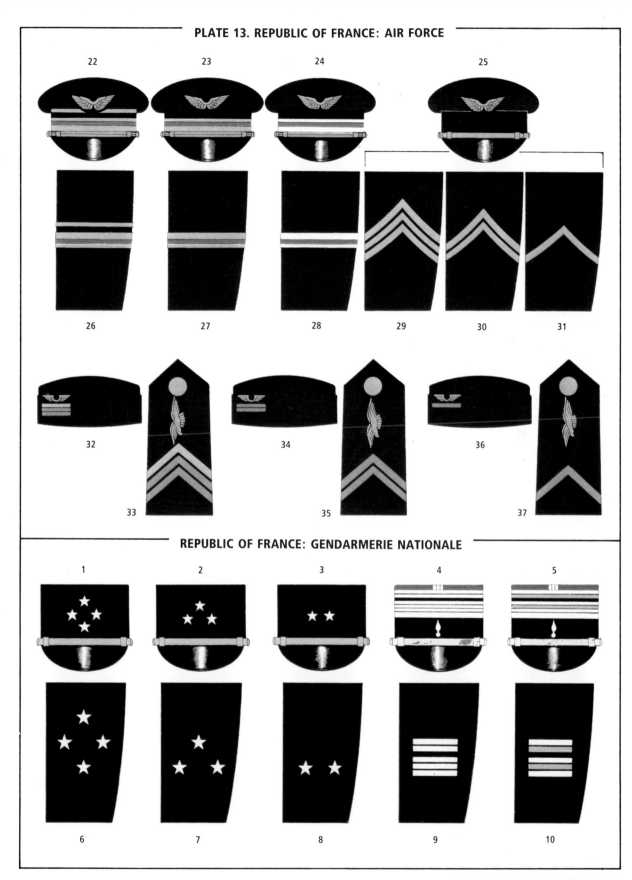

PLATE 13. REPUBLIC OF FRANCE: AIR FORCE

22   23   24   25

26   27   28   29   30   31

32   33   34   35   36   37

REPUBLIC OF FRANCE: GENDARMERIE NATIONALE

1   2   3   4   5

6   7   8   9   10

PLATE 14. REPUBLIC OF FRANCE: GENDARMERIE NATIONALE

11 Squadron Chief (rank 16).
12 Captain (rank 17).
13 Lieutenant (rank 18).
14 Second-Lieutenant (rank 19).
15 Sergeant-Major (rank 20).
16 Chef d'Escadron.
17 Capitaine.
18 Lieutenant.
19 Sous-Lieutenant.

20 Major.
21 Senior Sergeant (rank 25).
22 Sergeant (rank 26).
23 Lance-Sergeant (rank 27).
24 Constable (rank 28).
25 Adjudant-Chef.
26 Adjudant.
27 Maréchal des Logis-Chef.
28 Gendarme.

29 Kepi worn by remaining auxiliary personnel (ranks 30 to 33).
30 Shoulder-board for Maréchal des Logis.

31 Brigadier-Chef.
32 Brigadier.
33 1ère Classe.

Below: General Alfred M. Gruenther takes his leave of senior French officers at SHAPE on the eve of his retirement as Supreme Allied Commander Europe, November 1956.

PLATE 14. REPUBLIC OF FRANCE: GENDARMERIE NATIONALE

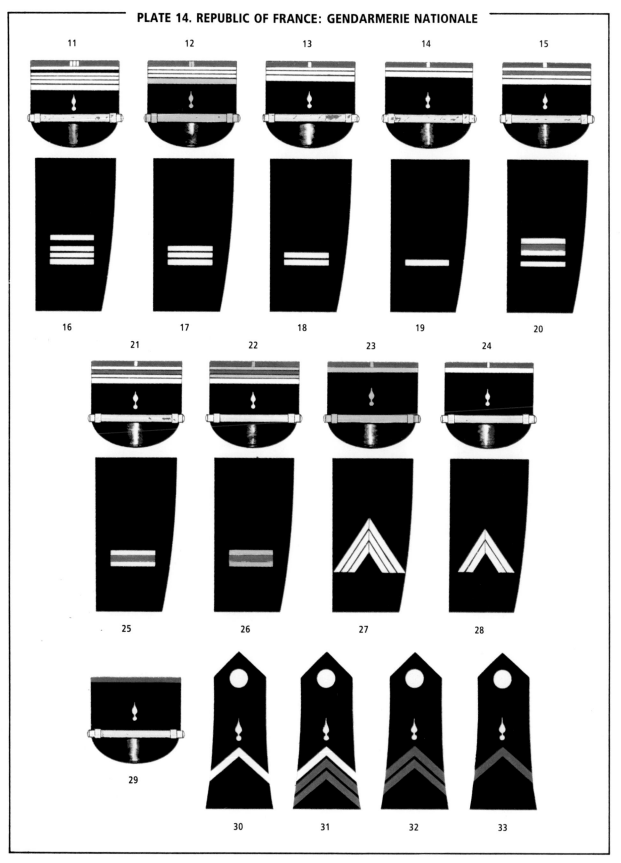

PLATE 15. FEDERAL REPUBLIC OF GERMANY: ARMY

The head-dress illustrated, items 1 to 4 and all the shoulder-boards, shoulder-straps and collar patches, with the exception of items 12 and 24, are of the type worn with the Uniform Dress. The green beret, item 5, is one of a range of coloured berets introduced into the West German Army during the 1970s. The colours employed correspond roughly to the arm-of-service colours used as piping to the shoulder-straps and shoulder-boards, and backing to the collar patches, other than those worn by General Officers.

Head-dress

1 Uniform peaked cap for General Officers (ranks 7 to 10).
2 Senior officers (ranks 12 to 14).
3 Junior officers (ranks 15 to 19).
4 Other Ranks.
5 Beret for wear by all ranks here shown for Jäger (Infantry) units.

Rank and Appointment Insignia

6 Collar patch worn by all General Officers (ranks 7 to 10).
7 Shoulder-board for rank of General.
8 General-Leutnant.
9 General-Major.
10 Brigade-General.
11 Design of collar patch worn by all officers. Background colour indicates arm-of-service, here shown for Infanterie (Infantry) a shade of green known as *Jägergrün*.
12 Shoulder-strap for the olive-green shirt or similar-coloured garment worn with a machine woven rank slip-on. Rank shown is that of Oberst. The narrow, coloured strip at the base of the strap is worn on certain items of work and combat dress to indicate the wearer's arm-of-service. The dark-green shown here is for Panzerjäger.
13 Shoulder-board for Oberst Leutnant of Fernmeldentruppen (signals communication troops).
14 Major, Heeresfliegertruppen (army flying branch).

15 Hauptmann, Panzeraufklarung-struppe, or Fernspähtruppe (FNT) (armoured reconnaissance troops and signals units).
16 Oberleutnant Panzergrenadiere (armoured-infantry).
17 Leutnant, Feldjäger (military police).
18 Oberfährich, Feldzugtruppen (field supply troops).
19 Fähnrich, Panzertruppen (armoured – tank – troops).
20 Fahnenjunker, Pioniertruppe (engineers).
21 Gefreiter OA, Artillerie (artillery).
22 Design of collar patch worn by all ranks below that of Ober-stabsfeldwebel (inclusive). As before, background colour indicates wearer's arm-of-service, here shown as 'Rosa' for Panzer and Panzerjägertruppen (armoured and armoured destroyer (hunter) units).
23 Oberstabsfeldwebel. Panzer-jägertruppen (armoured hunter troops).

24 Shoulder-strap with rank slip-on (machine woven) for Stabs-feldwebel, Panzergrenadiere (armoured-infantry).
25 Shoulder-board for Haupt-feldwebel, Heeresflugabwehr-truppen (army anti-aircraft defence troops).
26 Oberfeldwebel, Infanterie (infantry).

Above: German Army Guard of Honour parade at Bonn. This is an early photograph taken sometime in the late 1950s. When the new West German Army was established in 1955 a deliberate effort was made to create a new image for the troops. Gone were the style of uniforms associated with the Third Reich along with the old-style steel helmet and 'jackboots'. In their place were introduced a less militaristic-looking uniform and an American-style steel helmet. Insignia of rank was new and simplified, even more so than the insignia worn today. The photograph shows troops of the new German Army. All wear the short cross-over jacket, baggy trousers tucked into high ankle-boots. They are wearing the liner from their German-made steel helmets. The NCO on the left of the front rank is an Unteroffizier.

PLATE 15. FEDERAL REPUBLIC OF GERMANY: ARMY

PLATE 16. FEDERAL REPUBLIC OF GERMANY: ARMY AND NAVY

27 Feldwebel, Quartiermeister (quartermaster branch).

28 Stabsunteroffizier, ABC-Abwehrtruppe (atomic-bacterio-logical-chemical defence troops).

29 Unteroffizier, Fernmeldentruppe (signals communication troops).

30 Hauptgefreiter, Infanterie (infantry).

31 Obergefreiter, Feldjäger (military police).

32 Unteroffizieranwärter – Gefreiter (Quartiermeister).

33 Gefreiter, Pionere (engineers). Grenadier (no rank insignia worn).

Head-dress items 1 to 4 are normal wear for personnel of the West German Navy – the Bundesmarine – and are worn with the navy-blue uniform. Item 5, the fore and aft cap, known as the *Schiffchen* or 'little boat' cap is a style of head-dress worn by all ranks of the Navy, dif-ference in rank being indicated by the use of silver-aluminium or gold coloured piping around the upper part of the cap's curtain. The cap shown here is that worn by Junior NCOs, without piping. Not shown here is the cap (*mütze*) worn with a cap ribbon displaying the name of the wearer's vessel or shore estab-lishment.

Items 6 to 11 and 13 to 16 are the cuffs of the officer's navy-blue uniform with sleeve rings. Items 12 and 35 overleaf are shoulder-straps with slip-on rank insignia, while items 17, 19, and 21, 23, 25, 27, 29, 31, 33 and 38 overleaf are shoulder-boards worn on the navy-blue uniform for the ranks indicated. Alongside most of these boards are the arm badges (of rank) worn on those items of uniform dress without shoulder-boards or shoulder-straps. All officer ranks also wear shoulder-boards of the same shape as the lower ranks illustrated here. Their insignia is of the same configuration as that worn on their cuffs.

Head-dress

1 Uniform peaked cap for Flag Officers (ranks 6 to 9).

2 Senior Officers (ranks 10 to 12).

3 Commanders (ranks 13 to 16).

4 Warrant Officers, Naval (ranks 17 to 27).

5 Fore and aft cap for wear by junior NCOs and ratings.

Rank and Appointment Insignia

6 Sleeve ring rank for an Admiral. Five-pointed star indicates a Line Officer.

7 Vizeadmiral.

8 Konteradmiral.

9 Flottilenadmiral.

10 Kapitän zur See.

11 Fregattenkapitän.

12 Shoulder-strap for the olive-drab shirt or anorak worn with a machine-woven slip-on for the rank of Korvettenkapitän.

13 Sleeve ring rank for Kapitänleutnant.

14 Oberleutnant zur See.

15 Leutnant zur See.

16 Oberfähnrich zur See.

17 Shoulder-board for Fähnrich zur See.

18 Sleeve badge for Seekadett.

19 Shoulder-board for same.

Left: Members of the West German Bundesmarine. The man nearest the camera has the rank of Obermaat.

PLATE 16. FEDERAL REPUBLIC OF GERMANY: ARMY

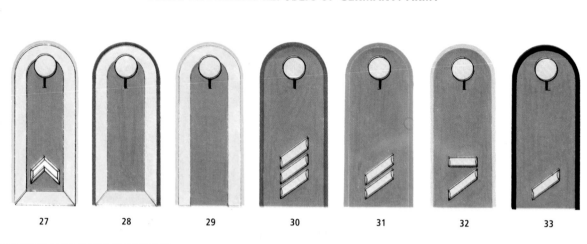

27   28   29   30   31   32   33

FEDERAL REPUBLIC OF GERMANY: NAVY

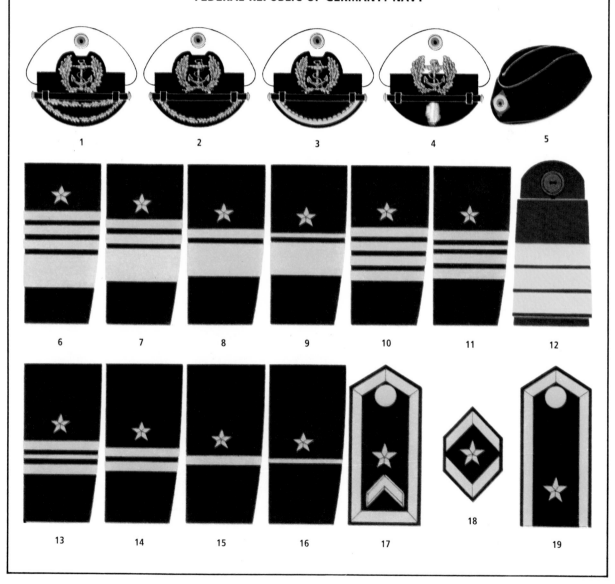

1   2   3   4   5

6   7   8   9   10   11   12

13   14   15   16   17   18   19

Left: Men of the Federal Border Guard – the Bundesgrenzschutz – were kitted out with uniforms almost identical with those worn during the Third Reich period.

The photograph shows men of the Bundesgrenzschutz on guard duty at the Presidential Chancellery, Bonn. The steel helmet (of post-war German manufacture), the dark-green collar to the greatcoat, the black leather rifle ammunition pouches and the black leather 'marching boots' are all reminiscent of the items worn during the Second World War. Today the Bonn Chancellery Guard wear slightly more modified dress, the dark-green beret in particular replacing the steel helmet.

Right: Major-General Hans Speidel (right) and General Lauris Norstad, SACEUR, photographed outside Supreme Headquarters April 1957.

Right: Hauptfeldwebel H. J. Rehm of the German Army Military Police (Feldjägertruppe). The blue-and-white NATO Military Police arm band is not worn when on duty in Germany.

PLATE 17. FEDERAL REPUBLIC OF GERMANY: NAVY AND AIR FORCE

20 and 21 Sleeve badge and shoulder-board for Offizieran-wärter Gefreiter (AO).
22 and 23 Oberstabsbootsmann.
24 and 25 Stabsbootsmann.
26 and 27 Hauptbootsmann.
28 and 29 Oberbootsmann.
30 and 31 Bootsmann.
32 and 33 Obermaat.
34 and 35 Maat.
36 Sleeve badge worn by Gefreiter (UA). A similar device is also worn on a plain navy-blue shoulder-board (not shown).
37 and 38 Sleeve badge and shoulder-board as worn by a Hauptgefreiter.
39 Sleeve badge for an Obergefreiter.
40 Gefreiter.
Matrose (no rank insignia worn).

The new German Air Force – the Bundes Luftwaffe – has chosen to use only one basic arm-of-service colour, that of gold-yellow, for all its personnel, with the exception of its General Officers, officers on the General Staff and Medical personnel (see plate 15). These gentlemen, like their opposite numbers in the West German Army, use bright red, carmine and cornflower blue respectively. Like the Army these three colours are employed as piping and underlay to the shoulder-boards, as background colour to the collar patches and, in a number of instances as given below, as piping to certain items of head-dress.

The range of ranks and the configuration of rank insignia, with the obvious exception of the basic Air Force collar patch, in use with the Luftwaffe are identical with those used by the West German Army, the Bundesheer.

Head-dress

1 Uniform peaked cap for Luftwaffe General officers (items 7 to 10).
2 Senior officers (ranks 12 to 14).
3 Junior officers (ranks 15 to 18).
4 Other Ranks (ranks 19 to 33).
5 Side cap for wear by all ranks. Other ranks below the rank of Oberstabsfeldwebel (inclusive) wear this cap as illustrated with gold-yellow piping. Officers below the rank of Oberst (inclusive) wear silver-aluminium piping to the cap and all General Officers have gold piping. This same arrangement holds true for the Uniform peaked cap.

Left: West German Army helicopter pilots. They are based at Fassberg, in the north-east of Germany, north of Celle and south of Münster. Their squadron badge, as worn on the grey leather flight jerkin, and also carried on their aircraft, depicts a helicopter above the castle of Celle, Celle being their first base before moving to Fassberg on 6 June 1987.

PLATE 17. FEDERAL REPUBLIC OF GERMANY: NAVY

21   22   23   24   25   26   27

28   29   30   31   32   33   34   35

36   37   38   39   40

FEDERAL REPUBLIC OF GERMANY: AIR FORCE

1   2   3   4   5

PLATE 18. FEDERAL REPUBLIC OF GERMANY: AIR FORCE

Rank and Appointment Insignia

6 Collar patch worn by all Luftwaffe General Officers (items 7 to 10).
7 Shoulder-board for General.
8 Generalleutnant.
9 Generalmajor.
10 Brigadegeneral.
11 Collar patch as worn by all Luftwaffe Officers. The design on the patch is hand embroidered in silver-aluminium threads.
12 Shoulder-board for Oberst.
13 Oberstleutnant.
14 Major.
15 Hauptmann.

16 Flying suit insignia for the rank of Oberleutnant. The sensible practice of wearing insignia of rank on the upper part of the sleeve at the point of the shoulder instead of on the shoulder itself is used in both the Army and the Air Force. In the Luftwaffe the patch of olive-green cloth is frequently worn surmounted by the national colours of the Federal Republic and a set of stylized wings of a design similar to the wings found on the Luftwaffe cuff titles.

17 Shoulder-board for Leutnant.
18 Oberfähnrich.
19 Fähnrich.
20 Fahnenjunker.
21 Gefreiter OA.
22 Collar patch worn by all remaining ranks from Oberstabsfeldwebel (inclusive). The design on the patch is machine woven in white threads.
23 Shoulder-board for Oberstabsfeldwebel.
24 Stabsfeldwebel.
25 Hauptfeldwebel.
26 Oberfeldwebel.

27 Combat sleeve insignia for Feldwebel.
28 Shoulder-board for Stabsunteroffizier.
29 Unteroffizier.
30 Hauptgefreiter.
31 Obergefreiter.
32 Unteroffizier Anwärter Gefreiter.
33 Gefreiter.
   Flieger (no rank insignia worn).

Left: Oberfeldwebel Gerhard Nicht, a Luftwaffe member and crew member of a Boeing E-3A Sentry aircraft, part of the NATO Airborne Early Warning Force. The rank insignia is worn stitched onto the shoulders of the flying overalls. The small pair of wings at the point of the shoulder indicate that the wearer is a member of the German Air Force. This fact is not obvious from the colour or insignia used as rank insignia worn on work clothing or shirt sleeve order, as both the Luftwaffe and the Army use identical insignia. The national flag badge is also worn on both shoulders.

PLATE 18. FEDERAL REPUBLIC OF GERMANY: AIR FORCE

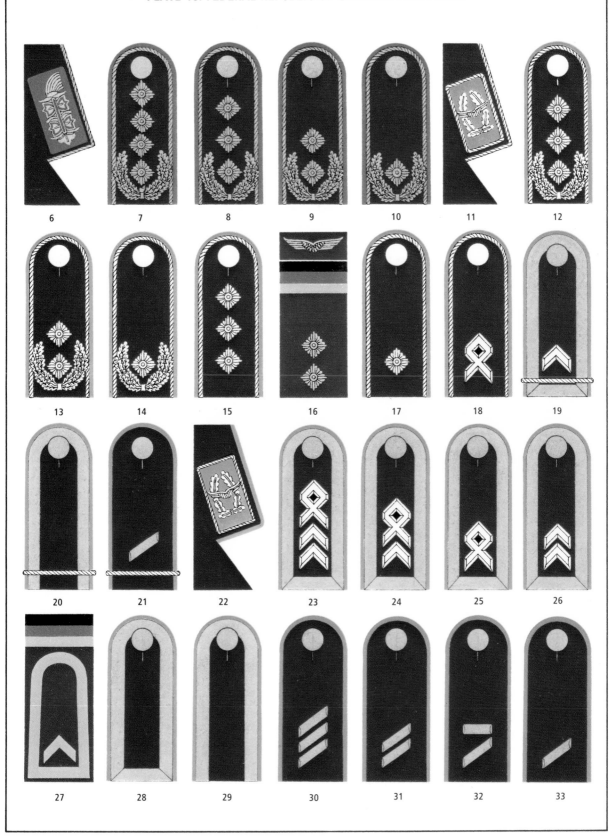

6   7   8   9   10   11   12

13   14   15   16   17   18   19

20   21   22   23   24   25   26

27   28   29   30   31   32   33

PLATE 19. FEDERAL REPUBLIC OF GERMANY: BORDER PROTECTION POLICE

Land-based Federal Border Protection Guards wear dark-green uniforms while the uniforms worn by members of the waterborne Marine section of the Border Guards are navy-blue.

The shoulder-boards and collar patches used by both formations are almost identical with the style of rank insignia that used to be used by some of the police formations operating in the different Landes of the Federal Republic prior to their unification. The Bundesgrenzschutz rank insignia is identical with the insignia that was used by the German 'Green Police' (Schutzpolizei) of the Third Reich period.

Head-dress
1 Uniform peaked cap for wear by personnel classed as Höherer Dienst – Senior or Higher Service officers, as for ranks items 7 and 8.
2 Uniform peaked cap for wear by BGS Officers (Gehöherer Dienst), items 10, 12 to 16, and 18.
3 Mittlerer Dienst – Middle Service personnel. Cap worn by remaining personnel other than Marine Section BGS.
4 Uniform peaked cap as worn by Middle Service personnel of the Marine Section of the BGS.
5 Beret worn by all ranks of the BGS. The beret badge changes to gilt metal for wear by Higher Service officers.

Rank and Appointment Insignia
6 Collar patch worn by Higher Service officers, items 7 and 8.
7 Shoulder-board for wear by Inspekteur des BGS.
8 Kommandeur im BGS.
9 Collar patch for wear by all other officers of the BGS.
10 Shoulder-board for Direktor im BGS.
11 Leiten der Polizeidirektor im BGS.
12 Polizeidirektor im BGS.
13 Polizeioberrat im BGS.
14 Fregattenkapitän im BGS (Marine).
15 Erste Polizeihauptkommissar im BGS.
16 Polizeihauptkommissar im BGS.
17 Kapitänleutnant im BGS (Marine).
18 Polizeikommisar im BGS.
19 Collar patch for wear by all remaining personnel of the BGS.
20 Oberstabsmeister im BGS.
21 Stabsmeister im BGS.
22 Polizeihauptmeister im BGS.
23 Oberbootsmann im BGS (Marine).
24 Polizeimeister im BGS.
25 Polizeihauptwachtmeister im BGS.
26 Maat im BGS (Marine).
27 Polizeiwachtmeister im BGS.
28 Polizeihauputwachtmeister Anwärter im BGS.

Left: An Oberfeldwebel of Jäger Troops from 5 Panzerdivision, wearing Service Uniform.

PLATE 19. FEDERAL REPUBLIC OF GERMANY: BORDER PROTECTION POLICE

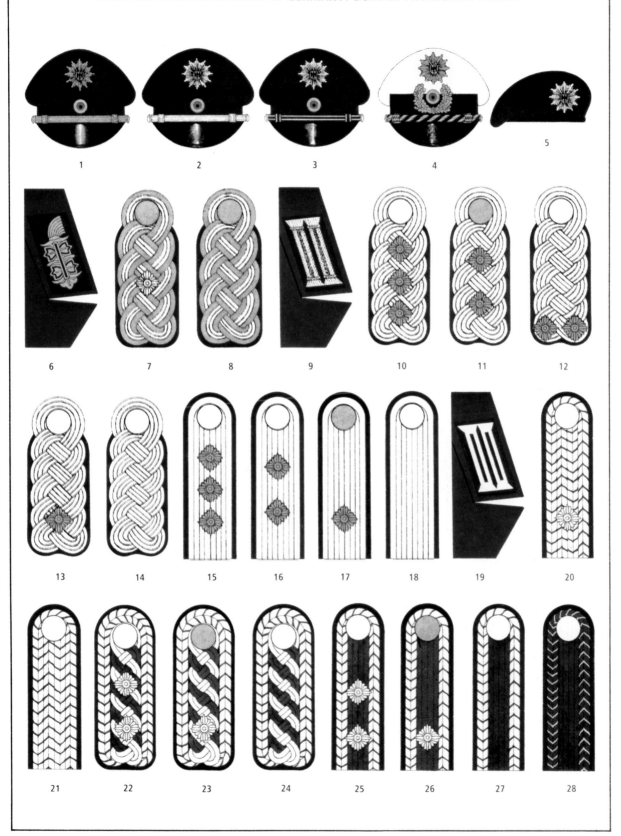

PLATE 20. FEDERAL REPUBLIC OF GERMANY: MEDICAL SERVICES

Each of the four West German services, Army, Navy, Air Force and the Border Protection Police, has its own uniformed, qualified medical and veterinary service personnel. They are distinguished by the insignia worn on their shoulder-boards and the rank terms used.

Four areas of skill are employed in the Federal services, those of Doctors, Dentists, Chemists (Pharmacists) and Veterinarians. However, not all four skills are employed in each branch of the German services; for example, the Bundesmarine does not have Vets among their number. All such qualified personnel are classed as officers of varying ranks. Their rank is displayed on the shoulder-boards and their particular skill is indicated by a small metal device. Doctors are distinguished by a snake and staff (Caduceus), the snake having four curves in its body. This distinguishes it from the insignia for a Dentist who has the same emblem but with only two curves to the snake's body. Veterinarians are indicated by the use of a serpent on its own, while Pharmacists use the same form of serpent but balanced on a small shallow dish.

Rank and Appointment Insignia

1 Shoulder-board for Oberstveterinär. Cornflower-blue being the Army Medical Service's branch colour.
2 Oberstleutnantarzt.
3 Majorapotheker.
4 Hauptmannzahnartz.
5 Shoulder-board for naval Oberstabsarzt.
6 Zahnarzt.
7 Apotheker.
8 Oberstleutnantarzt.
9 Majorapotheker.
10 San.OA. Here shown for Fähnrich in der Ausbildung zum Zahnarzt. An officer aspirant undergoing training to become a Dentist in the German Air Force.
11 Leitender Medizinaldirecktor im Bundesgrenzschutz. Senior medical director in the Federal Border Protection Police. The BGS does not have a special branch colour for its medical service. The special shoulder-board insignia distinguishes them from ordinary BGS personnel.
12 Medizinaldirecktor im BGS.
13 Medizinaloberst im BGS.
14 Medizinalrat im BGS.

Left: A Luftwaffe Leutnant of Reserve wearing Service Uniform. He wears a marksmanship lanyard on his right shoulder and the Military Service Achievement badge for Reservists on his left breast pocket.

PLATE 20. FEDERAL REPUBLIC OF GERMANY: MEDICAL SERVICES

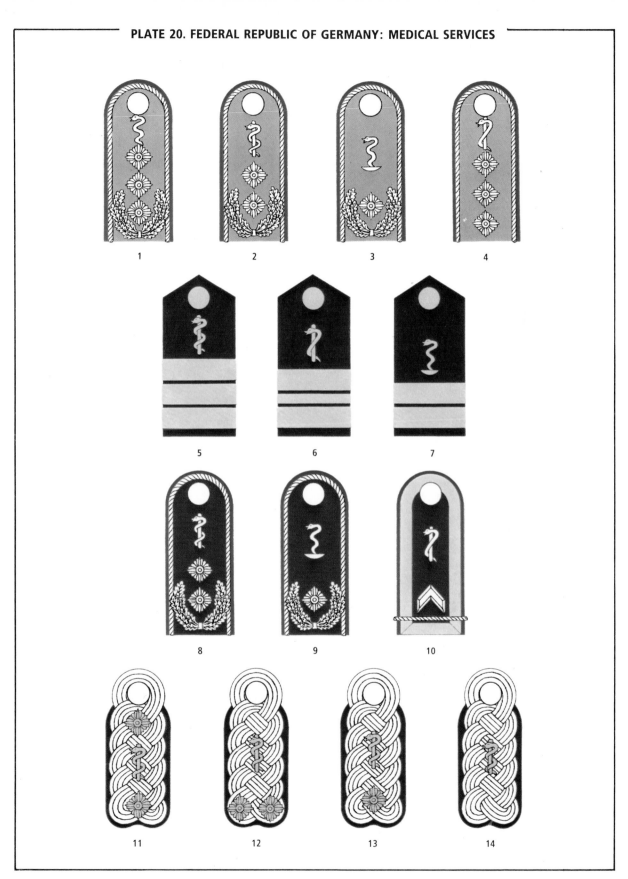

1

2

3

4

5

6

7

8

9

10

11

12

13

14

PLATE 21. HELLENIC REPUBLIC: ARMY

The State Arms appear on most forms of Greek military head-dress. It takes the form of a small blue shield bearing a white cross and surrounded by a wreath of golden laurel leaves. Rank displayed on Greek Army head-dress is restricted to two patterns of peak decorations. No other distinctions are made. Rank displayed on the uniform is by means of shoulder-boards, gorget patches in the case of General Officers, and rank chevrons.

Head-dress

1 Uniform peaked cap for wear by General Officer ranks (ranks 6 to 9).
2 Cap worn by Colonels, Lieutenant-Colonels and Majors (ranks 10 to 12).
3 Cap for Junior Officers, Warrant Officers and NCOs (ranks 13 to 20).
4 Beret as worn by paratroops.

Rank and Appointment Insignia

5 Gorget patch as worn by General officers (ranks 6 to 9).
6 Stratigos.
7 Antistratigos.
8 Ypostratigos.
9 Taxiarchios.
10 Syntagmatarchis.
11 Antisyntagmatarchis.
12 Tagmatarchis.
13 Lochagos.
14 Ypolochagos.
15 Anthypolochagos.
16 Anthypaspistis.
17 Archilochias.
18 Epilochias.
19 Lochias.
20 Decaneas.
21 Decaneas (Conscript).
22 Ypodecaneas (Conscript). Stratiotis (no rank insignia worn).

Above: A member of the Greek Army Military Police with the rank of Decaneas (conscript). The shoulder titles have yellow Greek lettering on a yellow-bordered black title. The cap cover is of royal-blue and the soldier wears a Greek national flag badge on his right upper arm.

PLATE 21. HELLENIC REPUBLIC: ARMY

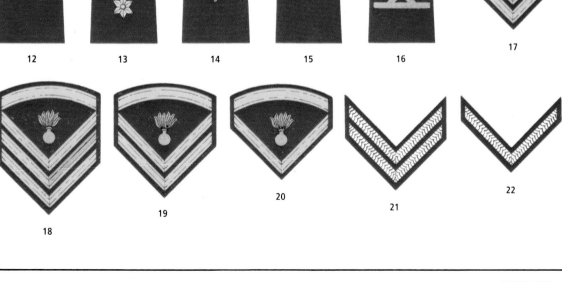

1 2 3 4

5 6 7 8 9 10 11

12 13 14 15 16 17

18 19 20 21 22

PLATE 22. HELLENIC REPUBLIC: NAVY

With the exception of the sailor's cap, Greek naval head-dress display the State Arms and rank is only indicated by peak decoration. In keeping with other European navies, rank is indicated by the use of sleeve rings for officers and warrant officers, shoulder-boards by officers of Flag rank and rank chevrons by Petty Officers and below.

Head-dress
1 Uniform peaked cap for Admirals (ranks 7 to 10).
2 Cap for Senior Officers (ranks 11 to 14).
3 Cap for Junior Officers and Warrant Officers (ranks 15 to 20).
4 Cap for Petty Officers (ranks 21 to 24).
5 Cap for Junior NCOs and Seamen (ranks 26 and 27).
6 Shipboard working cap for wear by personnel from Captains down to Seamen. The same State Arms badge is worn by all.

Rank and Appointment Insignia
7 Sleeve rings for Navarchos.
8 Antinavarchos.
9 Shoulder-board for Antinavarchos.
10 Yponavarchos.
11 Archipliarchos.
12 Pliarchos of Engineers.
13 Antipliarchos, Doctor.
14 Plotarchis.
15 Ypopliarchos, Pay Branch.
16 Shoulder-board for Ypopliarchos, Pay Branch.
17 Anthypopliarchos, Pharmacist.
18 Simaioforos.
19 Epikuros Simeoforos.
20 Anthypaspistis, Signalman.
21 Archikelefstis, Radar Operator.
22 Epikelefstis, Gunnery Engineer.
23 Kelefstis, Boatswain.
24 Dokimos Kelefstis, Engineer.
25 Diopos, Ordnance Artificer.
26 Naftis, Writer.
 Naftis (no rank insignia worn).

PLATE 22. HELLENIC REPUBLIC: NAVY

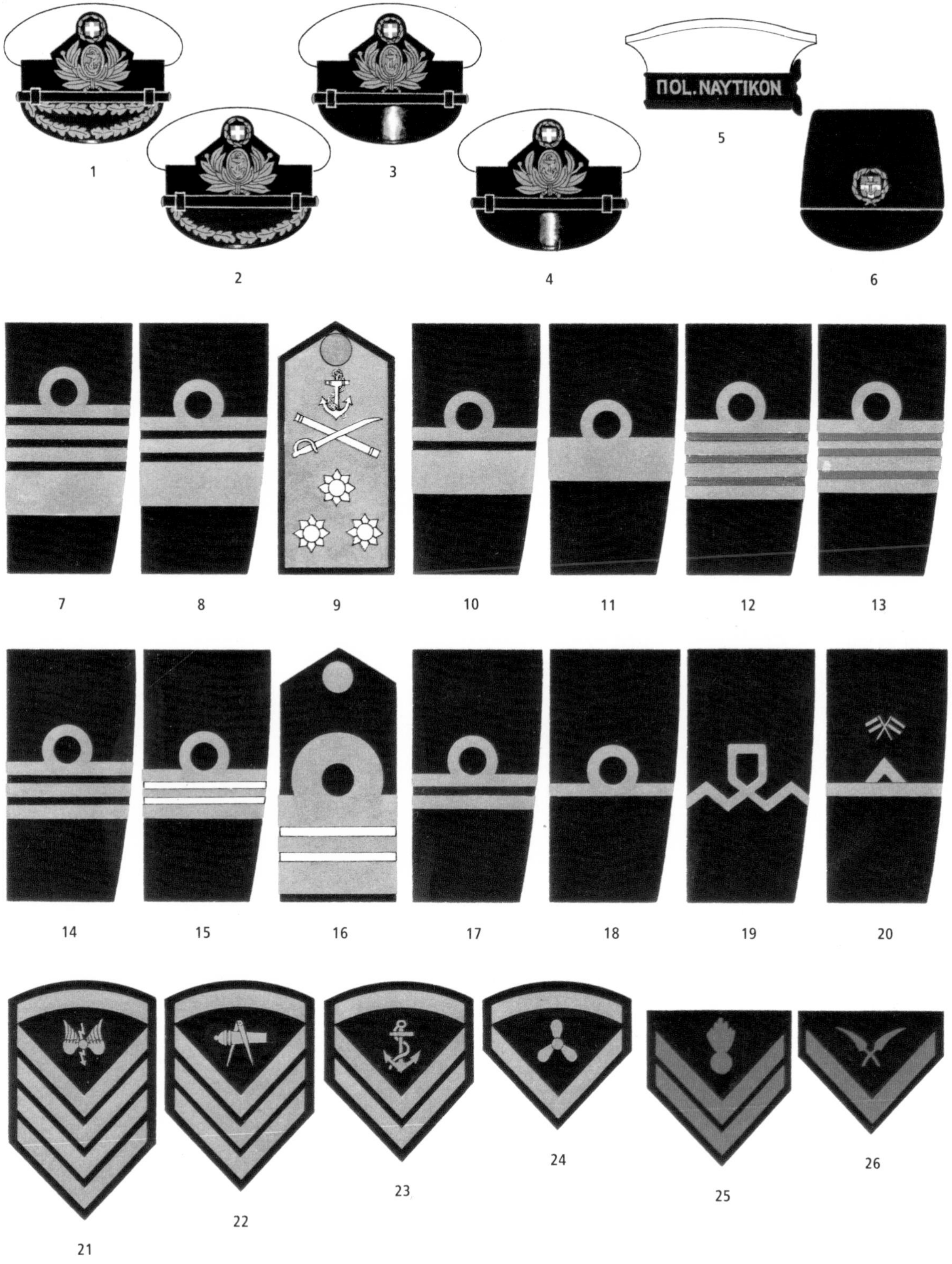

1

2

3

4

ΠΟΛ. ΝΑΥΤΙΚΟΝ

5

6

7

8

9

10

11

12

13

14

15

16

17

18

19

20

21

22

23

24

25

26

PLATE 23. HELLENIC REPUBLIC: AIR FORCE

Rank is displayed on Greek Air Force head-dress by the use of peak decoration and the difference in quality of the peak itself between officers and warrant officers. Rank indicated on the uniform takes the form of sleeve rings, and shoulder-boards for officers and sleeve chevrons for NCOs.

Head-dress
1 Uniform peaked cap for wear by Air Ranks (ranks 5 to 8).
2 Cap worn by Senior Officers (ranks 9 to 11).
3 Cap worn by Junior Officers (ranks 12 to 14).
4 Cap worn by Warrant Officers (rank 15).

Rank and Appointment Insignia
5 Sleeve rings for Pterarchos.
6 Antipterarchos.
7 Ypopterarchos.
8 Taxiarchos.
9 Sminarchos.
10 Antisminarchos.
11 Episminagos.
12 Sminagos.
13 Yposminagos.
14 Anthyposminagos.
15 Shoulder-board for Anthypaspistis.
16 Rank chevrons for Archisminias.
17 Episminias.
18 Sminias.
19 Efedrossminias.
20 Yposminias.
   Anthyposminias Sminitis (no rank insignia worn).

PLATE 23. HELLENIC REPUBLIC: AIR FORCE

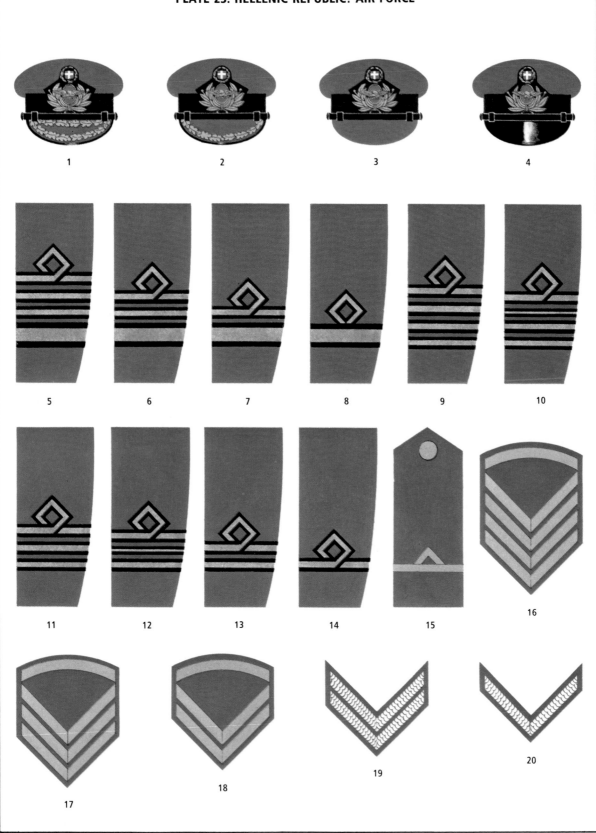

PLATES 24 AND 25. ITALIAN REPUBLIC: ARMY

An elaborate system of rank is displayed on Italian Army head-dress by means of the chin-cords and chin-straps. The range of ranks are indicated by the design of the cords or straps and specific ranks within each range are shown by the style of the loops on the chin-cords and chin-straps. There is also a difference in colour between the cap badge worn by Generals of Army Corps and those worn by other Generals. Rank insignia on the military uniform is extensive and elaborate. A number of methods exist for displaying the insignia, the most common of which is shown here, the use of shoulder-boards and arm chevrons.

Head-dress
1 Uniform peaked cap as worn by Generals of Army Corps and Generals of Army Corps with specific appointments. Cap shown here for the former.
2 Cap for other Generals, here shown for a Brigade General.
3 Cap for wear by Senior Officers, here shown for Colonel of Infantry.
4 Cap for Junior Officers, here shown for Captains of Artillery.
5 Cap for Senior Warrant Officers, here shown for Chief Warrant Officer of Tanks.
6 Cap for wear by Warrant Officers, here shown for Warrant Officer

of Anti-Aircraft Artillery.

Rank and Appointment Insignia
7 Shoulder-board for Generale di Corpo d'Armata con Incarichi Speciali.
8 Generale di Corpo d'Armata.
9 Generale di Divisione con Incarichi Speciali.
10 Generale di Divisione.
11 Generale di Brigata con Incarichi Speciali.
12 Generale di Brigata.
13 Colonnello con Incarichi Speciali.
14 Colonnello Comandante di Corpo.
15 Colonnello.
16 Tenente Colonnello con Incarichi Speciali.
17 Tenente Colonnello Comandante di Corpo.
18 Tenente Colonnello.
19 Maggiore.
20 Primo Capitano.
21 Capitano.
22 Tenente.
23 Sottotenente.
24 Aiutante di Battaglia.
25 Maresciallo Aiutante.
26 Maresciallo Maggiore.
27 Maresciallo Capo.
28 Maresciallo Ordinario.

Above: Italian, Greek and Turkish officers of Allied Forces Southern Europe, photographed in August 1955 at Lake Maggiore. It is possible to make out the AFSOUTH pocket badges on the Italian officer in the foreground and the Greek officer on the far right.

Left: A Sergente Paracadutista of the Italian Carabinieri, a qualified parachutist wearing the dark-blue/black service dress. The rank insignia used by the Carabinieri is identical to that used in the Italian Army. The Carabinieri was originally formed in 1814 with the task of maintaining law and order and the conservation of public and private security in peacetime and the defence of the Italian State in time of war. This still holds true today. Like the West German Bundesgrenzschutz, the French Gendarmerie Nationale and the Belgian Gendarmerie, the Italian Carabinieri, with a total strength of about 84,000 men, will take an important and active role alongside the Italian NATO forces should there be an external threat to the Alliance.

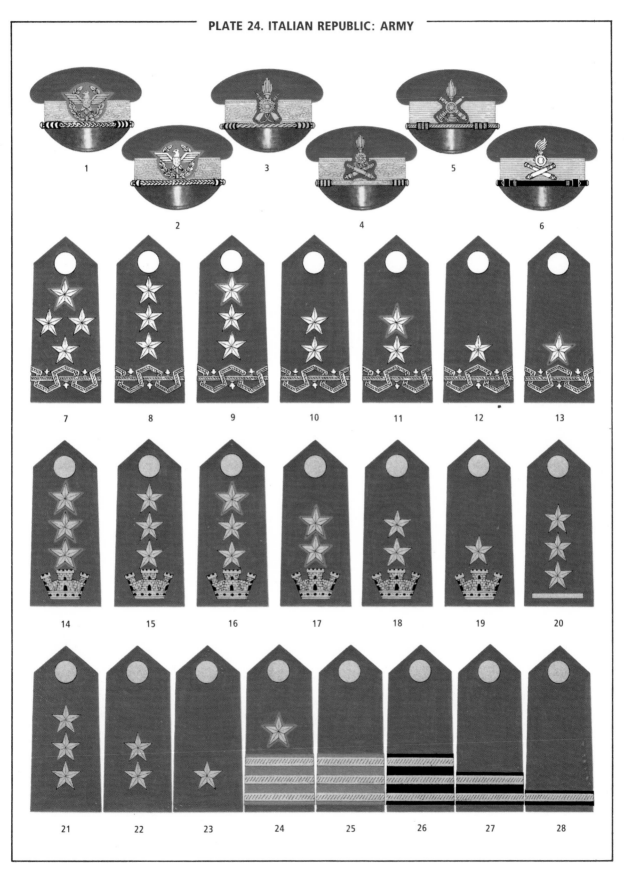

PLATE 24. ITALIAN REPUBLIC: ARMY

PLATE 25. ITALIAN REPUBLIC: ARMY AND NAVY

29 Rank chevrons for Sergente Maggiore.
30 Sergente Maggiore of Paratroops.
31 Sergente.
32 Sergente of Paratroops.
33 Caporale Maggiore.
34 Caporale Maggiore of Paratroops.
35 Caporale.
36 Caporale of Paratroops. Soldato (no rank insignia worn).

As with the Italian Army, rank in the Italian Navy is displayed on the head-dress by the use of chin-cords and chin-straps. Uniform ranks are indicated by sleeve rings, shoulder-boards and arm chevrons.

Head-dress
1 Uniform peaked cap for Admirals, here shown for Ammiraglio di Divisione.
2 Cap for senior naval officers, here shown for Capitano di Fregata.
3 Cap for junior officers, here shown for Sottotenente di Vascello.
4 Cap for Chief Petty Officers, here shown for Capo di 2ª classe.
5 Cap for Petty Officers, here shown for 2ª Capo.
6 Cap worn by sailors.

Rank and Appointment Insignia
7 Sleeve rings for Ammiraglio di Squadra con Incarichi Speciali.
8 Ammiraglio di Squadra.
9 Shoulder-board for Ammiraglio di Divisione. Two other similar shoulder-boards exist for the ranks of Ammiraglio di Squadra (three stars in a triangular group) and Contrammiraglio (a single star).
10 Contrammiraglio, Engineering branch.
11 Capitano di Vascello.
12 Capitano di Fregata, Commissariat branch.
13 Capitano di Corvetta. Shoulder Board.

Below: Parachutist Sergente Bonifazi of the Italian Carabinieri wearing camouflage combat clothing.

PLATE 25. ITALIAN REPUBLIC: ARMY

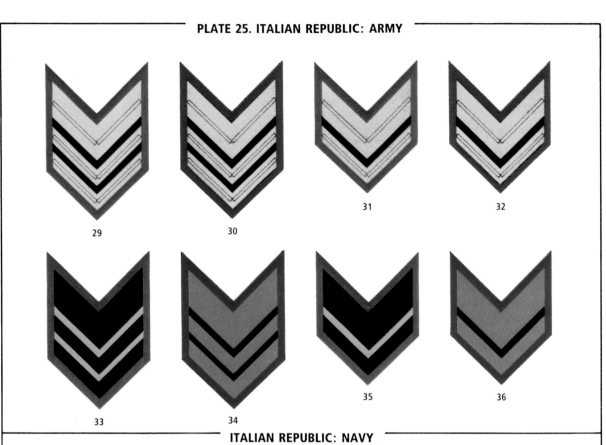

29 30 31 32

33 34 35 36

ITALIAN REPUBLIC: NAVY

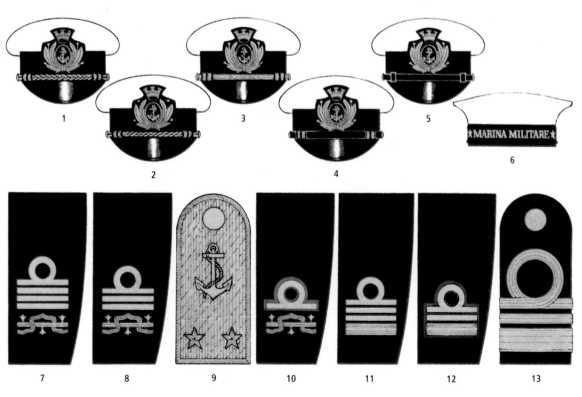

1 2 3 4 5 6

MARINA MILITARE

7 8 9 10 11 12 13

PLATE 26. ITALIAN REPUBLIC: NAVY AND AIR FORCE

14 Capitano di Corvetta.
15 Tenente di Vascello.
16 Sottotenente di Vascello.
17 Guardiamarina.
18 Aspirante.
19 Capo di 1ª Classe Scelto, Line.
20 Capo di 1ª Classe, Machinist.
21 Capo di 2ª Classe, Radar.
22 Capo di 3ª Classe, Musician.
23 Rank chevrons for Secondo Capo, Line.
24 Sergente, Radar.

25 Sottocapo, Machinist.
26 Comune di 1ª Classe, Line. Comune di 2ª Classe (no rank insignia worn).

The Italian Air Force relies on the system of differing chin-cords and chin-straps on their head-dress to indicate rank. Officers display their rank on their cuffs and by the use of shoulder-boards. Junior NCOs use rank chevrons.

Head-dress
1 Uniform peaked cap for Air Force Generals, here shown for Generali con Incarichi Speciali.
2 Cap for other Generals, here shown for Generale di Brigata Aerea.
3 Cap for wear by Senior Officers, here shown for Maggiore.
4 Cap for Junior Officers, here shown for Sottotenente.
5 Cap for wear by Ajutante di Battaglia. This rank no longer exists in the Italian Air Force, but it has been included here on the reasoning that there may still be a few 'old soldiers' still wearing it.
6 Cap for Warrant Officers, shown here for Maresciallo di 3ª classe.
7 Cap for wear by Sergeant Majors and Sergeants, shown here for Sergente Maggiore.

Left: Tenente Colonello Roberto De Gasperis of the Italian Air Force. He carries his rank insignia on the left breast of his orange-lined, olive-green flying-jerkin below which is his squadron badge. The Italian national title and tricolour is worn on the left shoulder.

PLATE 26. ITALIAN REPUBLIC: NAVY

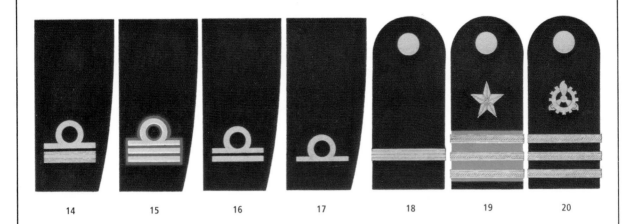

14 15 16 17 18 19 20

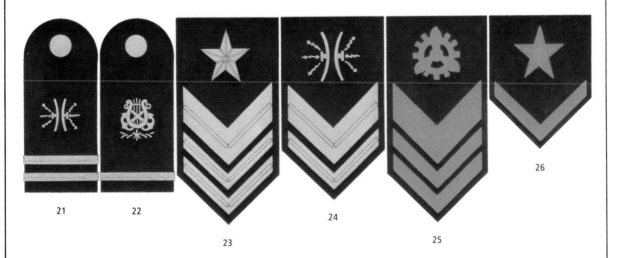

21 22 23 24 25 26

ITALIAN REPUBLIC: AIR FORCE

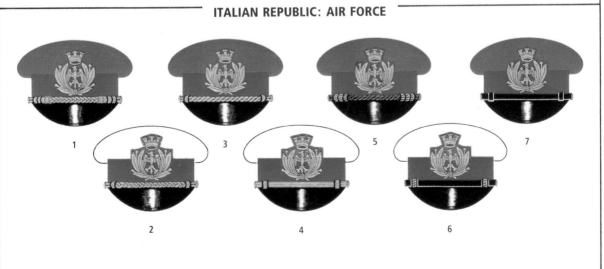

1 2 3 4 5 6 7

PLATE 27. ITALIAN REPUBLIC: AIR FORCE

8 Italian Air Force side cap (Bustina) as worn by Senior Officers.
9 Side cap for Junior Officers.
10 Side cap for wear by Other Ranks.

Rank and Appointment Insignia

11 Sleeve insignia for Generale di Squadra Aerea con Incarichi Speciali.
12 Generale di Squadra Aerea.
13 Generale di Divisione Aerea.
14 Shoulder-board for Generale di Divisione Aerea.
15 General di Brigata Aerea.
16 Colonnello.
17 Shoulder-board for Colonnello.
18 Tenente Colonnello.
19 Maggiore.
20 Capitano.
21 Tenente.
22 Sottotenente.
23 Shoulder-board for Maresciallo di 1ª classe Scelto.
24 Maresciallo di 1ª classe.
25 Maresciallo di 2ª classe.
26 Maresciallo di 3ª classe.
27 Rank chevrons for Sergente Maggiore.
28 Sergente.
29 1er Aviere.
30 Aviere Scelto.
Aviere (no rank insignia worn).

Above: Tenente Colonnello Antonio Stefanelli of the Italian Army, a member of a helicopter squadron. A similar arrangement applies for the Italian Army when it comes to wearing various badges and insignia of rank on flying overalls and work clothing. Rank insignia is displayed on the left chest and name tab on the right chest.

PLATE 27. ITALIAN REPUBLIC: AIR FORCE

8

9

10

11

12

13

14

15

16

17

18

19

20

21

22

23

24

25

26

27

28

29

30

Above: A Major (Maggiore) of the Italian Army helicopter force.

PLATE 28. GRAND DUCHY OF LUXEMBOURG: ARMY

Territorially the smallest country in NATO, Luxembourg has committed its battalion-size army to NATO ACE mobile force. Luxembourg does not possess a navy or an air force (disregarding the fleet of AWACS registered in Luxembourg.

Rank displayed on Luxembourg Army head-dress is a lot simpler than the army head-dress of other NATO member countries. Only the distinctive red cap band worn by the Colonel Commandant of the Army plus the quality of the cap badges used shows the differences in rank. The dark-blue beret is worn by Junior NCOs and other ranks.

The system of rank insignia worn on the uniform is in keeping with other NATO countries. Gorget patches, shoulder-boards and shoulder-strap slip-ons, sleeve badges and arm chevrons. The shape and design of the individual items is peculiar to the Luxembourg Army.

Head-dress

1 Uniform peaked cap worn by Colonel Commandant of the Army (ranks 5 and 7).
2 Cap worn by all other officers (ranks 7 to 13).
3 Cap worn by Senior NCOs (ranks 15 to 20).
4 Beret worn by remaining person-

nel, junior NCOs and other ranks (ranks 21 to 23).

Rank and Appointment Insignia

5 Gorget patch (worn with shoulder-board, item 7) for rank of Commandant de l'Armée.
6 Gorget patch for Colonel (worn with shoulder-board, item 7).
7 Shoulder-board worn by Commandant de l'Armée and by Colonel.
8 Shoulder-board for Lieutenant-Colonel.
9 Major.
10 Capitaine.
11 Shoulder-strap slip-on as worn on the summer, light-weight uni-

form for Premier Lieutenant.
12 Shoulder-board for Lieutenant.
13 Shoulder-board for Aspirant Officer.
14 Forearm insignia for Adjudant-Major and Adjudant de Corps.
15 Rank chevrons for Adjudant-Major.
16 Adjudant-Chef.
17 Adjudant.
18 Sergent-Chef.
19 Premier Sergent.
20 Sergent.
21 Caporal-Chef.
22 Caporal.
23 Soldat de première classe. Soldat (no rank insignia worn).

PLATE 28. GRAND DUCHY OF LUXEMBURG: ARMY

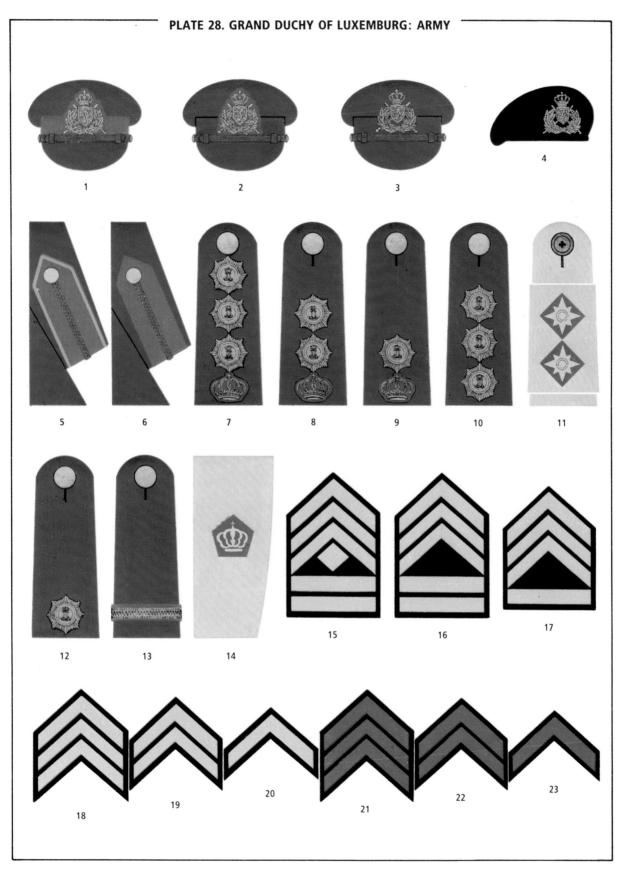

PLATE 29. KINGDOM OF THE NETHERLANDS: ARMY

Although the beret has become the everyday wear for troops of the Royal Netherlands Army, the uniform peaked cap continues to be worn in certain orders of dress and on particular occasions. With the obvious exception of the bright-red cap band worn by General Officers, the only other method of indicating rank on the head-dress is by the differences in the cap badges. Rank displayed on the uniform is by the use of shoulder-boards and shoulder-strap slip-ons by officers of all ranks, and badges of appoint-ment and chevrons worn on the sleeve and on the shoulder-strap by means of slip-ons.

Head-dress
1 Uniform peaked cap for General Officers (ranks 5 to 8).
2 Cap for wear by Officers (ranks 9 to 16).
3 Cap for Under Officers and Sergeants Major (ranks 17 to 20).
4 Cap for Sergeants, Corporals and Soldiers (ranks 21 to 25).

Rank and Appointment Insignia
5 Shoulder-board for Generaal.

6 Shoulder-strap slip-on for light tan shirt for Luitenant-generaal.
7 Generaal-majoor.
8 Brigade-generaal.
9 Kolonel.
10 Luitenant-kolonel, slip-on as worn on field uniform.
11 Majoor.
12 Kapitein and Ritmeester.
13 Eerste-luitenant.
14 Tweede-luitenant.
15 Kappelmeester.
16 Technisch opzichter.
17 Adjudant-onderofficier and Vaandrig/Kornet.

18 Sleeve badge worn on forearm by Komp.Sergeant-majoor.
19 Slip-on for Komp.Sergeant-majoor worn on the field uniform.
20 Rank chevrons for Sergeant-majoor and Opperwachtmeester.
21 Sergeant der 1e klasse and Wachtmeester der 1e klasse.
22 Sergeant and Wachtmeester, worn on the field uniform.
23 Korporaal der 1e klasse.
24 Korporaal.
25 Soldaat der 1e klasse. Soldaat (no rank insignia worn).

Left: Sergeant der 1e Klasse of the Netherlands Army. The medal worn on a ribbon around the neck is a commemorative medal struck to mark the occasion of the tenth anniversary of the Royal Military Police and City of Chichester March (1977–1988). A medal is awarded to each participant who successfully completes an endurance march of one of three lengths. The figure in the background is that of the Adjudant (warrant officer) of the Belgian Gendarmerie.

PLATE 29. KINGDOM OF NETHERLANDS: ARMY

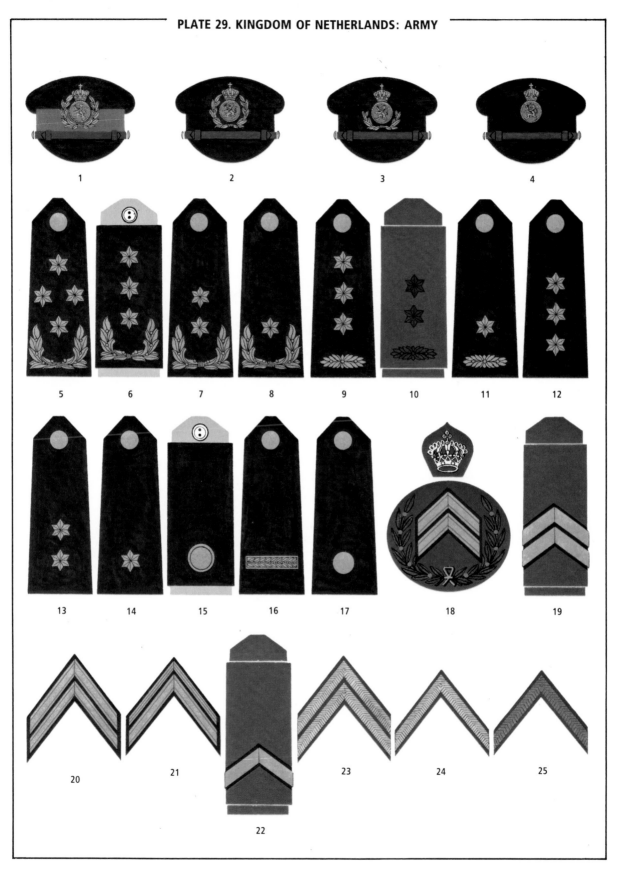

PLATE 30. KINGDOM OF THE NETHERLANDS: NAVY

Head-dress worn in the Royal Netherlands Navy follows the pattern found with many other European naval forces. Rank is displayed by means of peak decoration and differences of design and colour in the cap badges. Rank displayed on the naval uniforms takes the form of cuff rings, shoulder-boards and on certain forms of dress shoulder-strap rank slip-ons. Lower ratings wear arm chevrons.

Head-dress

1 Uniform peaked cap worn by Flag Officers (ranks 8 to 13).
2 Cap for wear by naval officers from Captains down to Lieutenant-Commander (ranks 14 to 16).
3 Cap for remaining officers (ranks 17 to 19).
4 Cap for Warrant Officers, Petty Officers and Sergeants (ranks 20 to 23).
5 Cap for Corporals (rank 24).
6 Cap for Seamen 1st class (rank 25).
7 Sailor's cap for seamen 2nd class and below (rank 26).

Rank and Appointment Insignia

8 Cuff rings and insignia for Admiraal.
9 Shoulder-board for Admiraal.
10 Cuff rings and insignia for Luitenant-admiraal.
11 Vice-admiraal.
12 Schout-bij-nacht.
13 Commandeur.
14 Kapitein ter zee.
15 Kapitein-luitenant ter zee.
16 Luitenant ter zee der eerste klasse.
17 Luitenant ter zee der tweede klasse oudste categorie.
18 Shoulder-strap slip-on worn on the orange flying overalls by helicopter crews for the rank of Luitenant ter zee der tweede klasse.
19 Luitenant ter zee der tweede klasse.
20 Luitenant ter zee der derde klasse.
21 Adjudant-onderofficier (opperschipper).
22 Sergeant-majoor (schipper). Rank chevrons.
23 Sergeant (bootsman).
24 Korporaal (kwartiermeester).
25 Matroos der 1e klasse.
26 Matroos der 2e klasse. Matroos der 3e klasse (no rank insignia worn).

Below: Sergeant Hooff of the Royal Netherlands Navy a member of an Air Sea Rescue helicopter squadron. Rank insignia is worn on the shoulder-straps of his bright orange flying overalls.

PLATE 30. KINGDOM OF NETHERLANDS: NAVY

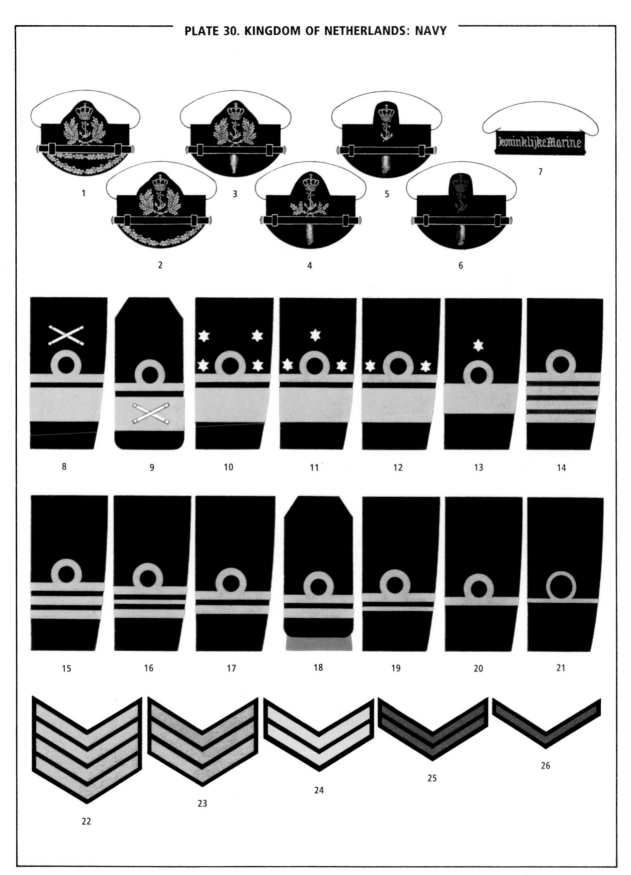

PLATE 31. KINGDOM OF THE NETHERLANDS: MARINE CORPS

Personnel of the Royal Netherlands Marine Corps wear head-dress very similar to that worn in the Royal Netherlands Navy. However, the Marine Corps head-dress is distinguished by the use of red piping to the upper and lower edges of the cap band on the uniform peaked cap. Marines of all ranks wear a dark-blue beret with a domed red cloth patch mounted behind the anchor beret badge. Rank is indicated on the uniform peaked cap, as it is on the Naval head-dress, by the use of oak-leaves as peak decoration and differences in design of the cap badges.

Rank worn on the uniform takes the form of shoulder-boards and cuff rings for officers, as well as shoulder-strap slip-ons and small gold metal insignia worn on the collar of the light-weight summer tan uniform. NCOs and Marines 1st and 2nd Class wear rank chevrons on the arm.

Head-dress
1 Uniform peaked cap for Marine Corps General Class Officers (ranks 8 to 12).
2 Field Officers (ranks 13 to 16).
3 Cap for remaining officers (ranks 17 to 20).
4 Cap for Warrant Officers (rank 21).
5 Cap for Sergeants and Corporals (ranks 22 and 23).
6 Cap for Corporals 1st and 2nd Class and Marines (ranks 24 to 26).
7 Beret worn by all ranks Netherlands Marine Corps.

Rank and Appointment Insignia
8 Sleeve rings for Generaal.
9 Shoulder-board for Generaal.
10 Sleeve rings for Luitenant-generaal.
11 Generaal-majoor.
12 Brigade-generaal.
13 Kolonel.
14 Luitenant-kolonel.
15 Shoulder-strap slip-on worn on the pullover by Luitenant-kolonel.
16 Majoor.
17 Kapitein.
18 Eerste luitenant.
19 Collar insignia for Eerste luitenant worn on the light khaki shirt.
20 Tweede luitenant.
21 Adjudant-onderofficier der mariniers.
22 Sergeant-majoor der mariniers rank chevrons.
23 Sergeant der mariniers chevrons worn on the light khaki shirt.
24 Korporaal der mariniers.
25 Marinier des 1e klasse.
26 Marinier der 2e klasse.

Left: A Korporaal of the Dutch Army Pay Corps (Militaire Administratie).

PLATE 31. KINGDOM OF NETHERLANDS: MARINE CORPS

PLATE 32. KINGDOM OF THE NETHERLANDS: AIR FORCE

Rank on Royal Dutch Air Force head-dress of the type illustrated here is only displayed as peak decoration. Rank displayed on the blue-grey uniform is in the form of sleeve rings and arm chevrons.

Head-dress
1 Uniform peaked cap for General officers (ranks 5 to 9).
2 Colonels (ranks 5 to 10).
3 Cap for Lieutenant-Colonels and Majors (ranks 11 and 12).
4 Cap for Junior Officers, Ensigns and Warrant Officers (ranks 13 to 18).
5 Side cap for NCOs and Airmen (ranks 19 to 14).

Rank and Appointment Insignia
6 Sleeve rings for Generaal.
7 Shoulder-board for Generaal.
8 Luitenant-generaal.
9 Generaal-majoor.
10 Commodore.
11 Kolonel.
12 Luitenant-Kolonel.
13 Majoor.
14 Kapitein.
15 Eerste Luitenant.
16 Tweede Luitenant.
17 Flying suit rank slip-on worn on shoulder-strap for Tweede Luitenant.
18 Adjudant Onderofficier and Vaandrig.
19 Shoulder-board for Adjudant Onderofficier and Vaandrig.
20 Rank chevrons for Sergeant-Majoor.
21 Sergeant der 1e klasse.
22 Sergeant.
23 Korporaal der 1e klasse.
24 Korporaal.
25 Soldaat der 1e klasse.
   Soldaat (no rank insignia worn).

Above: Members of the Netherlands Koninklijke Marechaussee, the equivalent of the Royal Military Police.

PLATE 32. KINGDOM OF NETHERLANDS: AIR FORCE

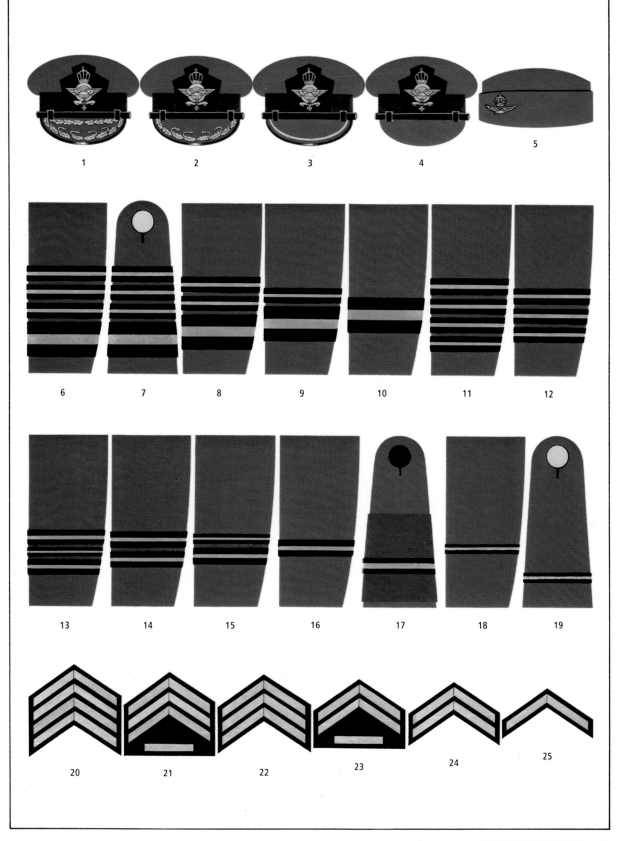

PLATE 33. KINGDOM OF NORWAY: ARMY

Only the red cap band distinguishes the head-dress worn by Generals of the Royal Norwegian Army from the head-dress worn by other Army officers. The cap badge worn in the peaked cap is also of a different pattern from that worn in the beret. Insignia of rank worn on the uniform consists of collar insignia with branch of service badges worn on the lapel.

Head-dress

1 Peaked cap worn by Officers of General rank and Officers of Colonel rank (ranks 6 to 11).
2 Cap for remaining officers (ranks 12 to 15).
3 Sergeants and Other Ranks (ranks 16 to 19).
4 Winter Cap for wear by all officers other than General Officers. This style of cap is available to be worn by all ranks, but with the appropriate form of cap insignia displayed on the front. For patterns of winter cap insignia see Norway Air Force plate 35 head-dress items 5 to 8.
5 Beret for wear by all Norwegian Army ranks.

Rank and Appointment Insignia

6 Collar insignia of rank and lapel branch-of-service insignia for General.
7 Generalløytnant.
8 Generalmajor.
9 Oberst I of the Infantry.
10 Oberst II of Field Artillery.
11 Oberstløytnant of the Infantry.
12 Major of the Infantry.
13 Kaptein of Engineers.
14 Løytnant of the Infantry.
15 Fenrik of Army Communications.
16 Sersjant of Army Transport Corps.
17 Korporal of Infantry.
18 Visekorporal of the Army Weapons Technical Corps.
19 Menig of the Infantry (no rank insignia worn).

Above: A Korporal of the Norwegian Army has his SHAPE pass checked by a lance-corporal of the Corps of Royal Military Police. In the background is a Sergent of the Danish Military Police.

PLATE 33. KINGDOM OF NORWAY: ARMY

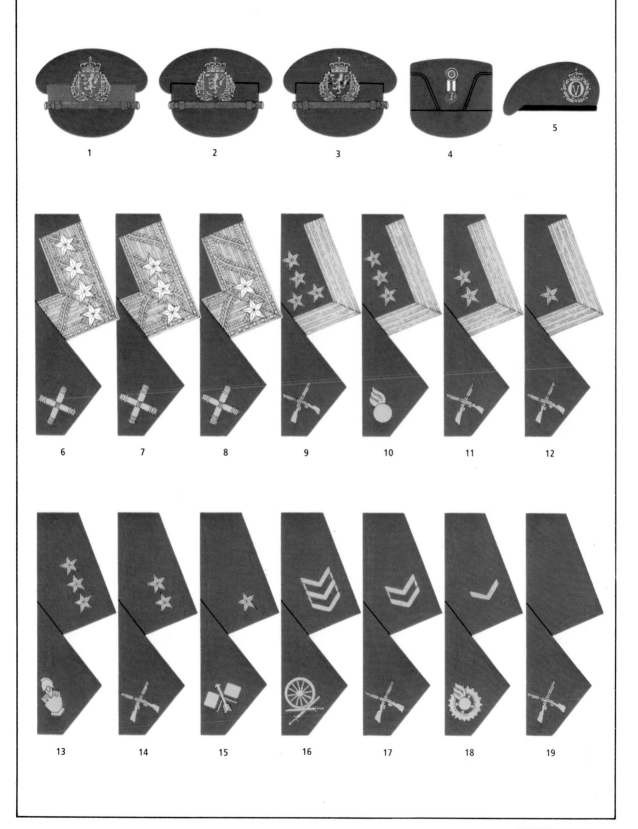

PLATE 34. KINGDOM OF NORWAY: NAVY

Differences in the cap badges and the decoration used on the peaks of the uniform caps is the means adopted to display rank on Norwegian naval head-dress. Sleeve rings and shoulder-boards are used on the uniforms of officers and rank patches by ratings to show rank.

Head-dress

1 Uniform peaked cap for Admirals (ranks 7 to 9).
2 Cap for wear by Senior Officers (ranks 10 to 13).
3 Cap for Junior Officers (ranks 14 to 16).
4 Cap for Chief Petty Officers (ranks 18 to 21).
5 Cap for Petty Officers (ranks 22 and 23).
6 Cap for seaman (rank 24).

Rank and Appointment Insignia

7 Shoulder-board for Admiral.
8 Sleeve rings for Viseadmiral.
9 Kontreadmiral.
10 Kommandør.
11 Kommandør Kaptein.
12 Orlogskaptein.
13 Kapteinløytnant.
14 Løytnant.
15 Fenrik.
16 Ustskrevet.
17 Kadett II Klasse.

18 Flaggkvartermester.
19 Kvartermester I Klasse (Mechanic).
20 Kvartermester (Artillery).
21 Kvartermester (Konstabel I Klasse) (Torpedo Mechanic).
22 Ledende Menig (Konstabel II Klasse) (Radar).
23 Menig 1 Saerklasse (Konstabel III Klasse) (Electrician).
24 Menig (Veiretmatros) (Mechanic).

Above: From 17 to 19 September 1956, General Gruenther, the outgoing Supreme Allied Commander Europe, paid a farewell visit to Norwegian and Danish government officials and military leaders. General Gruenther is seen here inspecting a parade of Norwegian naval and army personnel in Oslo. The SACEUR is accompanied by a Generalmajor of the Royal Norwegian Air Force and a Norwegian Army Kaptein.

PLATE 34. KINGDOM OF NORWAY: NAVY

PLATE 35. KINGDOM OF NORWAY: AIR FORCE

Royal Norwegian Air Force ranks, or rather groups of ranks, are indicated on the uniform peaked cap by means of peak decoration and differences in design and colour of the cap badge. The side caps worn also shown rank groupings by means of metallic and enamelled bosses and narrow strips of braid. Rank is indicated on the Air Force uniforms in two ways. Collar insignia, consisting of gold or silver braid for General and senior officers, with silver stars, and silver stars worn on the collar for remaining officers. All

other personnel wear small metal chevrons. This pattern of insignia is worn on the full-length Service tunic, while the same insignia worn on the shoulder-board is used on the short blouse.

Head-dress
1 Peaked cap worn by General Officers (ranks 9 to 11).
2 Cap for Colonels (ranks 12 and 13).
3 Cap for remaining officers (ranks 14 to 18).
4 Peaked cap for Sergeants (ranks 19 and 20).
5 Side cap for Air Force General officers (ranks 9 to 11).
6 Side cap for all other officers (ranks 12 to 18).
7 Side cap worn by Sergeants (ranks 19 and 20).
8 Side cap worn by Corporals and Airmen (ranks 21 and 22).

Rank and Appointment Insignia
9 Collar insignia of rank for a General.
10 Generalløytnant.
11 Generalmajor.

12 Oberst I.
13 Oberst II.
14 Oberstløytnant.
15 Major.
16 Kaptein.
17 Løytnant.
18 Fenrik.
19 Sersjant.
20 Shoulder-board insignia as worn on the Air Force blouse for Sersjant.
21 Korporal.
22 Vingsoldat.
  Flysoldat (no rank insignia worn).

Left: Kaptein Halvorsen of the Royal Norwegian Air Force, a pilot of a Northrop F-5 'Freedom Fighter' aircraft, hence the F-5 arm patch. The Norwegian Air Force pilot wings are worn on the right chest and rank and name patch on the left chest. This latter patch also displays the three rank stars for a Kaptein (Captain).

PLATE 35. KINGDOM OF NORWAY: AIR FORCE

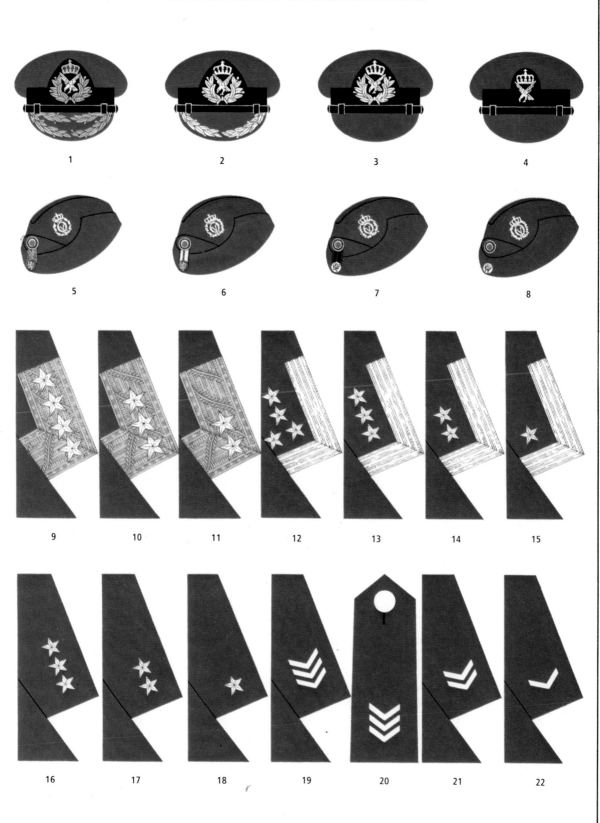

PLATE 36. PORTUGUESE REPUBLIC: ARMY

Rank in the Portuguese Army is shown on the head-dress by the use of peak decoration and chin-cords and chin-straps. Ranks displayed on the uniforms worn in the Army consists of gorget patches for General Officers and cuff bars for all officers on the pale-grey full dress uniform and shoulder-board slip-ons and arm chevrons on the olive-green Service Dress for all officers, warrant officers, NCOs and privates.

Head-dress

1 Uniform peaked cap worn by officers of General rank with pale-grey full dress uniform (ranks 8 to 10).
2 Cap for wear with the olive-green service dress by Colonels, here shown for Engineers (rank 11).
3 Cap for Lieutenant-Colonels and Majors (ranks 12 and 13).
4 Cap for Junior Officers and Senior Warrant Officers (ranks 14 to 19), here shown for Signals.
5 Cap for Sergeants, here shown for Cavalry.
6 Beret worn by all ranks, here shown for Artillery personnel.

Rank and Appointment Insignia

7 Gorget patch for wear by officers of General rank with the pale-grey full dress uniform (ranks 8 to 10).
8 Shoulder-board for the olive-green Service Dress for Generals.
9 General.
10 Brigadeiro.
11 Cuff bars worn on the pale-grey full dress uniform for Coronel.
12 Shoulder-board slip-on for Tenente-Coronel worn on the olive-green Service uniform.
13 Camouflage combat jacket shoulder-strap with slip-on rank for Major.
14 Capitao.
15 Tenente.

16 Alferes.
17 Rank chevrons and State Arms badge for Sargento-Mor.
18 Sargento-Chefe.
19 State Arms badge for Sergento-Ajudante.
20 Rank chevrons for Primerio-Sargento.
21 Segundo-Sargento.
22 Furriel.
23 Segundo Furriel.
24 Primeiro Cabo.
25 Segundo Cabo.
   Soldado (no rank insignia worn).
   Soldado Recruta (no rank insignia worn).

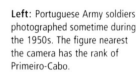

Left: Portuguese Army soldiers photographed sometime during the 1950s. The figure nearest the camera has the rank of Primeiro-Cabo.

PLATE 36. PORTUGUESE REPUBLIC: ARMY

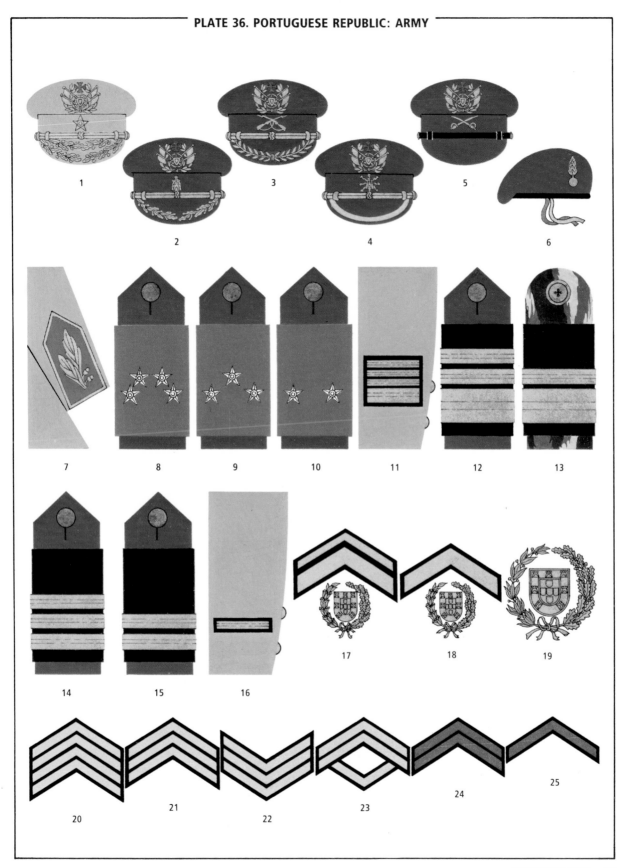

1
2
3
4
5
6
7
8
9
10
11
12
13
14
15
16
17
18
19
20
21
22
23
24
25

PLATE 37. PORTUGUESE REPUBLIC: NAVY

As befitting an ancient maritime nation, head-dress in the Portuguese Navy follows the pattern of other European maritime countries. Rank is shown on naval head-wear by peak decoration and to a limited extent by differences in cap badges and chin-cords. All peaked caps carry the State Arms above their cap badge. Rank displayed on naval uniform consists of sleeve rings for officers and rank chevrons and State Arms badges for all other ranks.

Head-dress
1 Uniform peaked cap as worn by Admirals (ranks 8 to 11).
2 Cap for wear by Captains and Commanders (ranks 12 and 13).
3 Cap for Lieutenant-Commander (rank 14).
4 Cap for remaining Junior Officers (ranks 15 to 17).
5 Cap worn by all Petty Officers (ranks 18 to 23).
6 Cap for Seamen.
7 Beret shown here for wear by Fuzileiro Especial.

Rank and Appointment Insignia
8 Sleeve rings for Almirante de Armada.
9 Almirante.
10 Vice-Almirante.
11 Contra-Almirante.
12 Capitao-de-Mar-e-Guerra.
13 Capitao-de-Fragata, Doctor.
14 Capitao-Tenente.
15 Primeiro-Tenente.
16 Segundo-Tenente.
17 Guarda-Marinha.
18 State Arms and chevrons worn by Sargento-Mor.
19 Sargento-Chefe.
20 State Arms for Sargento-Ajudante.
21 Rank chevrons for Primeiro-Sargento.
22 Segundo-Sargento.
23 Sub-Sargento.
24 Cabo.
25 Marinheiro.
   Primeiro Grumete (no rank insignia worn).
   Segundo Grumete (no rank insignia worn).

PLATE 37. PORTUGUESE REPUBLIC: NAVY

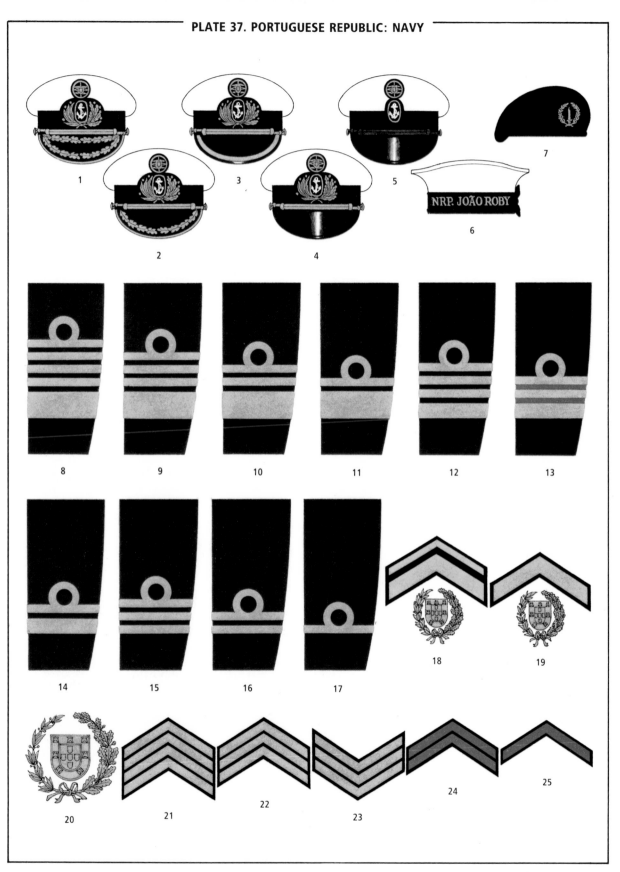

NRP. JOÃO ROBY

1
2
3
4
5
6
7
8
9
10
11
12
13
14
15
16
17
18
19
20
21
22
23
24
25

PLATE 38. PORTUGUESE REPUBLIC: AIR FORCE

Differences in Air Force rank displayed on head-dress is shown by the use of peak decoration and to a lesser extent by cap-cords and chin-straps. As with the head-dress of the Portuguese Navy, the Air Force also display the State Arms on their peaked caps for all ranks. Rank stars and sleeve rings are worn on the cuffs of Air Force Officers' uniforms and rank chevrons and State Arms badges are used by remaining personnel.

Head-dress

1 Uniform peaked cap for Air Officer ranks (ranks 7 to 10).
2 Cap for wear by Colonels, Lieutenant-Colonels and Majors (ranks 11 to 13).
3 Cap worn by Captains and First Lieutenants (ranks 14 and 15).
4 Cap for Pilot Officers (rank 16).
5 Cap for Sergeants-Major, Warrant Officers and Sergeants (ranks 17 to 23).
6 Beret worn by Lance-Corporals (ranks 24 and 25).

Rank and Appointment Insignia

7 Rank stars worn on the cuffs by Marechal.
8 General.
9 General.
10 Brigadeiro.
11 Coronel, sleeve rings.
12 Tenente-Coronel.
13 Major.
14 Capitao.
15 Tenente.
16 Alferes.
17 Chevrons and State Arms badge for Sargento-Mor.
18 Sargento-Chefe.
19 State Arms badge worn by Sargento-Ajudante.
20 Chevrons for Primeiro-Sargento.
21 Segundo-Sargento.
22 Furriel.
23 Segundo-Furriel.
24 Primeiro-Cabo.
25 Segundo-Cabo.
Soldado (no rank insignia worn).
Soldado Recruta (no rank insignia worn).

Above and left: Primeoro-Sargento Pia of the Portuguese Air Force's 501 Squadron. The primary mission of this squadron is tactical air transport and search and rescue operations. Its secondary mission is that of airlift operations, maritime patrols and fire-fighting. First Sergeant Pia wears his squadron patch on his right shoulder and the Portuguese national title and emblem on the left shoulder. His insignia of rank are worn stitched to both shoulders.

PLATE 38. PORTUGUESE REPUBLIC: AIR FORCE

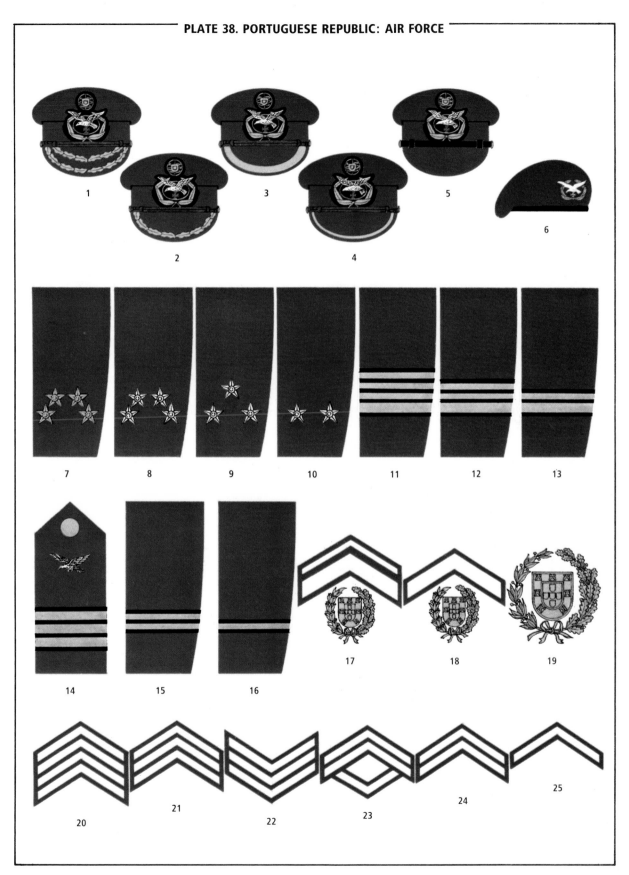

1

2

3

4

5

6

7

8

9

10

11

12

13

14

15

16

17

18

19

20

21

22

23

24

25

PLATE 39. KINGDOM OF SPAIN: ARMY

Until quite recently the Spanish Army operated an elaborate system of displaying rank both on its head-dress and its uniforms. Rank was carried on the cuffs of the Service Dress as well as on the front of the head-wear, which resulted in a range of head-dress that matched the range of individual ranks and appointments. With the restoration of the Spanish monarchy the opportunity has been taken to do away with the previous methods of displaying rank, but not the ranks themselves that pertained under the Franco era. Rank insignia displayed on all the head-dress as well as the cuff insignia and rhomboids worn by General Officers on the lapels of their tunics have been dropped.

Rank now displayed on the greatly reduced range of Uniform Peaked Caps consists of peak decoration only. Rank insignia worn on the uniform have been reduced to shoulder-boards only.

Head-dress

1 Uniform peaked cap for wear by General Officers (ranks 6 to 10).
2 Cap for Colonels, Lieutenant-Colonels and Majors (ranks 11 to 13).
3 Cap for Captains, Subalterns and First Lieutenants (ranks 14 to 17).
4 Cap for Warrant Officers (rank 18).
5 Beret worn by Privates, here shown for Mountain Troops. The beret is an item of head-dress available to officers, whose rank is distinguished by the badge.

Rank and Appointment Insignia

6 Shoulder-board for Capitan General.
7 Lapel insignia for all General Officers (ranks 6 to 10).
8 Teniente General.
9 General de Division.
10 General de Brigada.
11 Coronel.
12 Teniente Coronel.
13 Commandante.
14 Capitan.
15 Teniente.
16 Alferez.
17 Subteniente.
18 Brigada.
19 Sargento Primero.
20 Sargento.
21 Cabo Primero.
22 Cabo.
23 Soldado Primero.
   Soldado (no rank insignia worn).

Left: A Lieutenant-Colonel (Teniente Coronal) of the Spanish Army recently photographed. Clearly shown are the eight-pointed rank stars carried on the shoulder-straps and the simplified, post-Franco era, uniform cap.

PLATE 39. KINGDOM OF SPAIN: ARMY

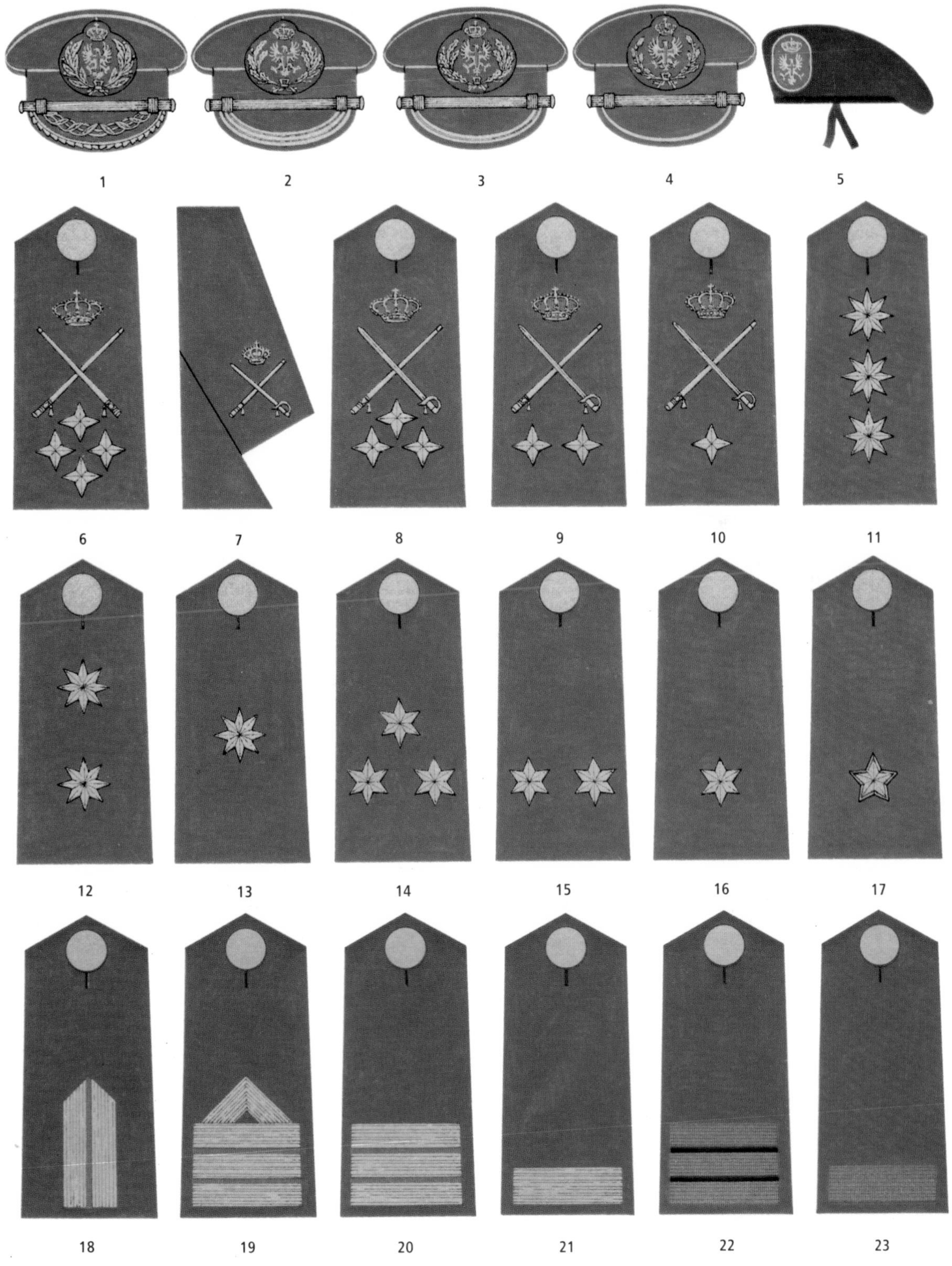

1

2

3

4

5

6

7

8

9

10

11

12

13

14

15

16

17

18

19

20

21

22

23

PLATE 40. KINGDOM OF SPAIN: NAVY

The amount of peak decoration and the use of chin-straps indicates rank displayed on naval head-dress. Background colour to the gold-coloured fouled anchor cap badge indicates branch of naval service. Shoulder-boards are worn by Spanish naval officers of flag rank. Cuff rings predominate on officers' uniforms and sleeve stripes are used by lower ranks.

Head-dress

1 Uniform peaked cap for wear by officers of flag rank (ranks 6 to 10), here shown.
2 Cap for wear by officers from rank of Captain to Lieutenant-Commander (ranks 11 to 13).
3 Cap for remaining officers (ranks 14–18). (Cap for naval warrant officers – ranks 19 & 20 – is identical to the cap – item 4 – worn in the Spanish Marines).
4 Cap for Chief and Petty Officers (ranks 21 to 24).
5 Cap for wear by seamen.

Rank and Appointment Insignia

6 Sleeve rings for Capitan General.
7 Shoulder-board for Capitan General.
8 Cuff rings for Almirante.
9 Vice-Almirante, here shown for Engineer Branch.
10 Contra-Almirante.
11 Capitan de Navio.
12 Capitan de Fragata.
13 Capitan de Corbeta.
14 Capitan, here shown Administration.
15 Capitan, here shown Machinist.
16 Capitan, here shown as Medical Branch.
17 Alferez de Navio.
18 Alferez de Fragata.
19 Subteniente.
20 Brigada.
21 Sleeve stripes for Sargento Primero.
22 Sargento.
23 Cabo Primero.
24 Cabo Segundo Especialista.
25 Cabo Segundo.
26 Marinero Distinguido Especialista.

PLATE 40. KINGDOM OF SPAIN: NAVY

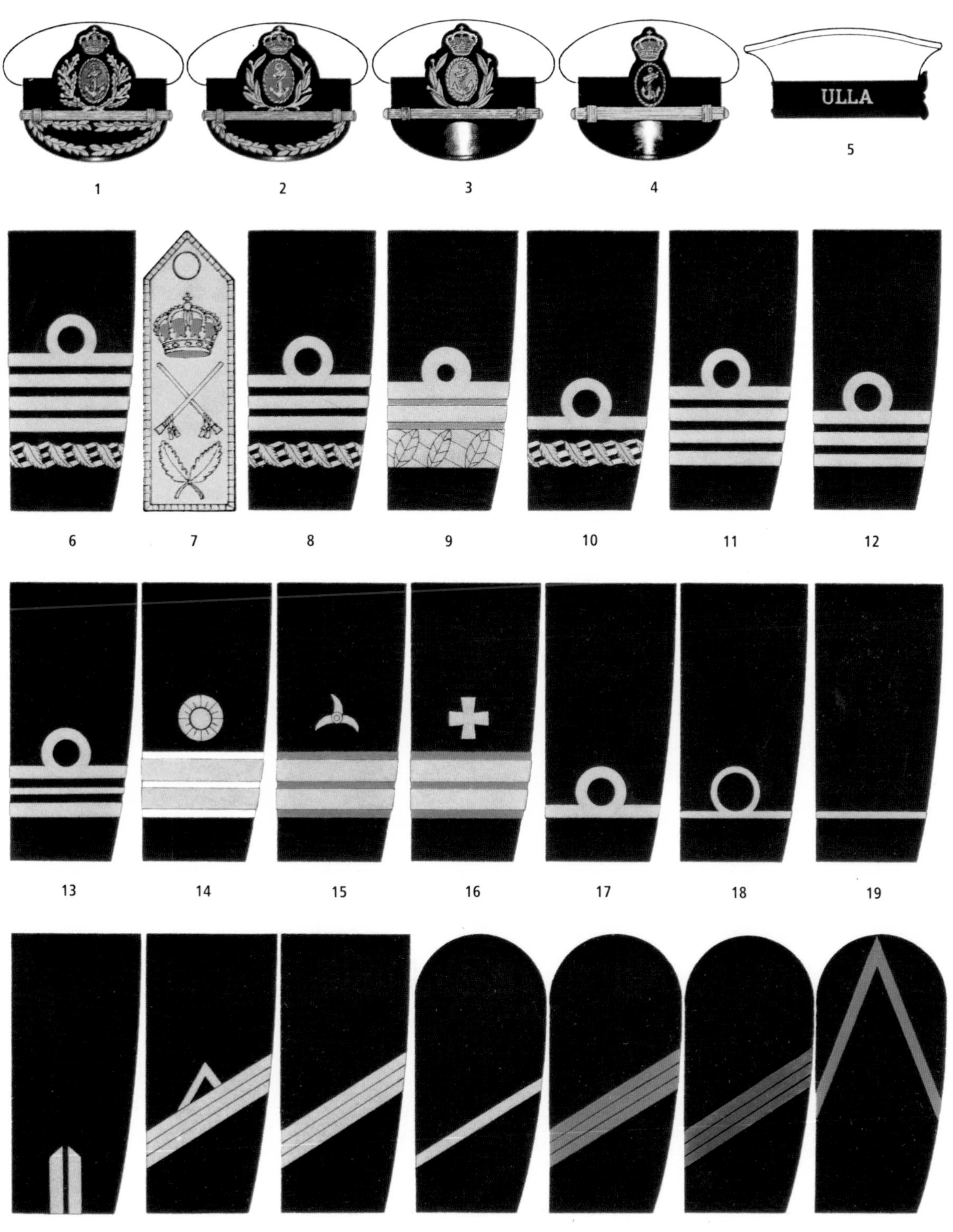

ULLA

1   2   3   4   5

6   7   8   9   10   11   12

13   14   15   16   17   18   19

20   21   22   23   24   25   26

PLATE 41. KINGDOM OF SPAIN: MARINES

The head-dress worn by officers, warrant officers and NCOs of the Spanish Marines is of the type worn by Spanish naval personnel. Both organizations display rank insignia in much the same way, with that of the Marines being slightly more extended, peak decoration and cap badges being the most notable. Cuff decorations, also carried onto shoulder-boards, are the main method of indicating ranks within the Marines.

Head-dress

1 Uniform peaked cap worn by Marine Generals (ranks 8 and 10).
2 Cap for wear by Colonels to Commandants (ranks 11 to 14).
3 Cap for Junior Officers (ranks 15 to 17).
4 Cap for Senior Warrant Officers (ranks 18 to 23).
5 Cap for wear by Junior NCOs (ranks 24 to 27).
6 Beret worn by qualified Marines, here shown for Commandante (rank 14).
7 Seaman's cap for wear by Apprentice (rank 28).

Rank and Appointment Insignia

8 Cuff decoration for General de División.
9 Shoulder-board for General de División.
10 General de Brigada.
11 Coronel.
12 Teniente Coronel.
13 Shoulder-board for Teniente Coronel.
14 Commandante.
15 Capitan.
16 Teniente. Rank insignia worn as a shoulder-strap slip-on on the camouflaged combat uniform.
17 Alferez.
18 Subteniente.
19 Guardia Marina. Shoulder-board as worn on the white uniform.
20 Brigada.
21 Shoulder-board for Brigada.
22 Sargento 1°.
23 Sargento.
24 Cabo 1°.
25 Cabo 2° Especialista.
26 Shoulder-board for Cabo (ranks 24, 25 and 27).
27 Cabo 2°.
28 Arm badge for Apprentice.

Left: Capitan Porras of the Spanish Air Force. The national flag patch is worn on the upper right shoulder and the wearer's rank insignia on a patch worn on the left breast.

PLATE 41. KINGDOM OF SPAIN: MARINES

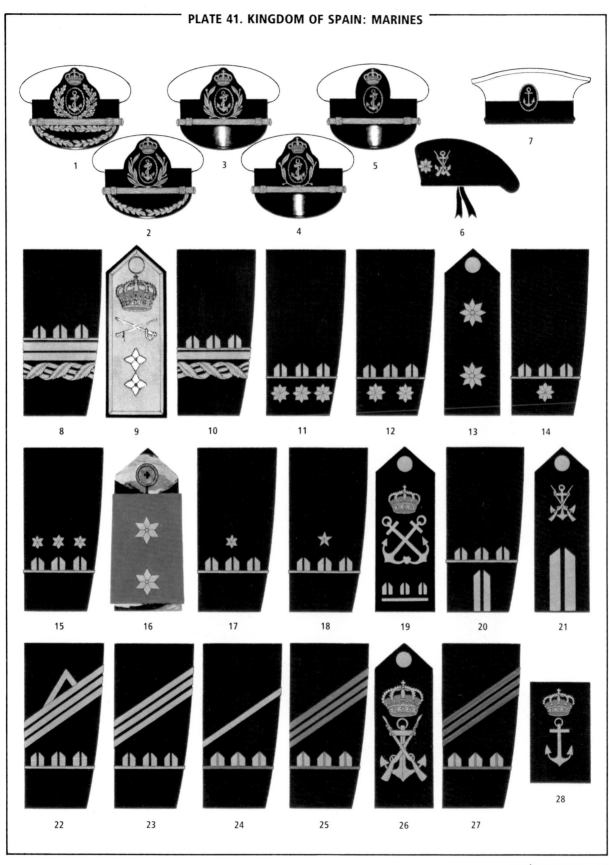

1

2

3

4

5

6

7

8

9

10

11

12

13

14

15

16

17

18

19

20

21

22

23

24

25

26

27

28

PLATE 42. KINGDOM OF SPAIN: AIR FORCE

Differences in Air Force rank as displayed on head-dress is shown by the amount of decoration to the peaks and the design of the cap badges. Rank shown on the Air Force uniform follows the style that has been in use for many years. Rank insignia for officers is worn on the cuffs of the tunics as well as on shoulder-boards. NCOs wear cuff stripes.

Head-dress
1 Uniform peaked cap worn by General Officers (ranks 6 to 10).
2 Cap for wear by Colonels, Lieutenant-Colonels and Commandants (ranks 11 to 13).
3 Cap for other officers (ranks 15 to 17).
4 Cap as worn by Warrant Officers and NCOs (ranks 18 and 22).
5 Cap for other ranks.

Rank and Appointment Insignia
6 Cuff insignia for Capitan General.
7 Shoulder-board for Capitan General.
8 Teniente General.
9 General de Division.
10 General de Brigada.
11 Coronel.
12 Teniente Coronel.
13 Commandante.
14 Shoulder-board for Commandante.
15 Capitan.

16 Teniente.
17 Alferez.
18 Subteniente.
19 Brigada.
20 Sargento 1º.
21 Shoulder-board for Sargento 1º.
22 Sargento.
23 Cabo 1º.
24 Cabo.
25 Soldado 1º.
26 Shoulder-board for Soldado 1º. Soldado (no rank insignia worn).

Left: Sargento Matias of the Spanish Air Force. Rank insignia is displayed on the left breast of the flying overalls above his name tab.

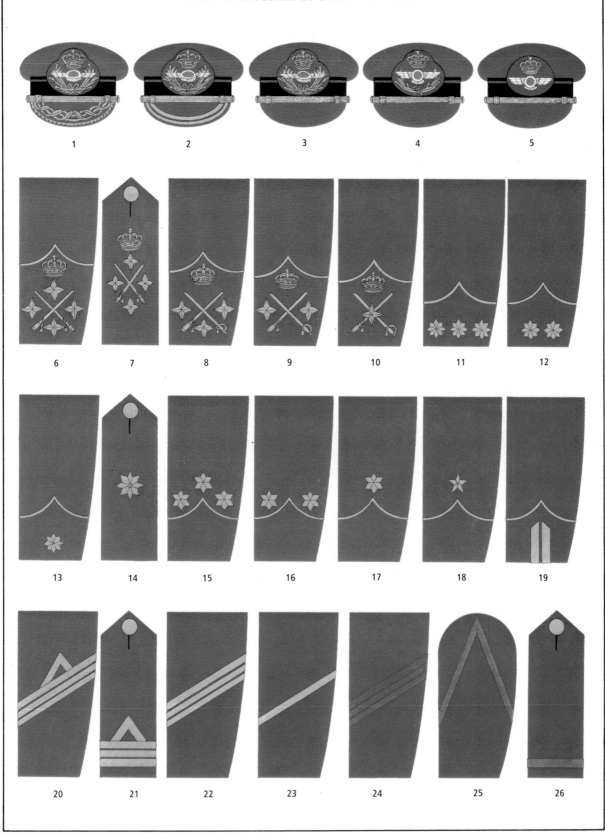

PLATE 42. KINGDOM OF SPAIN: AIR FORCE

1   2   3   4   5

6   7   8   9   10   11   12

13   14   15   16   17   18   19

20   21   22   23   24   25   26

PLATE 43. REPUBLIC OF TURKEY: ARMY

Both the Turkish Army and Air Force sport a range of rank insignia that is not only attractive but whose design has the appearance of being influenced by the insignia worn by the forces of the United States of America. Rank is indicated on the head-dress by the obvious differences in peak decoration and by the chin-straps. Officers' cap badges differ from those worn by the rank and file. Insignia of rank on the uniform is displayed by means of officers' shoulder-boards, gorget patches in the case of General Officers and arm 'chevrons' of a very distinctive pattern worn by NCOs.

Head-dress

1 Uniform peaked cap worn by General Officers (ranks 6 to 10).
2 Cap worn by Field Officers, here shown for an officer of the Tank arm (black as background to cap badge).
3 Cap for Company Officers, here shown for an infantry officer when wearing summer uniform.
4 Cap for NCOs here shown for a Cavalry NCO.

Rank and Appointment Insignia

5 Gorget patch as worn by all General Officers (ranks 6 to 10).
6 Shoulder-board for Maresal.
7 Orgeneral.
8 Korgeneral.
9 Tümgeneral.
10 Tüggeneral.
11 Albay (Signals).
12 Yarbay (Infantry), light-weight summer uniform.
13 Binbaşi (Artillery) (Dark blue as background to officer's shoulder-board wreath).
14 Yüzbasi.
15 Üsteğmen.
16 Teğmen.
17 Asteğmen.
18 Rank chevrons for Astsubay Kidemli Başçavuş.
19 Astsubay Başçavuş.
20 Astsubay Kidemli Ustçavuş.
21 Astsubay Ustçavuş.
22 Astsubay Kidemli Çavuş.
23 Astsubay Çavuş.
24 Çavuş.
25 Onbaşi.
Er (no rank insignia worn).

Above: An Onbasi of the Turkish Army acting as Colour-Bearer at the 1988 Royal Military Police and City of Chichester March.

PLATE 43. REPUBLIC OF TURKEY: ARMY

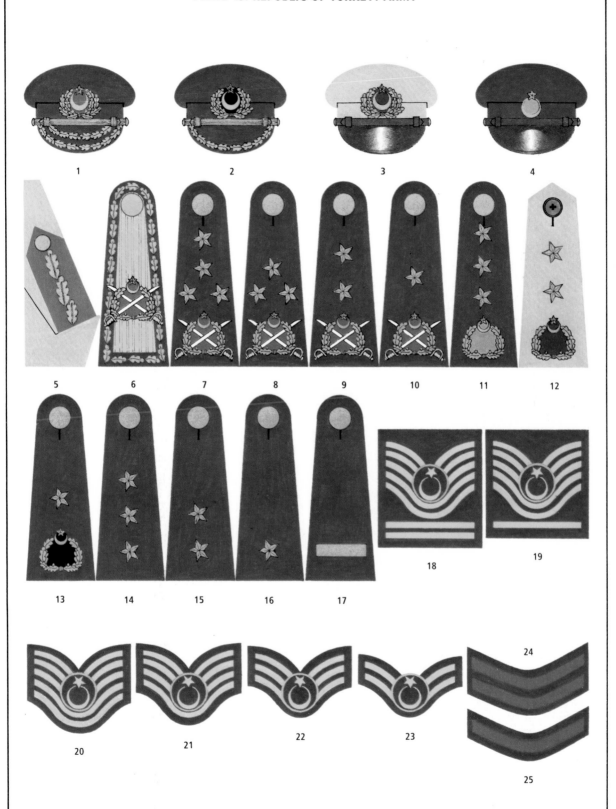

1

2

3

4

5

6

7

8

9

10

11

12

13

14

15

16

17

18

19

20

21

22

23

24

25

PLATE 44. REPUBLIC OF TURKEY: NAVY

Rank distinction is achieved on Turkish naval head-dress in the standard way, by differences in peak decorations, the use of chin-straps of different qualities and the cap badges. Rank is displayed on the naval uniforms in the traditional naval manner by the use of officers' sleeve rings and shoulder-boards, and rank chevrons for the lower ranks.

Head-dress
1 Uniform peaked cap for Flag Officers (ranks 6 to 11).
2 Cap for Senior Officers (ranks 12 to 15).
3 Cap for Junior Officers (ranks 16 to 19).
4 Cap for NCOs (ranks 20 to 25).
5 Cap for professional seamen (for those who do not wear rank insignia).

Rank and Appointment Insignia
6 Sleeve rings for Büyük Amiral.
7 Shoulder-board for Büyük Amiral.
8 Oramiral.
9 Koramiral.
10 Shoulder-board for Koramiral.
11 Tümamiral.
12 Tuğamiral.
13 Albay (Doctor).
14 Yarbay.
15 Binbaşi (Ordnance).
16 Yüzbasi.
17 Üsteğmen.
18 Teğmen.
19 Asteğmen.
20 Rank chevrons for Astsubay Kidemli Başçavuş.
21 Astsubay Başçavuş.
22 Astsubay Kidemli Ustçavuş.
23 Astsubay Ustçavuş.
24 Astsubay Kidemli Çavuş.
25 Astsubay Çavuş.
26 Mukellef Çavuş.
27 Onbaşi.
  Ikinci Yileri Er (no rank insignia worn).
  Birinci Yileri Er (no rank insignia worn).
  Egetem Eri Er (no rank insignia worn).

PLATE 44. REPUBLIC OF TURKEY: NAVY

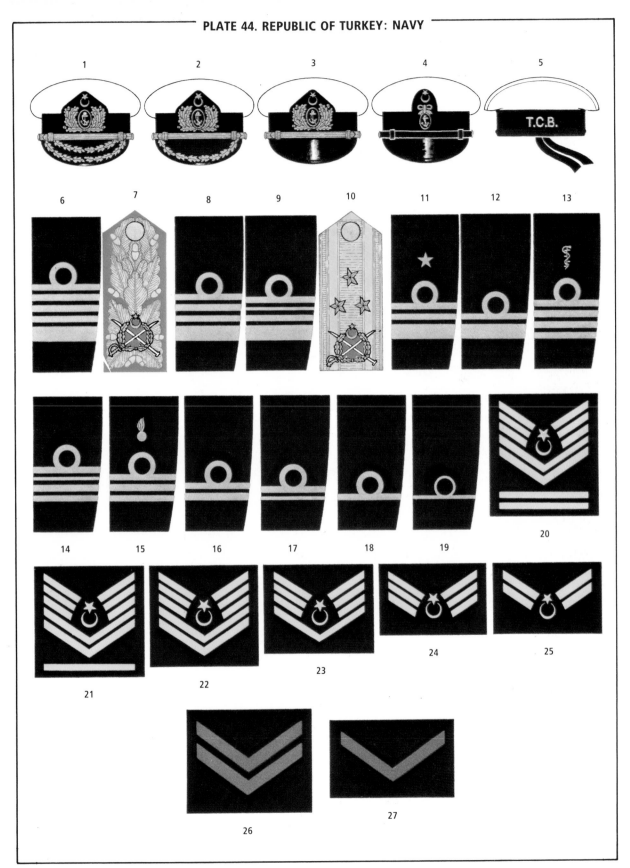

PLATE 45. REPUBLIC OF TURKEY: AIR FORCE

Peak decoration, differences in chin-straps and cap badges plus the introduction of background colour to these cap badges are all used to display rank on the head-dress of the Turkish Air Force. The type of rank insignia and the method of displaying such on the Air Force uniform is almost identical with that used in the Turkish Army.

Head-dress
1 Uniform peaked cap for General Officers (ranks 6 to 10).
2 Cap for Field Officers, here shown as a Staff Officer (ranks 11 to 13).
3 Cap for Junior Officers (ranks 14 to 17).
4 Cap as worn by NCOs and Men (ranks 18 to 25).

Rank and Appointment Insignia
5 Gorget patch as worn by all Air Force Generals (ranks 6 to 10).
6 Shoulder-board for Maresal.
7 Orgeneral.
8 Korgeneral.
9 Tümgeneral.
10 Tuğgeneral.
11 Albay on the General Staff.
12 Yarbay.
13 Binbaşi.
14 Yüzbasi.
15 Üsteğmen.
16 Teğmen.
17 Asteğmen.

18 Rank chevrons for Astsubay Kidemli Başçavuş.
19 Astsubay Başçavuş.
20 Astsubay Kidemli Ustçavuş.
21 Astsubay Ustçavuş.
22 Astsubay Kidemli Çavuş.
23 Astsubay Çavuş.
24 Çavuş.
25 Onbaşi.
   Er (no rank insignia worn).

Above: Turkish Air Force officers photographed in 1956.

PLATE 45. REPUBLIC OF TURKEY: AIR FORCE

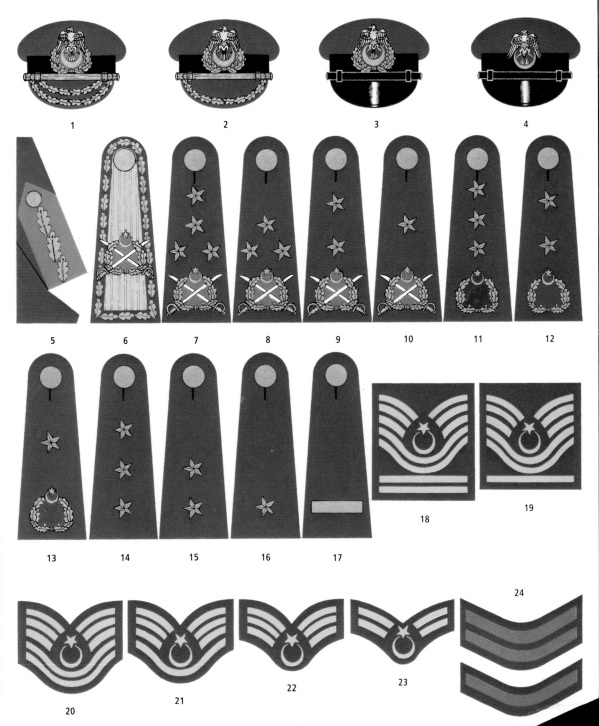

PLATE 46. UNITED KINGDOM OF GREAT BRITAIN AND NORTHERN IRELAND: ARMY

The style of head-dress shown as items 1 to 4 are the Forage Caps as worn by certain British Army officers. They are normal parade head-dress but they are also worn with No. 2 (Service) Dress, the temperate parade and ceremonial uniform.

These items of head-dress have been shown as they display rank by means of the cap badge and the peak decoration. The plain khaki peaked cap is more often worn with khaki Service Dress for minor parades and when undertaking duties inside barracks, and as normal wear by officers below the rank of Major (exclusive).

The badges of rank worn on British Army shoulder-straps can either be of metal or cloth, both qualities illustrated here. Metal rank badges can be of silver metal for Light Infantry, black metal for Rifle regiments or gilt and enamelled for all other regiments and corps. The rank star or 'pip' comes in a number of various designs as worn within certain regiments.

Head-dress

1 Forage Cap as worn by Field Marshals (rank 7).
2 Forage Cap as worn by General Officers (ranks 8 to 10).
3 Brigadiers and Colonels (ranks 12 and 13).
4 Royal Artillery field officer below the rank of colonel (ranks 14 and 15).
5 Beret worn by members of the Army Air Corps (A.A.C.) below the rank of Colonel. Other colours of berets exist for certain regiments.

Rank and Appoi

6 Gorget patch
  Service D
  shals
7 Sh

our is a relatively recent introduction. This pattern is worn on the shirt.
13 Shoulder-strap for No. 2 (Service) Dress for a Colonel.
14 Lieutenant-Colonel of either The Queen's Regiment or The Royal Regiment of Wales. The pattern of the rank star is the 'Eversleigh' Star.
15 Tank suit black denim shoulder-strap with black cloth rank slip-on as worn by a Major of the 3rd Royal Tank Regiment. The green braid at the base of the strap indicates members of 3 RTR, the yellow backing to the rank crown is the arm-of-service colour allo-

cated to the Royal Armoured Corps.
16 Captain. Shoulder-strap and rank loop of the DPM (Disruptive Pattern Material – camouflage), combat jacket.
17 Lieutenant of either The Life Guards, The Blues and Royals, Grenadier Guards, Coldstream Guards or Welsh Guards. The bronzed metal rank stars are the star of the Order of the Garter.
18 Second Lieutenant of the 16th/5th Lancers as worn on the olive-green denims.
19 Conductor, Royal Army Ordnance Corps, badge of appointment worn on both fore-

arms in No. 2 (Service) Dress.
20 Warrant Officer, Class I, Royal Arms badge of appointment, also worn on both forearms.
21 Quartermaster-Sergeant ranking as Warrant Officer, Class II, metal (brass) crown in wreath.
22 Warrant Officer, Class II, Light Infantry. The crown and edging to the maize-coloured backing being rifle-green.
23 Staff Sergeant, Service Dress chevrons.
24 Sergeant.
25 Corporal. Chevrons as worn in shirt-sleeve order.
26 Lance-Corporal.
   Private (no rank insignia worn).

'A' Squadron, The Royal Scots Dragoon Guards
...ia is worn on a leather wrist strap together with the regimental

PLATE 46. UNITED KINGDOM OF GREAT BRITAIN AND NORTHERN IRELAND: ARMY

1   2   3   4   5

6   7   8   9   10   11   12   13

14   15   16   17   18   19   20

21   22   23   24   25   26

PLATE 47. UNITED KINGDOM OF GREAT BRITAIN AND NORTHERN IRELAND: ROYAL NAVY

Differences in rank displayed on Royal Navy head-dress is shown by the use of oakleaf decoration to the peaks as well as the design and colour of the cap badge. A range of badges exist for wear in the naval beret, each one for a group of ranks. Two such badges are illustrated here. Insignia of rank worn on the uniform consists of cuff rings, shoulder-boards and sleeve badges many of which are also worn as a form of slip-on on the shoulder-straps of certain items of uniform dress and clothing.

Head-dress
1 Uniform peaked cap for wear by Royal Naval Flag Officers (ranks 8 to 12).
2 Cap for Commodores, Captains and Commanders (ranks 13 to 15).
3 Cap for all remaining officers (ranks 16 to 20).
4 Cap for wear by Warrant Officers (rank 21).
5 Cap for wear by Chief Petty Officers (ranks 22 and 23).
6 Beret worn by Petty Officers (rank 24).
7 Beret for wear by Leading Ratings and Seamen (rank 26).

Rank and Appointment Insignia
8 Sleeve rings for Admiral of the Fleet.
9 Admiral.
10 Vice-Admiral.
11 Shoulder-board as worn by a Vice-Admiral. Other shoulder boards exist for an Admiral of the Fleet (crown above a silver wreath containing crossed batons above royal cypher); an Admiral (similar to the shoulder-board for a Vice-Admiral but with three stars); and a Rear-Admiral (a large single star in place of the two stars illustrated here).
12 Sleeve rings for a Rear-Admiral, Medical Officer.
13 Commodore.
14 Captain.
15 Commander, Royal Corps of Naval Constructors (R.C.N.C.).
16 Lieutenant-Commander, Medical Services Officer or Medical Technician Officer.
17 Lieutenant, Dental Officer.
18 Sub-Lieutenant, Royal Naval Reserve.
19 Lapel patch for Midshipman.
20 Shoulder-strap slip-on rank badge for Midshipman worn on the white shirt.
21 Sleeve badge worn on the forearm by Warrant Officers.
22 Sleeve cuff with Chief Petty Officers' distinctive cuff buttons.
23 Chief Petty Officers' 'Woolley-Pully' shoulder-strap slip-on.
24 Petty Officers' rate arm badge.
25 Petty Officers' rate badge worn on blue working shirt as a shoulder-strap slip-on.
26 Leading Rate sleeve badge.
27 Leading Rate badge worn as a slip-on on the khaki shirt.
Able Seaman (no rank insignia worn).
Junior Rating (no rank insignia worn).

Left: Petty Officer Smyth, Royal Navy helicopter crew member.

Left: Flying Officer D. A. Hunter, Assistant Provost Marshal, Royal Air Force Police.

Below: A Senior Aircraftsman based at SHAPE. This airman wore two arm brassards both of which displayed the SHAPE badge. The left brassard, however, had the addition of a national emblem for Great Britain, as shown in the photograph. It is stated that this is an official badge and at the time the photograph was taken in the summer of 1986 the badge had been in use for at least two years.

Right: A Sergeant of the Royal Military Police. The rank insignia worn is the British Army sub-dued pattern of black insignia on an olive-green rectangle. It is worn here above the black on red 'MP' identification patch, all of which are stitched to a camouflaged arm brassard. This Sergeant wears a pair of West German parachute wings above the right breast pocket of his DPM jacket.
Below: A Gunner from the 148 (Meiktila) Forward Observation Battery of 29 Commando Regiment, Royal Artillery.

After the white pith helmet worn for ceremonial occasions, the red-and-white peaked cap is the most distinctive form of head-dress worn by all ranks of the Royal Marines. Peak decorations and cap badges are the means whereby rank is displayed on this form of head-dress. Rank groups are indicated on the green beret by the use of different badges. Royal Marine recruits who have not qualified to wear the green beret wear instead a dark-blue beret with a red cloth patch worn behind the badge. Insignia of rank is carried on the uniform by means of shoulder-boards, shoulder-strap slip-ons, badges of appointment worn on the forearm and rank chevrons on the upper arms.

Head-dress

1 Uniform peaked cap worn by Royal Marine General Officers (ranks 8 to 10).
2 Uniform peaked cap for Brigadiers and Colonels (ranks 12 and 13).
3 Cap for Lieutenant-Colonels and Majors (ranks 14 and 15).
4 Cap for all other officer ranks (ranks 15 to 18).
5 Green beret for Warrant Officers (ranks 19 and 20).
6 Green beret for NCOs and Men (ranks 21 to 24 plus Marines). The coveted green beret is worn only by those Royal Marines that have successfully completed the commando training. It is worn by all ranks with the appropriate cap badge.

Rank and Appointment Insignia

7 Gorget patch as worn on the Lovat-green uniform by General Officers (ranks 8 to 10).
8 Shoulder-board for the Lovat-green uniform for a General.
9 Lieutenant-General.
10 Major-General.
  The unique rank of Captain-General of Royal Marines has the same shoulder-board and peaked cap insignia as that worn by a Field Marshal of the British Army (see plate 46). It is worn by His Royal Highness, Prince Philip, Duke of Edinburgh in his capacity as Colonel-Commandant, Royal Marines.
11 Gorget patch (worn in matching pairs, one patch to each col-

lar) for Brigadiers and Substantive Colonels.
12 Shoulder-board as worn by Brigadiers.
13 Colonel.
14 Shoulder-board for Lieutenant-Colonel. Note that the five ranks from Lieutenant-Colonel to Second-Lieutenant (inclusive) have the added distinction of a bronze metal title 'RM' worn at the base of their Lovat-green shoulder-boards. These titles appear in gilt anodized for wear on the No. 1 Blue Dress Uniform and other forms of uniform.
15 Major.
16 Shoulder-strap slip-on as worn by a Captain on the 'Woolley Pully', the khaki-green wool knit long-sleeved jumper issued to all ranks of the Royal Marines.
17 Shoulder-strap 'camo' rank slip-

on as worn on the straps of the British Forces D.P.M. (Disruptive Patterned Material) combat jacket. The insignia displayed on this type of slip-on is normally machine embroidered. The slip-on is often worn attached on the front and back of the combat jacket suspended from a button so as to be visible when the wearer is carrying backpacks, the supporting straps of which cover the shoulders.
18 Lovat-green shoulder-board for Royal Marine Lieutenant.
19 Badge of Appointment as worn by Royal Marine Warrant Officer, Class I, Regimental Sergeant Major. Worn on the forearm of Lovat-green uniform.
20 Royal Marine Warrant Officer, Class II.
21 Rank chevrons worn on the

upper arm by Colour Sergeants of the Royal Marines. These and other RM chevrons worn on the Lovat-green uniform are distinctive in that the sides of the chevrons are not parallel, as is the case with most other British NCOs' chevrons.
22 Subdued rank chevrons worn on combat dress for the rank of Sergeant. These are similar to the standard pattern design subdued rank badges used throughout the British Forces and worn on combat dress, DPM jackets, overalls and some arm brassards. Royal Marine versions are, however, slightly smaller in overall size.
23 Corporal, rank chevron for Lovat-green uniform.
24 Lance-Corporal, Royal Marines.

Above: A close-up of the Army Air Corps emblem worn above the arm badge for No. 3 Commando Brigade, Air Squadron, Royal Marines.

PLATE 48. UNITED KINGDOM OF GREAT BRITAIN AND NORTHERN IRELAND: ROYAL MARINES

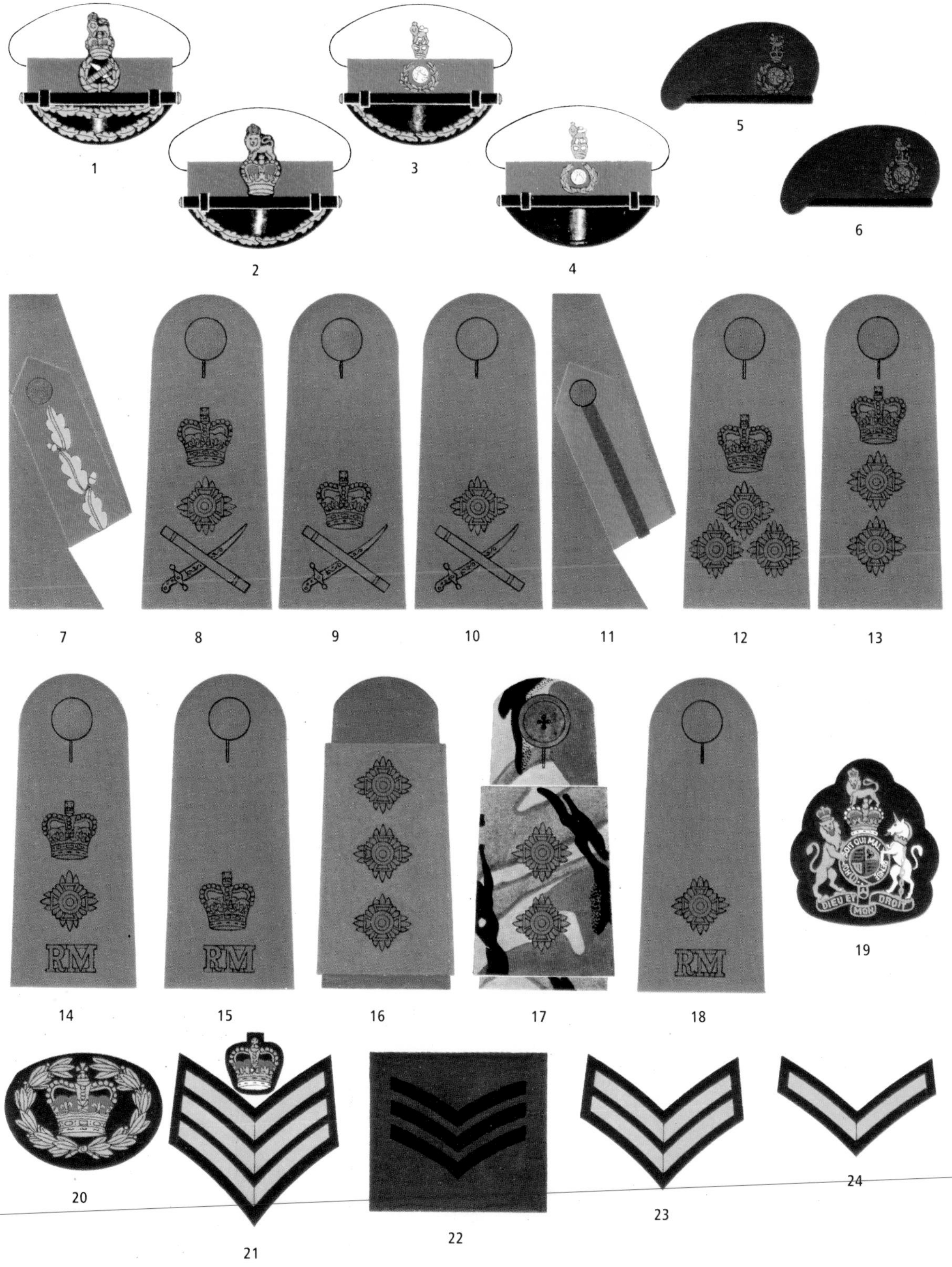

Different ranks, as displayed on the Uniformed Peak Cap, are indicated by the use of gold oakleaves on black patent leather peaks for officers of Air rank and Group Captains. Other officers have a cloth-covered peak to their caps. Air rank officers have a more elaborate cap badge than that worn by other officers. Personnel below officer status have black patent leather peaks to their caps as well as metal cap badges of a pattern peculiar to their rank group.

Sleeve rings indicating rank are worn by officers of all ranks on the Service Uniform. Shoulder-boards and shoulder-straps with slip-on rank loops are also worn, both of which display the wearer's rank. Warrant officers and Master Aircrew wear badges of appointment and rank on the forearm, while the remaining Royal Air Force personnel wear arm chevrons and arm badges.

Head-dress

1 Uniform peaked cap worn by 'Air' rank officers (ranks 6 to 10).
2 Cap worn by Group Captains (rank 11).
3 Cap for all remaining officers (ranks 12 to 16).
4 Peaked cap for Warrant Officers (rank 17).
5 Side cap for NCOs and other ranks (ranks 18 to 27 plus Airmen). The side cap is an item of head-wear worn by all ranks of the RAF. Quality of material, piping and cap badge design distinguish differences in rank. The blue beret is another item of head-dress widely worn throughout the RAF. The badge worn in the beret indicates the wearer's rank group.

Rank and Appointment Insignia

6 Sleeve rings for Marshal of the Royal Air Force.
7 Air Chief Marshal.
8 Air Marshal.
9 Air Vice-Marshal.
10 Air Commodore.
11 Group Captain.
12 Shoulder-strap slip-on for shirt, rank for Wing Commander.
13 Sleeve rings for Squadron Leader.
14 Flight Lieutenant.
15 DPM combat jacket shoulder-strap slip-on for Flying Officer.
16 Pilot Officer.
17 Warrant Officer, Class I badge of appointment. Worn on the forearm.
18 Arm badge for Master Aircrew.
19 Rank chevrons for Flight Sergeant.
20 Flight Sergeant Aircrew.
21 Chief Technician.
22 Sergeant.
23 Sergeant Aircrew.
24 Corporal rank slip-on shown here worn on olive working overalls.
25 Arm badge for Junior Technician.
26 Senior Aircraftsman.
27 Leading Aircraftsman. Aircraftsman (no rank insignia worn).

Above: Flight Lieutenant Richard Harrison, navigator of 70 Squadron, Royal Air Force. On the shoulder-straps of the olive-green flying-overalls are displayed the rank insignia. The Union Jack flag is worn as a national emblem on the left shoulder, and on the right upper arm are both the squadron emblem and the official RAF squadron patch. The navigator half brevet is combined as part of the name patch.

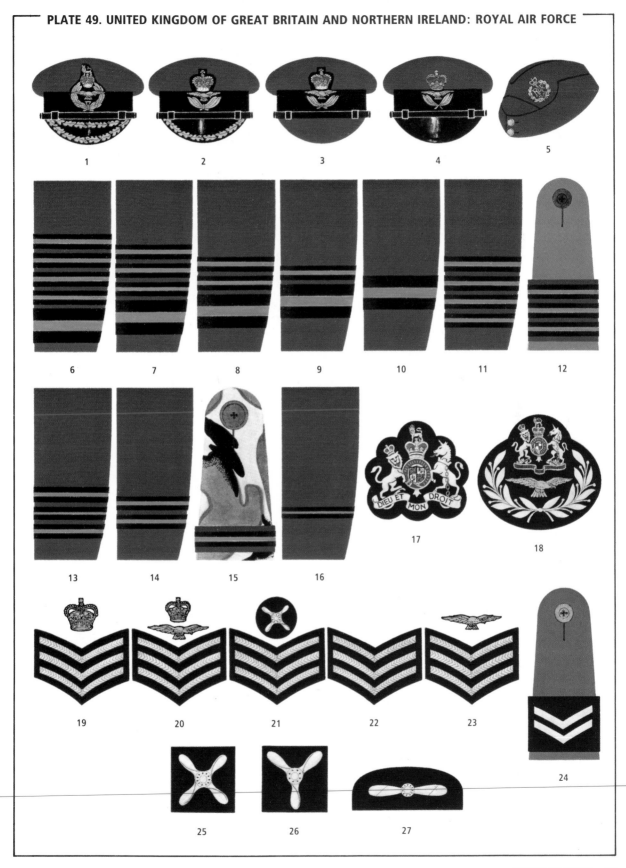

Above: Supreme Allied Commander Europe, General Lauris Norstad, and Deputy Supreme Allied Commander Europe, Field Marshal Viscount Montgomery, photographed in January 1957.
Left: Flight Lieutenant Derek Johnston, navigator of 43rd Fighter Squadron, Royal Air Force. The squadron emblem of a red aircraft on a black-and-white quartered diamond with black numbers '4' and '3' is echoed in the black-and-white chequered neck scarf worn.

Above: Sergeant First Class M. H. Johnson, Snr, US Army, receiving his certificate of honourable discharge from the Armed Forces of the United States of America from the hands of Captain K. E. Mirise, US Navy. Sergeant Johnson wears the pocket badge in the form of a pocket fob for the Headquarters United States European Command, a design which is carried on the drapes in the backdrop to the photograph. Sergeant Johnson, who qualified for his paratroop wings as well as the West German marksmanship lanyard, was a member of the US Army VII Corps.

Right: Close-up view of the NATO AWACS Training Centre patch.

Left: The design approved by the US Institute of Heraldry and used on the flag of the United States European Command. The emblem was also chosen as the Command's pocket badge but did not meet with the approval of the Commander-in-Chief USEUCOM and was therefore not used. It is instead worn as an unofficial pocket patch.

Far left: The design of the pocket badge used by Headquarters personnel of the United States European Command.

PLATE 50. UNITED STATES OF AMERICA: ARMY

The US Army provides its personnel with a range of uniforms, all of which are worn at various times for different reasons. The majority of the head-dress and shoulder-loops (shoulder-boards) illustrated on these plates are of the Army Green uniform. This uniform is authorized for year-round wear by all ranks and it is the normal service uniform worn during the winter season. It is also the prescribed general duty uniform and its use for social functions after retreat and outside normal duty hours is also permitted.

Head-dress
1 Uniform peaked cap, known as the Service Cap for wear by Generals and field grade officers (ranks 5 to 12).
2 Service Cap for all other (Company) officers (ranks 13 to 15).
3 Service Cap for Warrant Officers (ranks 16 to 19).
4 Cap for remaining personnel (ranks 20 to 33).

Rank and Appointment Insignia
5 Shoulder loop for a General of the Army.
6 General.

7 Lieutenant-General.
8 Major-General. Rank slip-on worn on the green shirt shoulder-loop.
9 Brigadier.
10 Colonel.
11 Lieutenant-Colonel.
12 Major.
13 Captain. Rank slip-on worn on the green shirt shoulder-loop.
14 First-Lieutenant.
15 Second-Lieutenant. Also worn on the shoulder-loop is the Combat Leader's Identification, a green cloth slip-on worn on all shoulder-straps by personnel

capable of leading troops in combat during an emergency.
16 Chief Warrant Officer W-4.
17 Chief Warrant Officer W-3.
18 Chief Warrant Officer W-2, slip-on worn on shoulder-loop of green shirt.
19 Warrant Officer W-1.
20 Arm rank chevrons for Sergeant-Major of the Army.
21 Command Sergeant-Major.
22 Sergeant-Major.
23 First Sergeant.
24 Master Sergeant.

Above: Private First Class Craft, 554th Military Police Company and Lieutenant-General Stone, Chief of Staff United States European Command, together cut a celebratory cake.

PLATE 50. UNITED STATES OF AMERICA: ARMY

1 2 3 4

5 6 7 8 9 10 11

12 13 14 15 16 17 18 19

20 21 22 23 24

PLATE 51. UNITED STATES OF AMERICA: ARMY AND NAVY

25 Platoon Sergeant or Sergeant 1st Class.
26 Staff Sergeant.
27 Sergeant. Chevrons are subdued pattern as worn on fatigues.
28 Corporal.
29 Private First Class.
30 Private E-2.
31 Specialist 6.
32 Specialist 5.
33 Specialist 4.
   Basic Private (no rank insignia worn).

On the peaked, or Combination Caps, worn in the United States Navy, rank is indicated by peak decoration for senior officers and cap badges of various sizes and designs for personnel of warrant officer rank and below. Chin-straps also indicate a certain degree of rank differentiation. Uniform rank insignia is displayed by the use of cuff rings, shoulder-boards and arm chevrons. The same insignia of rank worn on the khaki-tan uniform is by the use of shoulder-loops and shirt collar insignia.

Head-dress

1 Combination cap with white cover for Flag Officers (ranks 14 to 18).
2 Cap with khaki cover for Commodores and Captains worn as part of the light-weight khaki summer uniforms (ranks 19 and 20).
3 Combination cap for other officers and Commissioned Warrant Officers (ranks 21 to 28). Cap top in aviation-green.
4 Warrant Officer W-1 (rank 29).
5 Midshipman.
6 Cap worn by the Master Chief Petty Officer of the Navy (rank 30).
7 Master Chief Petty Officer, head-dress of light-weight khaki summer uniform (rank 32).
8 Senior Chief Petty Officer (rank 33).
9 Chief Petty Officer (rank 34), aviation-green cap cover.
10 Cap for Enlisted Men E1 to E6.
11 Command Ball Cap for Petty Officer 1st Class. Worn for work purposes (rank 35).
12 Command Ball Cap for Petty Officer 2nd Class (rank 36).
13 Command Ball Cap for Petty Officer 3rd Class (rank 37).

Above: Senior Petty Officer Warren Goins, US Navy, wearing summer working dress. The USEUCOM badge can be seen worn as a pocket fob suspended from the right breast shirt pocket.

PLATE 51. UNITED STATES OF AMERICA: ARMY

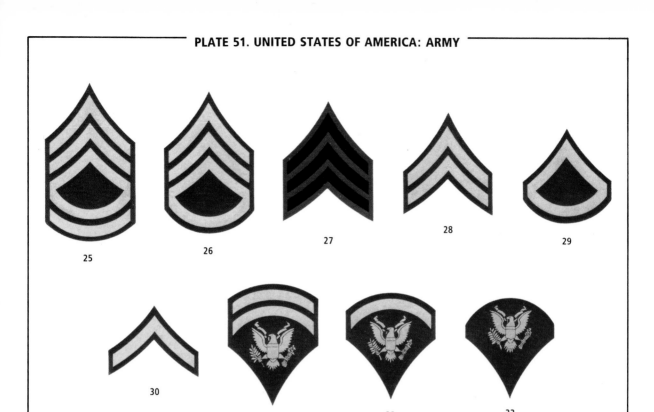

25

26

27

28

29

30

31

32

33

UNITED STATES OF AMERICA: NAVY

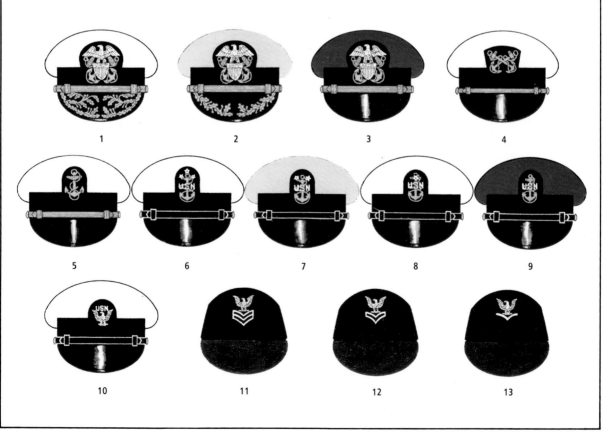

1

2

3

4

5

6

7

8

9

10

11

12

13

Left: Technical Sergeant Casino, US Air Force, wearing Air Force Service Uniform.

Left: A Staff Sergeant, US Air Force.

Above: Master-Sergeant Evans, US Air Force, wearing camouflage fatigues.

PLATE 52. UNITED STATES OF AMERICA: NAVY

Rank and Appointment Insignia

14 Sleeve rings for Fleet Admiral, Line Officer.

15 Shoulder-board for Fleet Admiral. Other shoulder-boards are used by Admirals (group of four stars), Vice-Admirals (triangle of three stars), Rear-Admirals (two stars one above the other) and Commodores (single star).

16 Sleeve rings for an Admiral, Line Officer.

17 Vice-Admiral, Line Officer.

18 Rear-Admiral, Line Officer.

19 Commodore, Line Officer.

20 Captain, Dental Corps.

21 Commander, Medical Service Corps.

22 Lieutenant-Commander, Line Officer.

23 Lieutenant, Judge Advocate General's Corps.

24 Lieutenant, Junior Grade, Supply Corps.

25 Ensign, Medical Corps.

26 Commissioned Warrant Officer

W-4, Ship's Clerk.

27 Commissioned Warrant Officer W-3, Ordnance Technician.

28 Commissioned Warrant Officer W-2, Repair Technician.

29 Warrant Officer W-1, Boatswain.

30 Arm chevrons for Master Chief Petty Officer of the Navy.

31 Fleet Forces Master Chief.

32 Master Chief Petty Officer, Boatswain's Mate.

33 Senior Chief Petty Officer, Signalman.

34 Chief Petty Officer, Gunner's Mate.

35 Petty Officer 1st Class, Photographer's Mate.

36 Petty Officer, 2nd Class, Radioman.

37 Petty Officer, 3rd Class, Aviation Ordnanceman.

38 Seaman, Torpedoman's Mate.

39 Seaman/Fireman Apprentice, here shown for Fireman.

Above: Staff Sergeant Snapp, US Army Military Police, US Army Europe. The word 'Customs' above the letters 'MP' on the arm brassard indicates that the function of this Military Police detachment is to check all items being sent from Germany to the United States in the same manner as a civilian customs control officer.

PLATE 52. UNITED STATES OF AMERICA: NAVY

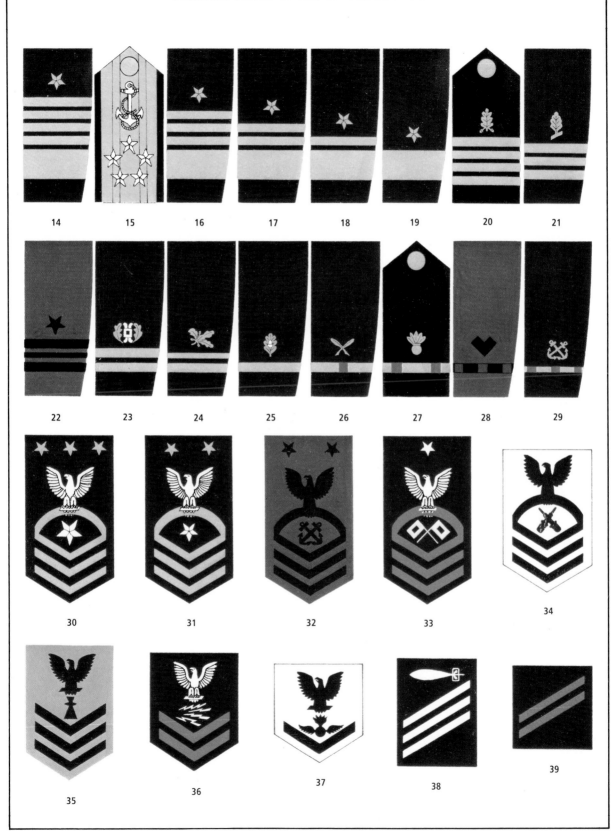

14   15   16   17   18   19   20   21

22   23   24   25   26   27   28   29

30   31   32   33

34

35   36   37   38   39

PLATE 53. UNITED STATES OF AMERICA: NAVY AND MARINE CORPS

40 Shoulder-loop for Fleet Admiral as worn on the blue raincoat. Seaman Recruit (no rank insignia worn).
41 Collar insignia for Admiral as worn on the khaki-tan shirt.
42 Vice-Admiral, shoulder-loop for khaki jacket.
43 Rear-Admiral, khaki jacket shoulder-loop.
44 Collar insignia for Commodore on the winter blue shirt.
45 Captain.
46 Commander.
47 Lieutenant-Commander.
48 Lieutenant.
49 Collar insignia for Lieutenant, Junior Grade, on the khaki tan shirt.

50 Ensign.
51 Collar insignia for Commissioned Warrant Officer W-4 as worn on the winter blue shirt.
52 Commissioned Warrant Officer W-3.
53 Commissioned Warrant Officer W-2.
54 Warrant Officer W-1.
55 Master Chief Petty Officer of the Navy, collar insignia as worn on the white shirt.
56 Fleet Force Master Chief.
57 Master Chief Petty Officer.
58 Senior Petty Officer, collar insignia as worn on the winter blue shirt.

In order to show the limited range of ranks displayed on US Marine Corps head-dress it is necessary to include the White Peaked Cap, normally worn with the white parade uniform. However, this style of head-dress is also worn with the green Service uniform and is therefore justifiably included here. Normal head-wear within the Corps is either the green peaked cap or the garrison cap. The former is worn by all ranks, officers' caps being distinguished by green tubular braid ornamentation on the crown of the cap (not illustrated). The garrison cap is also worn by all ranks. The wearer's rank insignia is shown on the right side and the US Marine Corps cap badge in bronze metal

on the left side. Marine Corps rank insignia worn on the uniform consists of shoulder-loops and arm chevrons.

Head-dress
1 Peaked cap for Generals (ranks 1 to 4).
2 Cap for Field Officers (ranks 5 to 7).
3 Cap for other officers (ranks 8 to 10).
4 Cap worn with the green uniform by officers and enlisted men.
5 Garrison Cap for Officers and Warrant Officers, right side shown here (ranks 1 to 14).
6 Garrison Cap for Enlisted Men, left side shown (ranks 15 to 25).

Left: Airman 1st Class Dougherty, a combat crew member of the US Air Force Para Rescue unit. He wears Air Force subdued insignia on his camouflaged fatigues.

PLATE 53. UNITED STATES OF AMERICA: NAVY

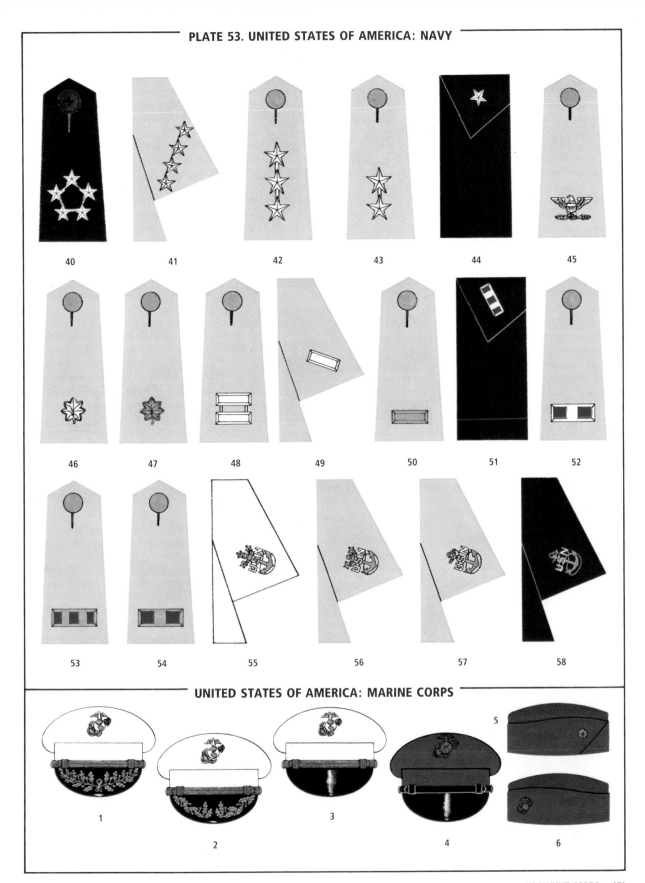

40

41

42

43

44

45

46

47

48

49

50

51

52

53

54

55

56

57

58

UNITED STATES OF AMERICA: MARINE CORPS

1

2

3

4

5

6

Above: Senior Airman Cressy, US Air Force Security Service.

Right: Private First Class Rodriguez, US Seventh Army.

Left: Second-Lieutenant O'Byrne, US Army. While this officer wears his gold-coloured metal rank bar on the front of his fatigue cap, the subdued insignia embroidered into the collar of his camouflaged jacket is in copper brown threads. This subdued colour represents the gold metal insignia, and black embroidery is used to represent silver rank insignia.

PLATE 54. UNITED STATES OF AMERICA: MARINE CORPS

Rank and Appointment Insignia

7 Shoulder-loop for the green uniform as worn by a General.
8 Lieutenant-General.
9 Major-General, khaki-tan uniform.
10 Brigadier-General, white summer uniform.

11 Colonel.
12 Lieutenant-Colonel.
13 Major.
14 Captain.
15 First Lieutenant.
16 Second Lieutenant.
17 Chief Warrant Officer 4.
18 Chief Warrant Officer 3.

19 Chief Warrant Officer 2.
20 Warrant Officer 1st Class.
21 Arm rank chevrons for Sergeant-Major of the Marine Corps.
22 Sergeant-Major.
23 Master Gunnery Sergeant.
24 First Sergeant.
25 Master Sergeant.

26 Gunnery Sergeant.
27 Staff Sergeant.
28 Sergeant.
29 Corporal.
30 Lance-Corporal.
31 Private 1st Class.
Private (no rank insignia worn).

Left: An Air Force Captain of the 57th Fighter Interceptor Squadron based at Reykjavik, Iceland. Metal rank insignia is frequently worn on US Air Force flying-overalls but is covered by a rectangle of clear plastic, as shown in this photograph.

PLATE 54. UNITED STATES OF AMERICA: MARINE CORPS

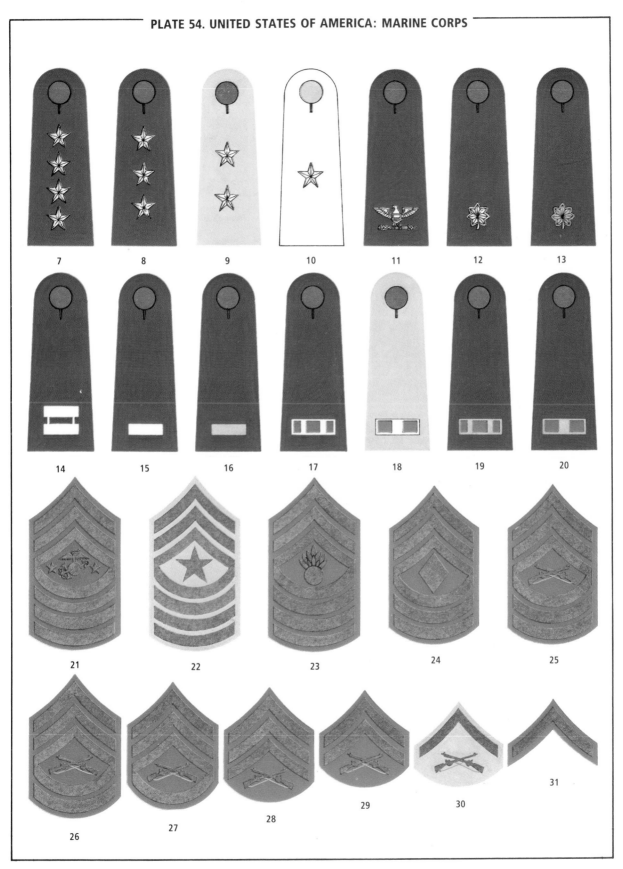

PLATE 55. UNITED STATES OF AMERICA: AIR FORCE

Uniform peaked caps worn in the USAF display the differences of rank by peak decoration and the amount of decoration as well as the cap badge. Rank insignia worn on the uniform takes the form of shoulder-loops, shoulder-strap slip-ons and arm chevrons. As with the US Army silver takes precedence over gold.

Head-dress
1 Uniform peaked cap for Generals (ranks 6 to 10).
2 Cap for wear by Colonels (rank 11).
3 Cap as worn by remaining officers (ranks 12 to 16) and Warrant Officers (ranks 17 to 20).
4 Cap for Chief Master Sergeant of the Air Force (rank 21).
5 Cap for remaining NCOs and Men (ranks 22 to 30).

Rank and Appointment Insignia
6 Shoulder-loop for General of the Air Force.
7 General.
8 Shoulder-loop slip-on for blue shirt worn by Lieutenants-General.
9 Major-General.
10 Brigadier-General.
11 Colonel.
12 Lieutenant-Colonel, worn on the blue shirt.
13 Major.
14 Captain.
15 First Lieutenant.
16 Second Lieutenant, as worn on the blue shirt.
17 Chief Warrant Officer W-4.
18 Chief Warrant Officer W-3.
19 Chief Warrant Officer W-2.
20 Warrant Officer W-1.
21 Arm chevrons for Chief Master Sergeant of the Air Force.
22 Chief Master Sergeant.
23 Senior Master Sergeant.
24 Master Sergeant.
25 Technical Sergeant plus First Sergeant's diamond.
26 Staff Sergeant, subdued pattern chevrons.
27 Sergeant.
28 Senior Airman.
29 Airman 1st Class.
30 Airman, subdued pattern. Basic Airman (no rank insignia worn).

Left: Master-Sergeant Cardiff, USAF.

PLATE 55. UNITED STATES OF AMERICA: AIR FORCE

1   2   3   4   5

6   7   8   9   10   11   12   13

14   15   16   17   18   19   20

21   22   23   24   25

26   27   28   29   30

PLATE 56. NATO BADGES

1 Metal and enamelled pin-on pocket badge worn by personnel on the International Military Staff. The NATO symbol surrounded by two fronds of laurel leaves crossed at their base and surmounted by an eagle with outstretched wings set on a fouled anchor on crossed swords represents the three branches of the military arm of NATO.

2 Metal and enamelled pin-on pocket badge worn by staff personnel of the NATO Defence School.

3 The Supreme Headquarters Allied Expeditionary Force (SHAEF) cloth shoulder-patch. Worn during the later part of the Second World War and early post-war period by Allied military personnel of all ranks on the staff of, or attached to, SHAEF. The badge was designed by a Corporal of the Auxiliary Territorial Service (A.T.S.), the British Army's women's military formation. The design and its use was authorized by General Eisenhower on 25 March 1944, and it was worn by all concerned at General Eisenhower's Supreme Headquarters in the United Kingdom, Versailles and Reims in France and Frankfurt-on-Main in Germany. It ceased to be used in 1946. The sword with silver blade ablaze with red flames represented the Crusader's sword of liberation with the flames of avenging justice. The black background was symbolic of the blackness of Nazi oppression. The blue arc stood for the skies of peace and tranquillity for the enslaved peoples of Europe, and the multi-coloured strip composed from the colours used on the various Allied flags represented a rainbow and was emblematic of hope. Although this patch and the next item, No. 4 are strictly not NATO badges they have been included here as it is felt they are of importance and should be recorded. The SHAEF patch has its echo in the US Army shoulder-sleeve insignia currently worn by personnel of US Army Europe and the US Army Berlin.

4 Allied Forces Western Europe. A cloth shoulder-badge described as having five gold links forming a pentagon on a blue background. The links represented the five nations of Great Britain, France, Belgium, the Netherlands and Luxembourg that made up the Western Union Powers of the Brussels Treaty (see page 10). Headquarters were at Fontainebleau, France. The first chairman was Field Marshal Viscount Montgomery of Alamein. The badge was worn by the joint staffs of the five countries concerned and all their military personnel, being adopted in January 1949.

5 and 6 Supreme Headquarters Allied Powers Europe (SHAPE), cloth shoulder-patch (5) and metal and enamelled pocket fob (6). Both items worn by all members on the staff of the Supreme Allied Commander Europe SACEUR. Authorized on 5 October 1951, the design of the SHAPE badge is officially described as: 'Two gold swords, unsheathed, are superimposed on a gold scroll, bearing the inscription "Vigillia Pretium Libertatis" (Vigilance is the Price of Liberty). Two sprays of olive leaves in gold at the bottom of the scroll indicate dedication of the NATO powers to peace, while the swords themselves indicate the necessity of armed strength in order to preserve that peace. The position of the swords produces the letter 'A', standing for the Allied Powers. Within the scroll and behind the swords twelve silver fronds stem from the olive sprays. These fronds represent the original signatories of the North Atlantic Treaty, and produce, by their position, rays of hope. The whole design is imposed on a shield of dark-green, the shield itself representing the crusading nature of SHAPE's mission and its colour signifying the peaceful woods and fields of Europe.'

7 Allied Forces Northern Europe (AFNORTH). A metal silver-edged blue-enamelled pin-on shield depicting a Viking Long Ship as seen from its port side. The ship, also in silver white metal, has a sail with alternating white metal and red-enamelled stripes.

8 Allied Forces North Norway (COMNON). Pocket badge as shown is a white-edged blue-enamelled shield displaying three upright unsheathed swords in silver white metal. The three swords represent the three branches of the Norwegian Forces that go to staff this tri-service headquarters. An embroidered shoulder-patch is also worn on the left shoulder by Other Ranks of this Command.

9 Allied Forces South Norway (COMSONOR). A pin-on pocket badge in metal and enamels of the same design as item 8, but with different colours. A blue-edged green shield with three silver white unsheathed upright swords.

10 This is the badge worn by personnel on the staff of the Allied Forces Baltic Approaches (BALTAP). It is also the basic design that is used for the four other badges of the Commands subordinate to BALTAP, items 11 to 14. The white-edged blue shield displays the NATO symbol set above three wavey lines representing the three Danish Straits, the Baltic Approaches of Lille Baelt, Store Baelt and Femer Baelt.

11 Allied Land Forces Schleswig-Holstein and Jutland (COMLANDJUT). The design of the badge worn by personnel on the staff of this Command is that of the BALTAP badge, but with the addition of gold-yellow crossed swords, indicative of the Danish Army role.

12 Allied Land Forces Zealand (LANDZEALAND). The same basic design as for item 10, but with a single, upright sword in gold-yellow.

13 Allied Naval Forces Baltic Approaches (NAVBALTAP). Same design as item 10, but with a gold-yellow fouled anchor, symbolic of the naval aspect of this Command.

14 Allied Air Forces Baltic Approaches (AIRBALTAP). Again, the same design as item 10, but with a pair of stylized gold-yellow wings, representing the air aspect of this Command.

PLATE 56. NATO BADGES

1

2

3

4

5

6

7

8

9

10

11

12

13

14

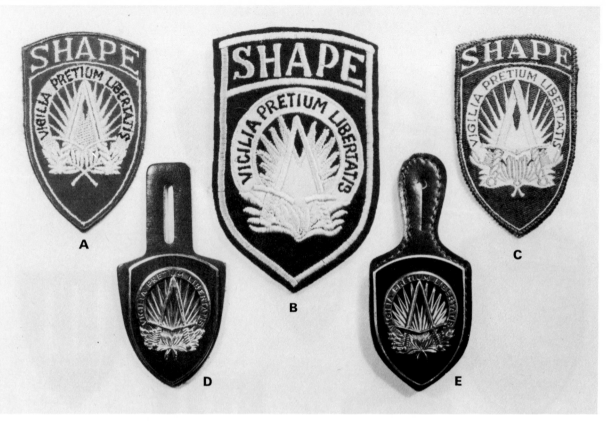

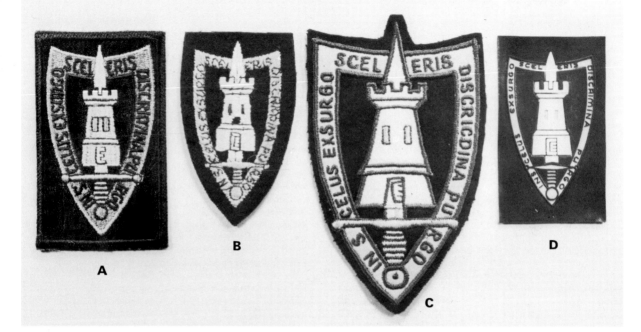

Top left: Versions of the SHAPE badge. Item A is machine stitched in cotton threads whereas item C is silk woven. Both versions were and are worn by troops of various nations serving at the Supreme Headquarters. Item B is of West German origin and as well as being larger than items A and C it is not so well produced. Item D is the more recent variant of the SHAPE pocket fob with the shallow relief of the enamelled badge. Item E is the superior quality, earlier version SHAPE pocket fob with the emblem in deep relief. Both badges are mounted on dark-green leather fobs or hangers.

Below left: Four versions of the Central Army Group badge. Items A and C are US shoulder-sleeve insignia worn by troops of the US Army Element CENTAG, item A being the coloured version worn on the US Army Green

Uniform and item C the subdued version for wear on fatigues. Item B is the enamelled pocket fob and item D is the West German cloth version.

Above: Four variants of the obsolete (green) HQ AFCE (Staff) badge. Item A is the US SSI, worn today by American troops of the US Support Group AFCENT; item B is a British-made badge; item C is West German and item D is a Belgian badge in plastic. Interestingly, the German item shown here has incorrect spelling to the motto around the edge of the shield.

Below: Four similar variants of the obsolete (red) HQ AFCE (Army) badge. Item A is the US Shoulder Sleeve Insignia. Item B is a French-manufactured woven badge. Item C is West German and item D is a plastic badge once worn by Belgian troops.

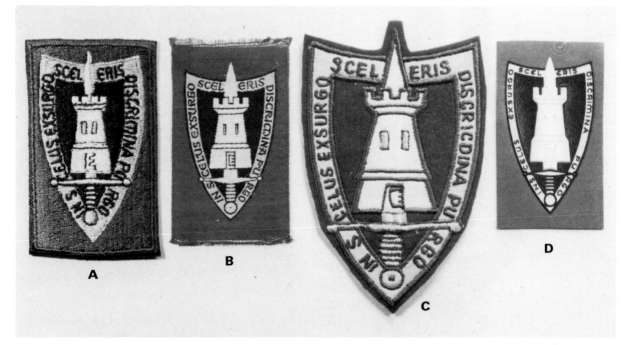

PLATE 57. NATO BADGES

Items 1 to 9, although separate badges issued for wear by various nationals at different times and thus having slightly differing designations, all have one thing in common, namely the central motif. The emblem adopted originally for wear by the personnel of the Headquarters Allied Forces Central Europe (HQ AFCE) and latterly by personnel of Allied Forces Central Europe (AFCENT) is the silver tower and sword set on a green shield, the gold-yellow edges of which bear the motto in black latin script 'In Scelus Exurgo Sceleris Discrimina Purgo'. Freely translated this is 'I Fight against Aggression and Punish the Aggressor'. This was the motto adopted in the year A.D. 800 by Charlemagne, King of the Franks and Emperor of the Occident.

The silver-white tower in the centre of the escutcheon symbolizes the European fortress and at the same time, the fortified city of Aix-la-Chapelle (Aachen) the capital of the ancient stronghold of Charlemagne. On the gateway to the tower are the letters 'CE' standing for 'Central Europe'. Set behind the tower and pointing straight up is the unsheathed, silver-white sword of Charlemagne. All these features combine to symbolize the strength of the Allied Armed Forces of Central Europe prepared to meet any eventuality.

Items 1 to 4 are US shoulder-sleeve insignia worn during the period 1951 to 1966 by American troops that served with HQ AFCE.

1 The US SSI with green background worn by personnel on the Staff of HQ AFCE.
2 Red background SSI worn by US Army personnel at HQ AFCE.
3 Light-blue background indicates US Air Force personnel serving under Headquarters Allied Forces Central Europe.
4 The dark-blue background indicates the naval element of HQ AFCE.

Items 5 to 8 are plastic shoulder-patches worn by Belgian troops serving with HQ AFCE during the period 1951 to 1966. The same individual designations apply to these Belgian shoulder-patches as for the US shoulder-sleeve insignia.

5 Belgian personnel on the Staff of HQ AFCE.
6 Belgian Army personnel under command of HQ AFCE.
7 Belgian Air Force personnel serving under HQ AFCE.
8 Belgian Naval personnel operating with naval elements of HQ AFCE.
9 Metal and coloured, enamelled pocket fob presently worn by personnel attached to Allied Forces Central Europe (AFCENT).

Northern Army Group (NORTHAG). The Francisca, the emblem of the Northern Army Group, is taken from a period of history with a marked similarity to the present day. In A.D. 451, Attila, with his Mongol army, had overrun a large part of western Europe. He was forced back and brought to battle at Châlons-sur-Marne by the Roman General Aetius, who was commanding an allied army of Gauls, Visigoths, Burgundians, Franks, Alans, Saxons and Britons. After a fierce battle, Attila was decisively defeated and as a result there were no further invasions from the East for five centuries.

In this battle the main missile weapon of the Frankish warriors forming the centre of the armies, was the Francisca – the throwing battleaxe. During the construction of the NORTHAG headquarters building a battleaxe of this type was found, and from then on the battleaxe symbol has been used as the badge of Northern Army Group.

10 NORTHAG pocket fob. A metal and enamelled badge mounted on a leather fob.
11 Cloth shoulder-patch of the type worn by West German troops serving with NORTHAG. This item is thought now to be obsolete.
12 Silk woven pattern worn on the right shoulder so that the throwing axe faces forward. For an as yet unexplained reason, this pattern of the NORTHAG badge is difficult to acquire. Most NORTHAG badges have the axe facing to the left.
13 Similar silk woven patch, axe faces to the left. This pattern of badge worn by Dutch and Belgian troops, was worn also by British forces when they wore formation signs on their uniform.

Left: Pocket fob and miniature lapel badge for AFCENT.

PLATE 57. NATO BADGES

1

2

3

4

5

6

7

8

9

10

11

12

13

PLATE 58. NATO BADGES

A series of NATO badges, each of which depicts a rampant lion superimposed on the NATO symbol, have been produced and worn at various times for a number of NATO Commands and military elements. Some of these commands no longer exist and information regarding the correct designation of certain of these badges is, surprisingly, sketchy.

1 A silver lion rampant superimposed on a black and silver countercharged compass rose NATO symbol set on a bright-red enamelled shield with silver metal edge. An obsolete badge of the pin-on type thought to have been used by personnel of the north-eastern Mediterranean Area based on Izmir, Turkey (see page 22).

2 A similar design, but with a yellow enamelled shield. Also an obsolete pin-on badge thought to have been for wear by personnel of the Mediterranean Command (see page 22).

3 A white enamelled shield with rampant lion and NATO symbol. Yet another obsolete badge, the designation for which has not been established.

4 A pin-on badge with a black enamelled shield, silver lion and black-and-silver compass rose thought to have been used by NATO personnel based on Bonn, the capital of the Federal Republic of Germany. The badge is obsolete.

5 A similar pin-on badge with brown enamelled shield, also obsolete. Thought to have been used by NATO personnel from the Gibraltar area.

A further lion rampant badge is known to exist, but is not illustrated here. It has a maroon enamelled shield. Its designation has not been established.

6 Badge of the pocket fob or pocket crest variety for wear by personnel of Allied Land Forces Central Europe (CENTAG) (see page 37). Whereas the significance of the shield colours of items 1 to 5 is unknown, no such problem presents itself with the background colour of this item. The dark-green of the CENTAG shield is said to be the colour traditionally used within NATO to represent its ground forces (see also items 13 and 14, plate 59). The lion, in a defensive striking posture, symbolizes both power and courage. The four points of the compass rose star represent the directions towards peace undertaken by all the NATO member nations. Black and silver used in this conjunction are said to be symbolic of wisdom and peace.

7 US Army Element Central Army Group (CENTAG). A shoulder-sleeve insignia worn by US Army troops operating with CENTAG. Badge approved on 7 January 1980.

8 A subdued version of item 7.

9 Pocket fob for wear by personnel of the 4th Allied Tactical Air Force (see page 38). The blue background to the enamelled shield represents the colour associated with the air element.

10 FOURATAF flying suit embroidered patch.

11 Pocket fob or crest for wear by Allied personnel of Allied Air Forces Central Europe (AAFCE). The official description of this badge is given as follows: 'A blue shield signifying air power upon which is featured the sword of the Emperor Charlemagne, he who first united Central Europe. This theme is further emphasized by the silver tower superimposed upon the sword in the centre of the shield and representing Charlemagne's capital at Aachen (Aix-la-Chapelle). In the upper right corner the NATO compass rose is depicted signifying command direction towards peace. The two stylized aircraft, with their contrails streaming down and to the right, are fixed in the upper left corner symbolizing Second Allied Tactical Air Force (TWOATAF) and Fourth Allied Tactical Air Force (FOURATAF), united under the common command of Allied Air Forces Central Europe, ready to protect and defend the peace, people and integrity of Central Europe'.

12 An embroidered pocket patch version of item 11 in true colours.

13 An embroidered pocket patch subdued version of item 11. Unlike the subdued badges used by the US Army, with their dark olive-green and black colouring, subdued badges used in the US Air Force employ dark-green, dark-blue, olive-drab and black for the designs of their insignia.

14 Metal and coloured enamelled pin-on badge for personnel of United Kingdom Air Forces (UKAIR) (see page 45). The central motif consists of a golden Astral Crown from behind which issue four bolts of red lightning. Piercing the crown is an unsheathed vertical golden sword. All these objects are placed on a white, blue-edged cloud which in turn is superimposed on the NATO compass rose, the whole design being raised from the surface of a sky-blue gold-edged shield which in turn bears the golden lettering 'United Kingdom' and 'Air Forces'.

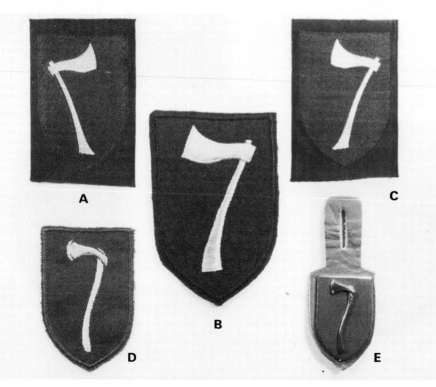

Left: Variants of the NORTHAG badge. Items A and C are a matching, mirror pair of the silk machine-woven shoulder-badges. Item B is a West German version. Item D is Dutch and item E is the gilt metal and blue enamelled version of the NORTHAG badge.

PLATE 58. NATO BADGES

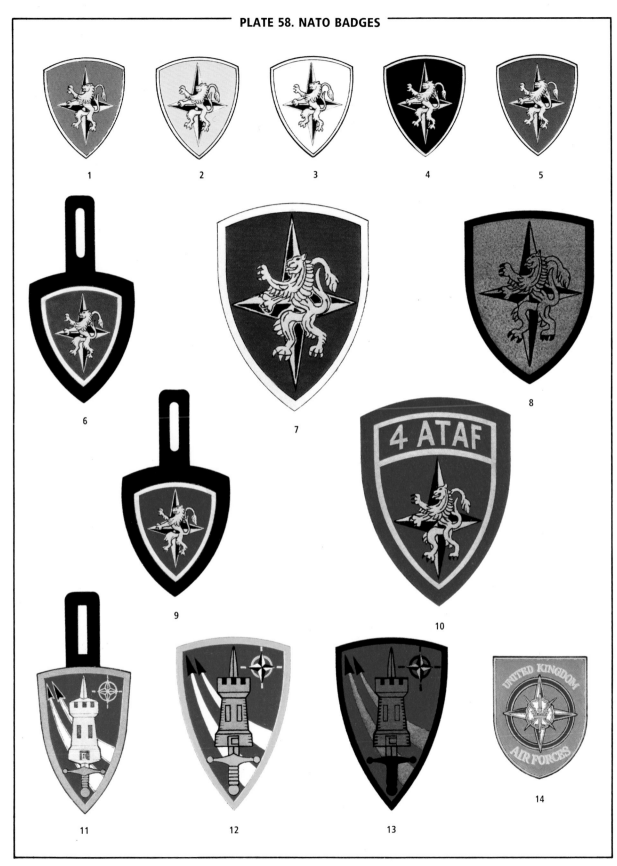

1

2

3

4

5

6

7

8

4 ATAF

9

10

11

12

13

14

UNITED KINGDOM

AIR FORCES

PLATE 59. NATO BADGES

1 Allied Air Forces Central Europe (AIRCENT) Headquarters, pocket patch. Pale-blue and royal-blue background for the central motif and surround are aptly chosen for this Air Forces badge. Rising from what is meant to be an Astral Crown are the seven national flags of the seven NATO member nations that formed the air element of AIRCENT. From left to right, top to bottom the flags are: Netherlands, Canada – the former Red Ensign flag – the United Kingdom, France, the United States, Federal Republic of Germany and Belgium.

2 Allied Air Forces Northern Europe. A pocket patch worn by personnel from the four countries contributing air force contingents to this early NATO organization. The four flags of the United States, Norway, Denmark and the United Kingdom represent the four participating NATO nations.

3 Second Allied Tactical Air Force (TWOATAF), pocket patch. The three golden bolts of lightning symbolize the three air forces that initially formed TWOATAF when first established in 1952, the crown signifies that it was the Kingdoms of Great Britain, Belgium and the Netherlands that placed their air forces under this joint command. A number of badges, each of which features the emblem of the Lion of St Mark, an ancient design often seen in Mediterranean countries,

and the traditional insignia associated with the sixteenth-century Republic of Venice, whose Patron Saint was the Apostle Mark, are worn by seven separate NATO Commands and Forces.

4 Headquarters Allied Forces Southern Europe (AFSOUTH). The Lion of St Mark is represented in the traditional manner holding a sword vertically in its right paw, resting on an open book on which appears the single word 'PAX' (peace). The winged lion, the sword, book and edging to the shield are gold-yellow, the background to the shield is carmine. The lion is said to represent power holding open 'the book of peace' with raised sword prepared to maintain that peace. The AFSOUTH insignia is worn as a shoulder sleeve insignia (cloth) and as a metal and enamelled pin-on or pocket-fob badge by all personnel assigned to Headquarters Allied Forces Southern Europe (see page 39).

5 Allied Land Forces Southern Europe (LANDSOUTH). Personnel of this command wear a badge very similar, both in design and colouring, to that worn by AFSOUTH (see page 40).

6 Naval Striking and Support Forces Southern Europe (STRIK-FORSOUTH). Personnel of this force wear a badge similar to AFSOUTH, but with a blue enamelled background (see page 43).

7 Allied Air Forces Southern Europe (AIRSOUTH). Another St Mark's Lion badge, but with a pair of stylized wings below the winged lion in place of the bar.

8 Fifth Allied Tactical Air Force (FIVEATAF). Very similar to the badge for AIRSOUTH, but with the addition of the number '5' set between the wings (see page 40).

9 Sixth Allied Tactical Air Force (SIXATAF). A silver-winged lion, sword and book set above stylized wings with the number '6' set between them, all on a shield with the left half in blue and the right half in red (see page 40).

10 Southern European Task Force (SETAF). The design for this badge was chosen for wear by troops of this task force because of the association between SETAF and LANDSOUTH, SETAF operating in support of LANDSOUTH. The shield represents the defensive nature of the Task Force, the red, white and blue sections symbolizing the American forces. The red of the band ('tab') above the shield is the heraldic colour for US artillery, the artillery being predominant in the composition of SETAF and its mission.

11 The subdued version of the Southern European Task Force badge minus the tab.

12 NATO Missile Firing Range, Crete. A red shield with gold-yellow inner border and NIKE Hercules

Missile. Top left-hand corner a white mountain goat leaping across white mountain rocks against a circular blue sky. In the lower portion of the shield a stylized version of the NATO star in white on a blue disc. The black Greek lettering translates as 'Accuracy-Speed'. Other versions of this cloth patch with slight colour differences are known to exist.

13 Mobile Land Force. The badge used by this force prior to the change in its title (see page 44).

14 Allied Command Europe (ACE) Mobile Force. The design of this metal and coloured enamelled badge consists of two mailed, clasped hands (silver) grasping a single lightning bolt (gold) beneath the silver initials 'AMF', all on a silver-edged green shield. The clasped hands symbolize the fraternity and solidarity of the NATO countries. The hands are armoured as befits a military force. The bolt of lightning represents the mobility of AMF and its speed of deployment. The green background to the shield signifies the Land Component of the Force.

15 Allied Command Europe (ACE) Mobile Force (Air). The sky-blue background to this shield signifies the Air element of the AMF.

PLATE 59. NATO BADGES

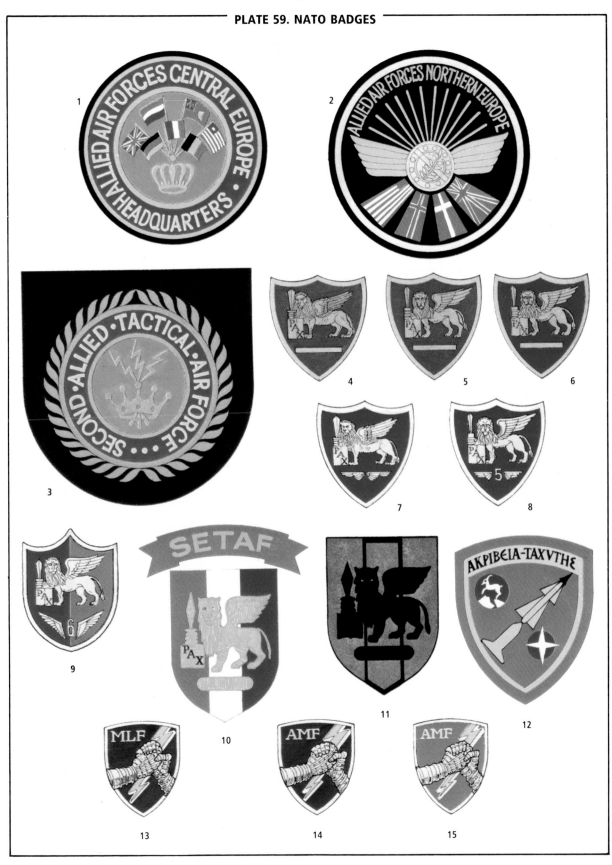

1

2

3

4

5

6

7

8

9

10

11

12

13

14

15

PLATE 60, NATO BADGES

1 Allied Land Forces South-eastern Europe (LANDSOUTHEAST). The insignia is in the form of a shield divided into four quarters with diagonal quarters displaying elements of the flags of Greece and Turkey. Top left and bottom right show the white cross on a blue background of the Hellenic flag; the white crescent and star on a red background in the top right and bottom left quarters represents Turkey. The yellow border to the shield echoes the border used on the insignia of AFSOUTH (see plate 59), the senior NATO Organization in southern Europe based in Naples, Italy.

The design of this badge was selected by the first LAND-SOUTHEAST Commander, Lieutenant-General Willard G. Wyman (USA) from a series of designs proposed by AFSOUTH. The Hellenic authorities approved the design on 15 October 1952 and the Turkish authorities approved it on 21 October 1952. CINCSOUTH, Admiral Robert Carney (USA), gave final approval for the badge a few days later.

2 The original insignia used by LANDSOUTHEAST has undergone a change of design due to the withdrawal of Greek military participation in the integrated command (see page 27 and elsewhere). The new badge now features the NATO compass rose symbol in the diagonally opposite quarters that previously displayed the Greek white cross on a blue field taken from the Greek flag.

Both this and the previous LANDSOUTHEAST badge (item 1) are, or were, worn as a metal pocket fob emblem by officers and NCOs of the Italian, British, American, Turkish, and – previously – Greek military personnel. The original LANDSOUTHEAST insignia was also produced as a cloth shoulder sleeve insignia for wear on the uniform, mainly by personnel of the lower ranks.

3 Allied Forces Mediterranean. A gilt metal shield, the border of which is polished and the dimpled shield in frosted gilt finish. The slightly raised, convex circular motif shows a surprisingly detailed map of the Mediterranean Sea and the land mass surrounding it, a credit to the skills of the Italian badge manufacturer. The land areas, including

all the islands shown, are in frosted gilt metal with the sea areas shown in light-blue coloured enamels. At the base of the central motif is a silver-white fouled anchor, a separate component set diagonally into the badge and raised from the surface of the motif. Directly atop the central motif is a frosted gilt eagle with outstretched wings in an attitude of flight. On a royal-blue enamelled band is the gilt legend 'ALLIED FORCES MEDITERRANEAN'. This pin-on badge is no longer in use and has been superseded by the next item.

4 Allied Naval Forces Southern Europe (NAVSOUTH). With the disestablishment of Allied Forces Mediterranean (AFMED) on 5 June 1967 and the establishment on the same day of Allied Naval Forces Southern Europe (see page 41), a new badge was introduced for wear by personnel of the new Command. The new pin-on pocket badge had a change of lettering which now read 'ALLIED NAVAL FORCES SOUTHERN EUROPE'.

5 Allied Naval Forces Central Europe (NAVCENT). An embroidered cloth pocket patch, the item illustrated here is thought to be for German naval personnel, worn by naval forces subordinate to the Commander-in-Chief Central Army Group (CINCENT). With the removal of NAVCENT Headquarters from French soil in October 1966, Allied Naval Forces Central Europe together with Allied Land Forces and Allied Air Forces Central Europe ceased to exist as separate entities when their headquarters were merged with those of Allied Forces Central Europe (AFCENT) (see page 27). This badge therefore became obsolete at that same time.

6 Allied Command Atlantic (ACLANT). A gilt metal and dark-blue enamelled pin-on pocket badge featuring a design consisting of a trident overlaying two crossed swords over a pair of wings. At the base of the shield is a short yellow ribband on which, in dark-blue lettering, is the acronym 'ACLANT'. The three symbols of the trident, the crossed swords and the wings represent the three services which form Allied Command Atlantic, the main one naturally being the naval element. It is of interest to note the

use of the trident as a symbol used on NATO badges to represent naval Commands or units rather than an anchor, fouled or clear which is heraldically a more traditional emblem (see page 46).

7 Submarines Allied Command Atlantic (SUBACLANT). A badge, similar in size, shape, quality and colouring to the last item, but with a different design. A submarine seen in profile overlaying two crossed torpedoes behind which appears an upright trident. The ribband at the base of the pin-on shield displays the word 'SUBACLANT' (see page 47).

8 Commander-in-Chief Iberian Atlantic Area (CINCIBERLANT). A pin-on pocket badge identical in all features with item number 6, the ACLANT badge, other than the lettering on the ribband (see page 48).

9 Standing Naval Force Atlantic (STANAVFORLANT). Another metal and coloured enamelled pin-on pocket badge the design of which shows the NATO symbol set against a sky-blue background above dark-blue and white wavey lines representing the waters of the North Atlantic. On the dark-blue upper portion of the shield-shaped badge appears the acronym 'STANAVFORLANT' (see page 47).

10 Standing Naval Force Channel (STANAVFORCHAN). Almost identical with the design used for the previous described badge, the dark-blue and white wavey lines on this item represent the waters of the English Channel and the southern part of the North Sea, STANAVFORCHAN's area of responsibility (see page 49). The lettering at the top of the shield displays the acronym used by this Force.

11 Supreme Allied Commander Atlantic (SACLANT). A circular metal and enamelled pin-on pocket badge, the central motif of which features the tri-service emblems of a trident, crossed swords and wings. This is superimposed on a representation of sea (light-blue) and land (dark-blue) areas of the North Atlantic and the surrounding land masses. The wide gold-coloured border to this circular badge is decorated with laurel leaves and has at its top and base the acronyms 'NATO' and 'SACLANT' (see page 47).

12 Striking Fleet Atlantic (STRIKFLTANT). Identical with item 11, but with the lettering 'STRIKFLTANT' at the base (see page 47).

13 NATO North Atlantic Command (NORLANT). This badge is thought to be for personnel operating under NATO's North Atlantic Command. This is further borne out by the central motif which features the waters of the North Atlantic and the Western Approaches (light-blue) and the land areas (dark-blue) of Greenland, the British Isles and western Europe The emblem of a trident and wings indicates only two participating services.

14 Allied Command Channel (CHANCOM), first pattern. A shield-shaped gilt metal and enamelled pin-on pocket badge. The design shows the English Channel stylistically represented by the light-blue and white wavey lines covering the field of the bend sinister on each side of which are the green lands of England and France. Although the 'bend sinister' is frequently stated in heraldry to be the mark of illegitimacy, its use here is apt in representing this stretch of waterway as geographically the lie of the English Channel can be said to be from the North Sea (upper right) towards the North Atlantic (lower left). Interestingly the fouled anchor and an eagle in flight are used to represent the naval and airforce element of this Command, while at the same time the trident symbol has also been incorporated. The four-pointed star above the prongs of the trident is a poor representation of the NATO symbol. This badge has been superseded by a better-designed version.

15 Allied Command Channel (CHANCOM), second pattern. Very similar to the previously described item, but with stronger design features. Made in white metal with coloured enamels, the new version of the badge has a central diagonal bar with a more pronounced pale-blue and white wavey field. The fouled anchor and eagle-in-flight emblems are in white, while the silver trident now reaches to the upper edge of the shield, with the improved NATO symbol set in the centre of the badge in its correct colours of white and dark-blue. It is believed that this badge is in current use.

PLATE 60. NATO BADGES

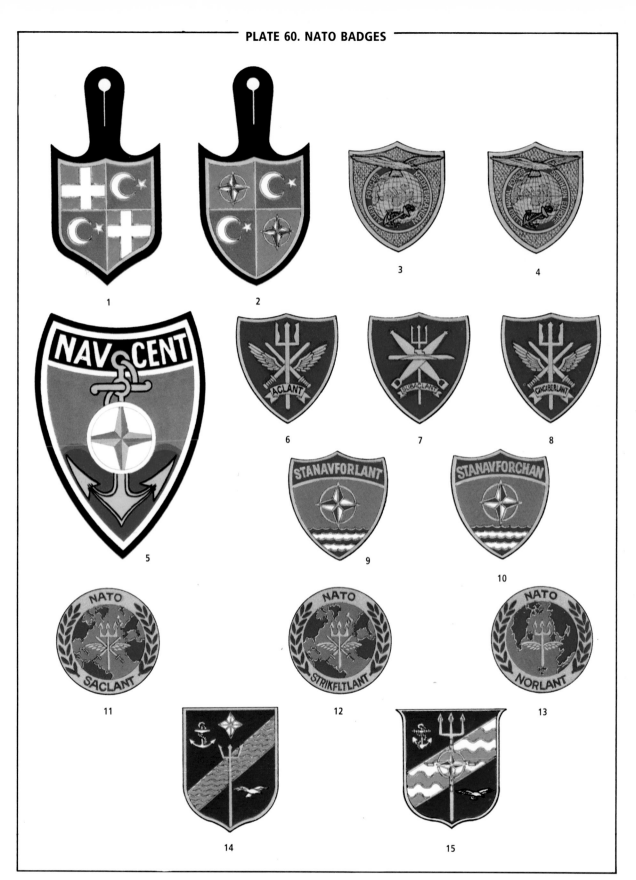

1

2

3

4

5

6

7

8

9

10

11

12

13

14

15

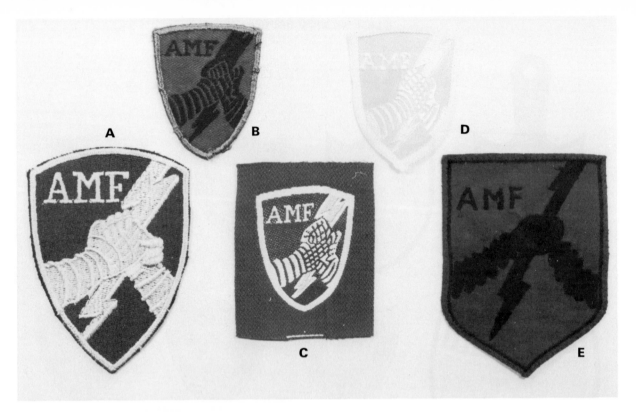

Above: Five versions of the cloth ACE Mobile Force badge. Item A is the US coloured SSI for wear on the US Army Green Uniform. Item D is the West German version for wear on the shirt and item C for wear on the field uniform. Item B is worn by both British and US troops on the field uniform and item E is an Italian version of the subdued patch.

Left: Mark McKinnon of the 32nd Tactical Fighter Squadron, United States Air Force Europe, based at Soesterberg, the Netherlands. He wears the new-pattern Squadron patch.

Top right: The two patterns of the USAFE 32nd Tactical Fighter Squadron patch. Left is the former pattern (see colour plate 64 item 13) and right the new, heraldically correct version.

Right: US Air Force flying-suit patches. Items A and D are US Tactical Air Command patches, both coloured and subdued. Item B is the US Air Forces in Europe patch; items C and E are the US Strategic Air Command patch, coloured and subdued.

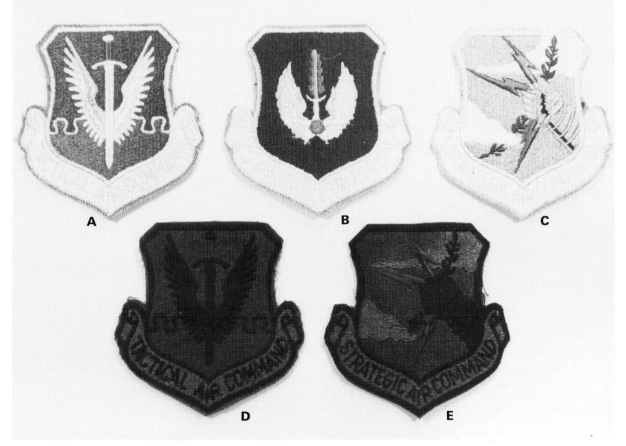

A   **B**   **C**

D   **E**

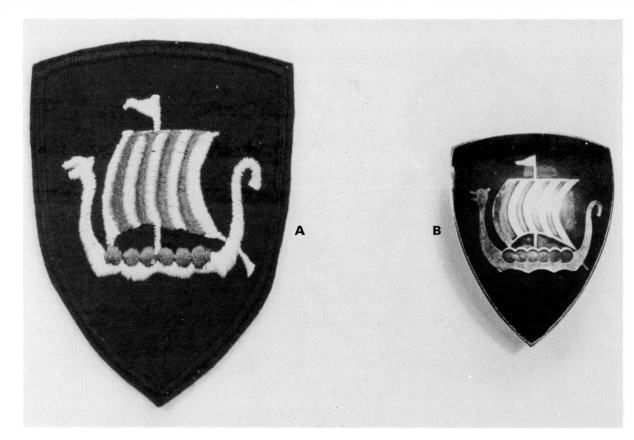

Above: AFNORTH badges. Item A is a West German cloth patch; item B the pin-on enamelled badge.

PLATE 61. BADGES OF NATIONAL UNITS ASSIGNED TO NATO

Belgium
1 1st Belgian Army Corps.
2 1st Belgian Infantry Division.
3 16th Belgian Armoured Division.
4 Belgian Home Defence Forces.
Canada
5 National flag identifying emblem

worn on certain uniform items.
6 4 Canadian Mechanized Brigade Group.
Denmark
7 National identifying emblem worn on certain uniform items. The title 'Danmark' and the

Dannebrog emblem are always worn together.
8 1st Sjaellandske Brigade.
9 2nd Sjaellandske Brigade.
10 Royal Danish Helicopter Squadron No. 722.
11 Badge of the Danish Naval

Home Guard.
Italy
12 Mechanized Infantry Brigade 'Granatieri di Sardegna'.
13 Alpine Brigade 'Tridentina'.
14 Alpine Brigade 'Orobica'.
15 Alpine Brigade 'Cadore'.

PLATE 61. BADGES OF NATIONAL UNITS ASSIGNED TO NATO

1

2

3

4

5

6

7

8

9

10

11

12

13

14

15

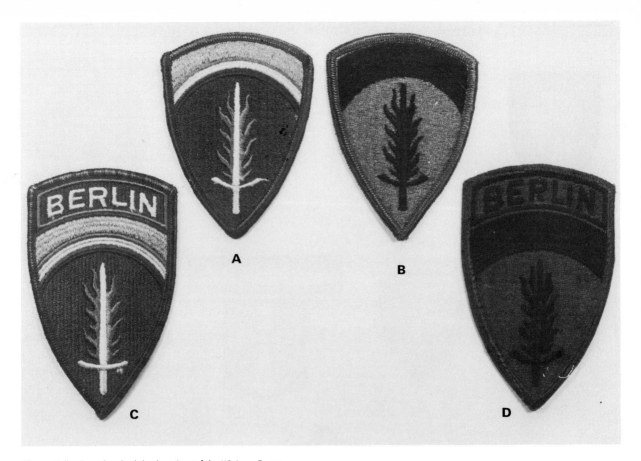

Above: Full-coloured and subdued versions of the US Army Europe –
USAREUR – patches (items A and B) and the US Army Berlin patches (items
C and D).

PLATE 62. BADGES OF NATIONAL UNITS ASSIGNED TO NATO

Germany
1 Military District I.
2 1st Corps, Münster.
3 17th Panzer-Grenadier Brigade, Hamburg-Rahlstedt.
4 21st Panzer Brigade, Augustdorf.
5 23rd Mountain Brigade, Bad Reichenhall.
6 1st Air Landing Division HQ, Bruchsal.
7 28th Panzer-Grenadier Brigade.
8 31st Panzer-Grenadier Brigade, Oldenburg.
9 Territorial Command 'North'.
10 Home Defence Command 51.
11 Home Defence Command 53.
12 Home Defence Command 56.
13 2nd Air Force Division, pocket patch.
14 Federal Republic of Germany identifying flag worn on most forms of combat clothing and work uniforms.
15 Pocket patch badge for Staff of 'Immelmann' Reconnaissance Squadron '51'.

PLATE 62. BADGES OF NATIONAL UNITS ASSIGNED TO NATO

1

2

3

4

5

6

7

8

9

10

11

12

13

14

15

Above: Badges of the Headquarters Allied Forces Southern Europe (items A, B and C) and the Fifth Allied Tactical Air Force (items D, E and F). Item A is the machine-woven cloth shoulder-patch and items B and C are two versions of the gilt metal and enamelled badges; item B being a pin-on badge and item C a pocket fob. Item D is a screen-printed plastic badge bonded to serge material. Items E and F are two versions of the same pin-on enamelled badge, item E being made in two parts with the silver metal Lion of St Mark and the wings below mounted onto the blue enamelled shield whereas item F is a blue enamelled and silver metal one-piece badge.

PLATE 63. BADGES OF NATIONAL UNITS ASSIGNED TO NATO

The Netherlands

1 National title for Dutch Army personnel.

2 Flag of the Netherlands identifying badge.

3 Staff of 1st Army Corps.

4 1st Corps Troops.

5 1st Division.

6 4th Division.

7 5th Division.

8 Territorial Defence Troops. Worn during period 1946 to 1970s.

Norway

9 National title for Norwegian military personnel, Army.

United Kingdom

The practice of wearing formation signs on the uniforms of the British Army has greatly diminished since the withdrawal of the Battle-Dress in the 1960s. The signs shown here were just some of the many that were being worn by British Troops committed to NATO in north-west Europe and the United Kingdom. Although no longer worn, the signs live on as emblems used on notice boards, camp signs and on letterheadings.

10 Rhine Army Troops.

11 I Army Corps.

12 1st Infantry Division.

13 2nd Infantry Division.

14 4th Infantry Division.

15 Flying suit patch for personnel of Second Tactical Air Force, Royal Air Force Germany.

PLATE 63. BADGES OF NATIONAL UNITS ASSIGNED TO NATO

Above: Three slightly differing versions of the West German Federal Border Guard shoulder insignia. Items A are worn on the greatcoat, items B are for wear on the shirt and items C on the Service tunic.

PLATE 64. BADGES OF NATIONAL UNITS ASSIGNED TO NATO

United States of America

Because of the enlightened attitude of the American military authorities towards shoulder-sleeve insignia and the fact that the US armed forces are vast compared to the armed forces of other NATO member countries, and possessing many and varied types of military formations, all its personnel are authorized to wear specially designed unit badges. The shoulder-sleeve insig-

nia illustrated here are just a few of the many items that are worn by the personnel serving, or who have served, with the US Army and Air Forces in Europe, and committed to NATO.

1 32nd Air Defense Command.
2 1st Infantry Division, the 'Big Red One'.
3 2nd Support Command.
4 VII Corps.
5 11th Armoured Cavalry

Regiment.
6 Seventh Army, subdued version.
7 21st Support Command.
8 3rd Infantry Division.
9 7th Medical Command.
10 72nd Field Artillery Brigade.
11 3rd Armoured Division 'Spearhead'.
12 3rd Air Force.
13 32nd Tactical Fighter Squadron, United States Air Force in Europe. Based at Soesterberg

Royal Netherlands Air Force base, the US Air Force personnel wear this unique 'Dutch' style squadron patch on their flying suits. It is, however, on the point of being re-designed in order to produce a heraldically correct badge. The wreath and crown will be re-designed in keeping with other Royal Netherlands Air Force badges (see page 190).

PLATE 64. BADGES OF NATIONAL UNITS ASSIGNED TO NATO

1

2

3

4

5

6

7

8

9

10

11

SPEARHEAD

12

13

Left: NATO Military Police arm brassard. The badge is white on mid-blue, the letters 'MP' are white and both are sewn to a black cloth brassard. This item is worn by Military Police when on duty at CENTAG Headquarters.

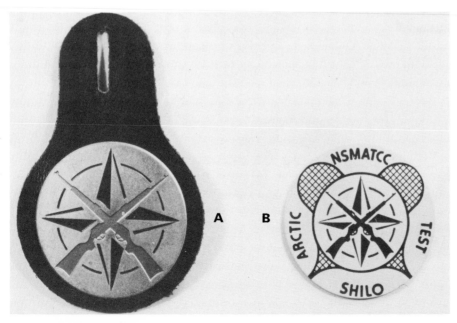

Left: NATO Small Arms Test Control Commission (NSMATCC) badges. This Commission was set up in order to conduct a series of technical and field tests with a selection of rifles and light machine-guns together with the appropriate ammunition. A comprehensive field test was conducted by a multi-national group, of which 29 were Canadians, at Hammelburg, FRG from June 1978 to June 1979. The pocket fob badge (item A) was worn during these tests. A more limited cold weather test was conducted by a largely Canadian group at Camp Shilo, Manitoba, Canada. The personnel of this group wore the ivorene with black design pin-on badge as shown by item B.

Right: Two versions of the badge worn by troops of the Belgian Support Element to NATO. The NATO symbol is in black-and-white on a broad white circle set on a representation of the Belgian national colours of black, yellow and red. Item A is machine-stitched onto khaki serge material and item B is in coloured plastics. An enamelled pin-on version also exists. This badge was worn by Belgian forces assisting in the re-location of NATO and SHAPE when these headquarters moved from France to Belgium. These badges ceased to be used after 1963.

A   **B**

Right: The Canadian Armed Forces national emblem badges. The small-size badge is normally worn on the shirt, while the larger version is used on the combat jacket and flying-overalls.

Right: The Danish Army national emblem badge with national title. The Dannebrog emblem and Danmark title are worn together on the Service tunic and combat jacket. While the white cross on the red shield is standard, the colouring of the national title changes according to the uniform item upon which it is worn. Items A are for use on the field uniform, the title being grey letters on olive-drab background. Item B is worn on the Service tunic and here the title has white letters on a red background.

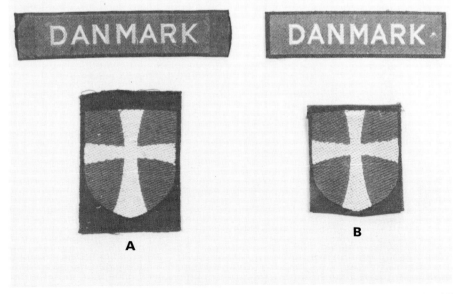

A   **B**

Appendix 1. Acronyms and Abbreviations

AAFCE — Allied Air Forces Central Europe
ACCHAN — Allied Command Channel
ACE — Allied Command Europe
ACLANT — Allied Command Atlantic
AEW — Airborne Early Warning
AFCE* — Allied Forces Central Europe
AFCENT — Allied Forces Central Europe
AFMED* — Allied Forces Mediterranean
AFNORTH — Allied Forces Northern Europe
AFSOUTH — Allied Forces Southern Europe
AGARD — Advisory Group for Aeronautical Research and Development, later changed to Advisory Group for Aerospace Research and Development
AIRBALTAP — Allied Air Forces Baltic Approaches
AIRCENT* — Allied Air Forces Central Europe
AIRNON/AIRNORNOR — Allied Air Forces North Norway
AIRSONOR — Allied Air Forces South Norway
AIRSOUTH — Allied Air Forces Southern Europe
AMF — ACE Mobile Force
AMF(A) — Allied Command Europe Mobile Force (Air)
AMF(L) — Allied Command Europe Mobile Force (Land)
ATAG — Air Training Advisory Group
ATS* — Auxiliary Territorial Service
AWACS — Airborne Warning and Control System
BALTAP — Baltic Approaches Command
BAOR — British Army of the Rhine
BENECHAN — Benelux Sub-Area Channel
BGS — BundesGrenzSchutz (German) Federal Border Protection (Police)
1 CAG — 1 Canadian Air Group
CENTAG — Central Army Group, Central Europe
CFE — Canadian Forces Europe
CHANCOM — Channel Committee, also Allied Command Channel
CHOD NORWAY — Chief of Defence Norway
CINCAFMED — Commander-in-Chief Allied Forces Mediterranean
CINCEASTLANT — Commander-in-Chief Eastern Atlantic Area
CINCENT — Commander-in-Chief Allied Forces Central Europe
CINCHAN — Commander-in-Chief Channel and Southern North Sea
CINCIBERLANT — Commander-in-Chief Iberian Atlantic Area
CINCNORTH — Commander-in-Chief Allied Forces Northern Europe

CINCSOUTH — Commander-in-Chief Allied Forces Southern Europe
CINCUKAIR — Commander-in-Chief United Kingdom Air Forces
CINCWESTLANT — Commander-in-Chief Western Atlantic Area
4 CMBG — 4 Canadian Mechanized Brigade Group
COMAAFCE — Commander Allied Air Forces Central Europe
COMAIRBALTAP — Commander Air Forces Baltic Approaches
COMAIRNON — Commander Allied Air Forces North Norway
COMAIRNORTH* — Commander Air Forces North Europe
COMAIRSOUTH — Commander Allied Air Forces Southern Europe
COMBALTAP — Commander Allied Forces Baltic Approaches
COMCENTAG — Commander Central Army Group
COMGIBMED — Commander Gibraltar-Mediterranean
COMIBERLANT — Commander Iberian Atlantic Area
COMNORTH* — Commander North European Region
COMNORTHAG — Commander Northern European Army Group
COMLANDDENMARK* — Commander Land Forces Denmark
COMLANDJUT — Commander Allied Land Forces Schleswig-Holstein and Jutland
COMLANDNON — Commander Allied Land Forces North Norway
COMLANDNORWAY* — Commander Land Forces Norway
COMLANDSOUTH — Commander Allied Land Forces Southern Europe
COMLANDZEALAND — Commander Land Forces Zealand and Bornholm
COMNAVBALTAP — Commander Naval Forces Baltic Approaches
COMNAVSOUTH — Commander Allied Naval Forces Southern Europe
COMNAVNON — Commander Allied Naval Forces North Norway
COMNON — Commander Allied Forces North Norway
COMSONOR — Commander Allied Forces South Norway
COMSUBMED — Commander Submarines Mediterranean
COMSTRIKFORSOUTH — Commander Naval Striking and Support Forces Southern Europe
CUSRPG — Canada-US Regional Planning Group
DEFCOMNON — Defence Command North Norway
DEFCOMSONOR — Defence Command South Norway
DEPCOMSTRIKFORSOUTH — Deputy Commander Naval Striking and Support Forces Southern Europe

DPC	Defence Planning Committee	NAVSONAR	Allied Naval Forces South Norway
DPM	Disruptive Patterned Material	NAVSOUTH	Allied Naval Forces Southern Europe
EASTLANT	Eastern Atlantic Area	NAVOCFORMED	Naval On-Call Force Mediterranean
EDC	European Defence Community	NMR	National Military Representative (at SHAPE)
ENJJPT	Euro-NATO Joint Jet Pilot Training		
ENTAG	Euro-NATO Training Group	NORAD	North American Air Defence System
EUROGROUP	Informal Group of NATO European Defence Ministers	NORLANT	North Atlantic Command
		NORTHAG	Northern Army Group, Central Europe
FIVEATAF	Fifth Allied Tactical Air Force, also shown as 5ATAF	OTAN	Organization du Traité de l'Atlantique Nord
FOB	Forward Operating Base	PSC	Principal Subordinate Command
FOURATAF	Fourth Allied Tactical Air Force, also shown as 4ATAF	PTC	Programme Training Centre
		RAF	Royal Air Force
FRG	Federal Republic of Germany	RAFG	Royal Air Force Germany
GSG 9	Federal Border Group 9 Special	RDF	Rapid Deployment Force
IBERLANT	Iberian Command Atlantic	RM	Royal Marines
IMS	International Military Staff	RN	Royal Navy
LANDCENT*	Allied Land Forces Central Europe	SAC	Strategic Air Command
LANDJUT	Allied Land Forces Schleswig-Holstein and Jutland	SACEUR	Supreme Allied Commander Europe
		SACLANT	Supreme Allied Commander Atlantic
LANDNON	Allied Land Forces North Norway	SACLANTCEN	Supreme Allied Commander Atlantic (Anti-Submarine Warfare Research) Centre
LANDSONOR	Allied Land Forces South Norway		
LANDSOUTH	Allied Land Forces Southern Europe		
LANDSOUTHEAST	Allied Land Forces South-eastern Europe	SASWREC	Supreme Allied Commander Atlantic Anti-Submarine Warfare Research Centre
LANDZEALAND	Allied Land Forces Zealand		
LLRS	Low Level Reporting System		
MAIRCHAN	Allied Maritime Air Forces Channel	SETAF	Southern European Task Force
MARAIRMED	Maritime Air Forces Mediterranean	SHAFE*	Supreme Headquarters Allied Forces Europe
MC	Military Committee		
MCM	Mine Counter-Measures	SHAPE	Supreme Headquarters Allied Powers Europe
MEDCENT	Central Mediterranean		
MEDEAST	Mediterranean East	SIXATAF	Sixth Allied Tactical Air Force, also shown as 6ATAF
MILREP	Military Representative		
MLF	Multilateral Forces, also Mobile Land Force	SSI	Shoulder Sleeve Insignia
		STC	SHAPE Technical Centre
MNC	Major NATO Commander	STANAVFORCHAN	Standing Naval Force Channel
MEDNOREAST	Mediterranean North-east	STANAVFORLANT	Standing Naval Force Atlantic
MoD	Ministry of Defence	STRIKFLTANT	Striking Fleet Atlantic
MRCA	Multi-Role Combat Aircraft	STRIKFORSOUTH	Naval Striking and Support Forces Southern Europe
MSC	Major Subordinate Command		
NAC	North Atlantic Council	SUBACLANT	Submarines Allied Command Atlantic
NADEFCOL	NATO Defence College	SUBMED	Allied Submarine Forces Mediterranean
NAEW	NATO Airborne Early Warning	TAF	Tactical Air Force
NADGE	NATO Air Defence Ground Environment (System)	TWOATAF	Second Allied Tactical Air Force, also shown as 2ATAF
		UK	United Kingdom
NAMFI	NATO Missile Firing Installation	UKADR	United Kingdom Air Defence Region
NAPMA	NATO Airborne Early Warning and Control Programme Management Agency	UKAIR	United Kingdom Air Forces
		UN	United Nations
		USA	United States of America
NAPMO	NATO Airborne Early Warning and Control Programme Management Organization	USAREUR	United States Army in Europe
		USAF	United States Air Force
		USAFE	United States Air Force Europe
NATO	North Atlantic Treaty Organization	USMC	United States Marine Corps
NATOSCH	NATO School (SHAPE)	WESTLANT	Western Atlantic Area
NAVBALTAP	Allied Naval Forces Baltic Approaches	WEU	Western European Union
NAVCENT*	Allied Naval Forces Central Europe	*Obsolete	
NAVNON	Allied Naval Forces North Norway		

Appendix 2. The NATO Military Structure: Formations and Locations

Military Committee	Brussels, Belgium
International Military Staff	Brussels, Belgium
Allied Communications Security Agency	Brussels, Belgium
Allied Long Lines Agency	Brussels, Belgium
Allied Radio Frequency Agency	Brussels, Belgium
Allied Naval Communications Agency	London, England
Allied Tactical Communications Agency	Brussels, Belgium
NATO Defence College	Rome, Italy
Military Agency for Standardization	Brussels, Belgium
Advisory Group for Aerospace Research and Development	Paris, France
Canada-United States Planning Group	Washington, USA and Ottawa, Canada
Supreme Headquarters Allied Powers Europe (SHAPE)	Mons, Belgium
Allied Forces Northern Europe	Oslo, Norway
Allied Forces North Norway	Bodø, Norway
Allied Forces South Norway	Oslo, Norway
Allied Forces Baltic Approaches	Karup, Jutland (Denmark)
Allied Forces Zealand	Ringsted, Denmark
Allied Naval Forces Baltic Approaches	Karup, Jutland, Denmark
Allied Air Forces Baltic Approaches	Karup, Jutland, Denmark
Allied Forces Schleswig-Holstein and Jutland	Rendsburg, Germany
Allied Forces Central Europe	Brunssum, The Netherlands
Northern Army Group	Mönchen-Gladbach, Germany
Central Army Group	Heidelberg, Germany
Second Allied Tactical Air Force	Mönchen-Gladbach, Germany
Fourth Allied Tactical Air Force	Heidelberg, Germany
Allied Forces Southern Europe	Naples, Italy
Allied Land Forces Southern Europe	Verona, Italy
Allied Land Forces South-eastern Europe	Izmir, Turkey
Allied Air Forces Southern Europe	Naples, Italy
Fifth Allied Tactical Air Force	Vicenza, Italy
Sixth Allied Tactical Air Force	Izmir, Turkey
Allied Naval Forces Southern Europe	Naples, Italy
Naval Striking and Support Force Southern Europe	Naples, Italy
Allied Submarine Forces Mediterranean	Naples, Italy
Maritime Air Forces Mediterranean	Naples, Italy
Naval On Call Force Mediterranean	Afloat
Mediterranean East	Holargos, Greece
Mediterranean North-east	Ankara, Turkey
Central Mediterranean	Rome, Italy
Gibraltar Mediterranean	Gibraltar
United Kingdom Air Forces	High Wycombe, England
Allied Command Europe Mobile Force (Land)	Heidelberg, Germany
Allied Command Atlantic	Norfolk, Virginia, USA
Western Atlantic Area	Norfolk, Virginia, USA
Island Commander Bermuda	Hamilton, Bermuda
Island Commander Greenland	Gronnedal, Greenland
Island Commander Azores	San Miguel, Azores
Submarine Forces Western Atlantic	Norfolk, Virginia, USA
Ocean Sub-Area	Norfolk, Virginia, USA
Canadian Atlantic Sub-Area	Halifax, Nova Scotia, Canada
Submarine Allied Command Atlantic	Norfolk, Virginia, USA
Eastern Atlantic Area	Northwood, Middlesex, England
Submarine Forces Eastern Atlantic Area	Gosport, Hampshire, England
Bay of Biscay Sub-Area	Northwood, Middlesex, England
Island Commander Iceland	Keflavik, Iceland
Island Commander Faroes	Thorshavn, Faroes
Striking Fleet and Special Task Forces	when assigned
Maritime Air Eastern Atlantic	Northwood, Middlesex, England
Northern Sub-Area	Rosyth, Scotland
Maritime Air Northern Sub-Area	Rosyth, Scotland
Central Sub-Area	Plymouth, England
Maritime Air Central Sub-Area	Plymouth, England
Standing Naval Force Atlantic	afloat
Iberian Command Atlantic	Freire, Portugal
Island Commander Madeira	Funchal, Madeira
Striking Fleet Atlantic	afloat
Carrier Striking Force	afloat
Carrier Striking Group One	afloat
Carrier Striking Group Two	afloat
Anti-Submarine Warfare Research Centre	La Spezia, Italy
Allied Command Channel	Northwood, Middlesex, England
Benelux Sub-Area	The Hague, the Netherlands
Nore Sub-Area	Rosyth, Scotland
Allied Maritime Air Force Channel	Northwood, Middlesex, England
Maritime Air Force Nore Sub-Area	Rosyth, Scotland
Plymouth Sub-Area	Plymouth, England
Standing Naval Force Channel	afloat
Programme Training Centre	Glons, Belgium
SHAPE Technical Centre	The Hague, the Netherlands

Index

ACE Mobile Force (AMF), 29, 44
Acheson, Dean (USA), 10
Advisory Group for Aeronautical Research and Development (AGARD), 23
Agreement for the establishment of an integrated military force, 14
Airborne Early Warning Force (NAEW), 51
Airborne Warning and Control System (AWACS), 51
Air Defence Ground Environment system, NATO, (NADGE), 25, 26, 38, 50
Air Training Advisory Group (ATAG), 23
Algeria, independence of and effects on North Atlantic Treaty, 12
Allied Air Forces Central Europe (AIRCENT), 21, 29; AAFCE, 37
Allied Air Forces Northern Europe, 21
Allied Air Forces North Norway (AIRNON), 33
Allied Air Forces South Norway (AIRSONOR), 33
Allied Air Forces Southern Europe (AIRSOUTH), 22, 39
Allied Command Atlantic (ACLANT), 14, 21, 29
Allied Command Channel (ACCHAN), 14, 29
Allied Command Europe (ACE), 14, 21, 29
Allied Commander-in-Chief Channel (CINCHAN), 14
Allied Forces Baltic Approaches (BALTAP), 33
Allied Forces Central Europe (AFCENT), 21, 27, 29, 36
Allied Forces Mediterranean (AFMED), 22, 41
Allied Forces Northern Europe (AFNORTH), 21, 29, 33
Allied Forces North Norway (DEFCOMNON), 33
Allied Forces Southern Europe (AFSOUTH), 22, 29, 39
Allied Forces South Norway (DEFCOMSONOR), 33
Allied Land Forces Central Europe (LANDCENT), 21, 27
Allied Land Forces Denmark, 21
Allied Land Forces North Norway (LANDNON), 33
Allied Land Forces Norway, 21
Allied Land Forces Schleswig-Holstein and Jutland, 34
Allied Land Forces South-eastern Europe (LANDSOUTHEAST), 22, 39, 40, 41
Allied Land Forces Southern Europe

(LANDSOUTH), 22, 39, 40
Allied Land Forces South Norway (LANDSONOR), 33
Allied Maritime Air Force Channel Command, 49
Allied Naval Forces Central Europe (NAVCENT), 21, 27
Allied Naval Forces Northern Europe, 21
Allied Naval Forces North Norway (NAVNON), 33
Allied Naval Forces Southern Europe (NAVSOUTH), 39, 41
Allied Naval Forces South Norway (NAVSONOR), 33
Allied Submarine Forces Mediterranean (SUBMED), 42
Andersen, General Tage (Denmark), first Commander Baltic Approaches (COMBALTAP), 34
Andrews, Vice-Admiral Sir William (UK), Commander-in-Chief American and West Indies Station and Deputy Supreme Commander Atlantic, 46
Anti-Submarine Warfare Centre, La Spezia (Italy), 26
Anti-Submarine Warfare Force, US Sixth Fleet, 32
Armaments, Standardization and Inter-operability Division, IMS, 14
Assassination attempt on General Haig, SACEUR, 19
Assistant Directors, International Military Staff, 14

B
Baele, Lieutenant-Général Etienne (Belgium), Chairman NATO Military Committee, 21
Baltic Approaches Command (BALTAP), 34
Bech, Joseph (Luxembourg), 10
Benediktsson, Bjarni (Iceland), 10
Benelux Channel Command, 49
Berlin Air Lift, 1948, 32
Bermuda, Azores and Greenland Island Commands, Western Atlantic Command, 47
Bevin, Ernest (UK), 10
'Black September' Palestine terrorist attack on Israeli athletes at Munich Olympics, 26 September 1972, 24
Boothman, Air Marshal Sir John (UK), Air Commander-in-Chief Channel and

Southern North Sea, and Chief, RAF Coastal Command, 22
Bradley, General Omar N. (USA), Chairman, NATO Military Committee, 21
Brind, Vice-Admiral Sir Patrick (UK), Commander-in-Chief Northern Europe, 20
Brosio, Signor, (Italy) NATO Secretary-General, 26, 49
Brussels, Treaty of, 10

C
Camp Guynemer, Headquarters of Allied Air Forces Central European Command, Fontainebleau, France, 21
Canada-United States Regional Planning Group, 23
Canadian Atlantic Sub-Area, Western Atlantic Command, 47
Canadian Forces Europe, Headquarters at Lahr, (FRG), 32
Canadian-US Regional Planning Group, 14, 21
Carney, Admiral (USA), Commander-in-Chief Allied Forces Southern Europe (CINCSOUTH), 41
Carrier Strike Force, Striking Fleet Atlantic Command, 47
Carrier Strike Groups One and Two, Striking Fleet Atlantic Command, 47
Carter, President James E. (USA), 19
Cassady, Vice-Admiral J. H., Commander of US Sixth Fleet and Commander of Naval Striking and Support Forces, Southern Europe, 43
Central Europe Air Defence Region, 45
Central Mediterranean Area, part of NAVSOUTH, 22, 42
Central Sub-Area Air Command, North Atlantic, 47
Central Sub-Area, Eastern Atlantic Command, 47
Central Sub-Area, North Atlantic Command, 47
Chairman, Military Committee, 14
Channel Command, 22, 48
Channel Committee, 21, 22
Chief of Defence Norway (CHOD Norway), 35, 36
Chiefs of Staff, the Military Committee, 13
Clerides, Glafkos, President of Cyprus, 27
Collins, General J. Lawton (USA), NATO

Standing Group, 21
Commander Allied Air Forces Baltic
    Approaches (COMAIRBALTAP), 35
Commander Allied Air Forces Central Europe
    (COMAAFCE), 38
Commander Allied Air Forces North Norway
    (COMAIRNON), 36
Commander Allied Air Forces Southern
    Europe (COMAIRSOUTH), 39
Commander Allied Forces North Norway
    (COMNON), 35
Commander Allied Forces North Norway
    (COMNON), 35
Commander Allied Forces South Norway
    (COMSONOR), 36
Commander Allied Land Forces North
    Norway (COMLANDNON), 36
Commander Allied Land Forces Schleswig-
    Holstein and Jutland (COMLANDJUT), 35
Commander Allied Land Forces Southern
    Europe (COMLANDSOUTH), 40
Commander Allied Naval Forces Baltic
    Approaches (COMNAVBALTAP), 35
Commander Central Army Group
    (COMCENTAG), 37
Commander Land Forces Zealand and
    Bornholm (COMLANDZEALAND), 35
Commander North-eastern Mediterranean
    (COMEDNOREAST), 42
Commander Northern European Army Group
    (COMNORTHAG), 37
Commander-in-Chief Allied Forces Central
    Europe (CINCENT), 36
Commander-in-Chief Allied Forces
    Mediterranean (CINCAFMED), 41
Commander-in-Chief Allied Forces Northern
    Europe (CINCNORTH), 36
Commander-in-Chief Allied Forces Southern
    Europe (CINCSOUTH), 39
Commander-in-Chief British Army of the
    Rhine, 37
Commander-in-Chief Channel (CINCHAN),
    48
Commander-in-Chief United Kingdom Air
    Forces (CINCUKAIR), 45
Commander-in-Chief Western Atlantic
    (CINCWESTLANT), 46
Command, Control and Communications
    Division, IMS, 14
Creasy, Admiral Sir George (UK), Naval
    Commander-in-Chief Channel and
    Southern North Sea, and Commander-in-
    Chief Portsmouth, 22
Crepin, Général Jean (France), Commander-
    in-Chief, Headquarters Allied Forces Central
    Europe, 25
Crete, Guided Missile Firing Range on, 52

D
Defence College, NATO, 14, 22, 49
Defence Committee, NATO, 15
Defence Planning Committee, 12
Defence Production Board, 15
De Gaulle, President Charles (France), 24
Denterghem, Count de Kerckhove de, 24
Deputy Chairman, the Military Committee,
    14

Deputy Secretary General of NATO, 13
Director International Military Staff, 14
Dunkirk, Treaty of, 10

E
Eastern Mediterranean Area, part of
    NAVSOUTH, 22, 42
Eaton, Major-General Robert E. (USA),
    Commander of SIXATAF, 40
Eaton, Vice-Admiral J. W. M. (UK), Deputy
    Supreme Commander Atlantic, 22
Eisenhower, General Dwight D. (USA), later
    President of USA, 10, 15, 16
Ely, Général Paul (France), Joint Chairman
    NATO Military Committee, 21
Embry, Air Marshal Sir Basil (UK),
    Commander of Allied Tactical Air Forces,
    Central Europe, 21

F
Faeroes, Island Commander, 47
Fechteler, Admiral (USA), Commander-in-
    Chief Allied Forces Southern Europe
    (CINCSOUTH), 22
Fifth Allied Tactical Air Force (FIVEATAF), 40
Financial Controller, the International Staff,
    13
First Canadian Air Group (1 CAG), 32, 33
Flag, NATO, 54
Fleet Ballistic Missile Submarine Force (US
    Sixth Fleet), 32
Ford, President Gerald (USA), 16
Foreign troops, first under SHAPE command
    in Europe, December 1950, 20
Foulkes, Lieutenant-General Charles
    (Canada), Chairman NATO Military
    Committee, 21
Fourth Allied Tactical Air Force (4ATAF), 25,
    33, 36, 37, 38
Fourth Canadian Mechanized Brigade Group
    (4 CMBG), 32
France withdraws from NATO, 24, 26
French First Tactical Air Command in France
    and Germany, 25

G
Galvin, General John (USA), SACEUR, 19
Geilenkirchen (FRG) operating base for
    NAEW, 51
'General Order No. 1', 2 April 1951, 20
German Border Protection Police
    (Bundesgrenzschutz, BGS), 24
German Federal Republic enters NATO, 23
Gibraltar Area, 22
Gibraltar Mediterranean Command, part of
    NAVSOUTH, 42
Gonzales, Felipe, Prime Minister of Spain, 28
Goodpaster, General Andrew J. (USA),
    SACEUR, 16
Görtz, Lieutenant-General Ebbe, C-in-C
    Danish Army and Commander of Allied
    Army Forces in Denmark, 20
Grantham, Admiral Sir Guy (UK),
    Commander-in-Chief Allied Forces
    Mediterranean (CINCAFMED), 22
Greece joins NATO, 27
Gröben, Major-General Peter von der (FRG),

Deputy Commander Baltic Approaches, 34
Gruenther, General Alfred M. (USA),
    SACEUR, 16, 23
GSG9, 24
Guided Missile Firing Range, Crete, 52
Guillaume, Général (France), Joint Chairman
    NATO Military Committee, 21

H
Haig, General Alexander M. (USA), SACEUR,
    19
Havana Conference, 1940, 11
Headquarters Allied Air Forces Central
    Europe (AAFCE), 36, 37, 38
Headquarters Allied Air Forces Southern
    Europe, 39
Headquarters Allied Command Atlantic,
    Norfolk, Virginia (USA), 22
Headquarters Allied Forces Baltic Approaches
    established 8 January 1962, activated 1 July
    1962, 34
Headquarters Allied Forces Central Europe,
    25, 26, 36
Headquarters Allied Forces North Norway, 35
Headquarters Allied Forces Northern Europe,
    33
Headquarters Allied Forces Southern Europe,
    39
Headquarters Allied Land Forces Southern
    Europe, 40
Headquarters Allied Powers Europe,
    Rocquencourt, France, 16, 25
Headquarters British Army of the Rhine (HQ
    BAOR), 37
Headquarters Central Army Group
    (CENTAG), 36, 37
Headquarters, NATO, 20
Headquarters Northern Army Group
    (NORTHAG), 36
Headquarters Royal Air Force Germany (HQ
    RAFG), 37
Headquarters Royal Canadian Air Force Metz
    and Marville, 25
Headquarters, SHAPE, 16, 20
Heusinger, General, Inspector General of
    Bundeswehr, 23

I
Iberian Atlantic Command, 47
Iceland Defence Force, 9
Iceland, Island Commander, 47
Intelligence Division, IMS, 14
International Military Staff (IMS), 14
International Staff, 13
Inter-Allied Confederation of Reserve Officers
    (CIOR), 50
Island Command of Madeira, Iberian Atlantic
    Command, 47
Island Commanders of Iceland and the
    Faeroes Eastern Atlantic Command, 47

J
Janjard, Vice-Amiral Robert (France), Naval
    Flag Officer Central Europe, 20, 21
Johnson, President Lyndon B. (USA), 24
Joint Jet Pilot Training (Programme), Euro-
    NATO (ENJJPT), 52

Juin, Général d'Armée Alphonse (France), Commander-in-Chief Allied Army Forces in Central Europe, 19, 21, 22

K

Karamanlis, Konstantinos, Prime Minister of Greece, 27, 28
Kennedy, President John F. (USA), 16
Kleist, Oberstleutnant Karl-Wilhelm von, Commanding Officer 84th Panzer-Battalion, 24
Kragh, Major-General E. (Denmark), Commander Land Command East Denmark (COMLANDZEALAND), 34

L

Lange, Halvard (Norway), 10
Larsen, Major-General F. B. (Denmark), Commander Land Forces Jutland, Funen and Schleswig-Holstein (COMLANDJUT), 34
Lehr, Général (France), 23
Lemonnier, Vice-Amiral André (France), NATO Deputy Naval Supreme Commander and first Commandant, NATO Defence College, Paris, 19, 21, 49
Logistics and Resources Division, IMS, 14
Lovett, Robert, US Secretary of Defence, 16
Low-level reporting system (LLRS), 38
Luftwaffe Squadron, first to be raised for operational use with NATO, 23
Luns, Dr Joseph, Secretary General of NATO, 28
Lemnitzer, General Lyman L. (USA), SACEUR, 16, 26, 49

M

McCormick, Admiral Lynde D. (USA), Commander-in-Chief US Atlantic Fleet and Supreme Allied Commander Atlantic (SACLANT), 46
Madeira, Island Command of (Iberian Atlantic Command), 47
Makarios, Archbishop, President of Cyprus, 27
Management, the International Staff, 13
Mansergh, General Sir Robert (UK), Commander-in-Chief Allied Forces Northern Europe (CINCNORTH), 21, 22
Maritime Air Central Sub-Area, Eastern Atlantic Command, 47
Maritime Air Eastern Atlantic Area, Eastern Atlantic Command, 47
Maritime Air Forces Mediterranean (MARAIRMED), subordinate to NAVSOUTH, 42
Maritime Air Northern Sub-Area, Eastern Atlantic Command, 47
Mata, Dr José Caeiro de (Portugal), 10
'Matchmaker' Naval Training Squadron, 47
Massu, Général Jacques (France), French Commander-in-Chief in Germany, 25
Mediterranean Command, 41
Military Agency for Standardization, London, 22
Military Committee, 13, 21
Military Production and Supply Board, 15
Miller, Rear-Admiral Edwin S. (USA), 47

Mintoff, Dominic (Dom), leader of the Maltese Labour Party and Prime Minister of Malta, 41
Mobile Land Force (MLF), 43, 44
Monroe Doctrine, 11
Montgomery, Field Marshal Viscount (UK), Chairman, Commanders-in-Chief of Western Union land, air and sea forces, 10; as Deputy Supreme Allied Commander, SHAPE, 19, 20
Moro, Aldo (Italy), Prime Minister, 49
Mountbatten of Burma, Earl, Commander-in-Chief British Mediterranean Fleet and NATO Commander-in-Chief Mediterranean, 22, 41
Mutual and Balanced Force Reductions (MBFR), 14

N

National Military Representative, 29
NATO School (SHAPE) (NSS), 49
NATO Weapons Systems Department, 50
NATO Weapons Systems School, 50
Naval On-Call Force Mediterranean (NAVOCFORMED), 42
Naval Striking and Support Forces Southern Europe (STRIKFORSOUTH), 22, 39, 43
Nixon, President Richard M. (USA), 16
Nore Channel Command, 49
Norstad, General Lauris (USA), Commander-in-Chief Allied Air Forces in Central Europe; as Air Deputy Supreme Allied Commander, SHAPE, 21; as SACEUR, 16, 23, 34, 43, 45
North Atlantic Treaty, 10, 16; articles of, 11–12
North Atlantic Command, 46
North Atlantic Council, 12, 14, 15
North Atlantic Ocean Planning Group, 23
Northern Approaches, 47
Northern Europe Air Defence Region, 45
Northern European Planning Group, 23
Northern European Sub-Area, North Atlantic Command, 47
North-east Atlantic Sub-Area, North Atlantic Command, 47
North-eastern Mediterranean Area, part of NAVSOUTH, 22, 42
Northern Sub-Area Air Command, North Atlantic, 47
Northern Sub-Area, Eastern Atlantic Command, 47
Northern Sub-Area, North Atlantic Command, 47
Norwegian Home Guard, 36
Nuclear Planning Group, 13

O

Ocean Sub-Area, Western Atlantic Command, 47
Operational Research Group, 50
Operations Division, IMS, 14
Outlaw, Rear-Admiral Edward C. (USA), Commander MARAIRMED, Maritime Air Forces Mediterranean, 42

P

Pacciardi, Signor, Italian Defence Minister, 20

Padandreou, Dr, Greek Defence Minister, 28
Pagh, Major-General H. J. (Denmark), Commander Air Forces Baltic Approaches (COMAIRBALTAP), 34
Paris Agreements of 1954 (German and Italian accession to Brussels Treaty), 10
Pearson, Lester (Canada), 10
Perez-Llorca, José Pedro, Spanish Foreign Minister, 28
Permanent Military Representative, the Military Committee, 13
Permanent Representatives and National Delegations at NATO Headquarters, 13
Plans and Policy Division, IMS, 14
Plymouth Channel Command, 49
Power, Admiral Sir Arthur (UK), Commander-in-Chief Portsmouth and Commander-in-Chief Home Station (designate) appointed Commander-in-Chief Channel Command (CINCHAN), 48

Q

Qadhafi, Colonel Moamar el, 41
Qvistgaard, Admiral E. J. C. (Denmark), Chairman NATO Military Committee, 21

R

Rasmussen, Gustav (Denmark), 10
Reagan, President Ronald (USA), 19
Ridgway, General Matthew B. (USA), SACEUR, 16, 41, 49
Rio de Janeiro, Treaty of, 10
Rogers, General Bernard (USA), SACEUR, 19, 28
Roster, Air Marshal Sir Robert (UK), Commander 2nd Allied Tactical Air Force, 38
Royal Air Force Fighter Command, 45
Royal Air Force Strike Command, 45

S

SACEUR, 29
SACLANT Anti-Submarine Warfare Research Centre, 47
Sampson, Nicos, Former EOKA gunman and extremist Greek-Cypriot politician, 27
Sanders, Air Chief Marshal Sir Hugh (UK), Deputy Supreme Allied Commander (Air) SHAPE, 19, 21
Saragat, President (Italy), 49
Schuman, Robert (France), 10
Second Allied Tactical Air Force (2ATAF), 36, 38
Secretary General of NATO, 13
Security Council, NATO, 12
Sforza, Count Carlo (Italy), 10
SHAPE Air Defence Technical Centre, 50
SHAPE, Mons, Belgium, 29
SHAPE Technical Centre, 50
SHAPE Technical Research Centre, The Hague, 26
Sheppard US Air Force Base, Texas (USA), 52
Sixth Allied Tactical Air Force (SIXATAF), 40
Sixth Fleet, Mediterranean (US Navy), 22
Smallwood, Air Chief Marshal Sir Denis, Air Officer Commander-in-Chief RAF Strike Command and Commander-in-Chief UK Air

Forces (CINCUKAIR), 45

Smirnovsky, Mikhail, Sovet Ambassador in London, 41

Sotgiu, Admiral Luciano (Italy), Commander Allied Naval Forces Southern Europe (COMNAVSOUTH), 41

South-east Mediterranean, under direct command of COMNAVSOUTH, 42

South-eastern Mediterranean Area, 22

Southern Europe Air Defence Region, 45

Southern European Task Force (SETAF), 40, 43

Southern European-Western Mediterranean Planning Group, 23

Spaak, Paul-Henri (Belgium), 10

Spain joins NATO, 30 May 1982, 28

Special Weapons Branch, US Army School, Oberamergau (FRG), 50

Speidel, Major-General Hans (FRG), former Chief of Staff to Field Marshal Erwin Rommel and Commander of Allied Land Forces Central Europe 1957, 23

Standing Naval Force Atlantic (STANAVFORLANT), 47

Standing Naval Force Channel (STANAVFORCHAN), 49

Steven, Air Marshal A. G. (UK), Air Officer Commander-in-Chief RAF Coastal Command and Commander-in-Chief Air, Eastern Atlantic (designate), appointed Allied Air Commander-in-Chief Channel Command, 21 February 1952, 48

Stikker, Dr Dirk (Netherlands), 10

Stoessel, Walter, US Deputy Secretary of State, 28

Striking Fleet Atlantic Command, 47

Struther, Major-General Dean C. (USA), Commander 4th Allied Tactical Air Force, 38

Submarine Force Eastern Atlantic Area, Eastern Atlantic Command, 47

Submarine Force Western Atlantic Area, Western Atlantic Command, 47

Supreme Allied Command Atlantic (SACLANT), 14, 21, 47

Supreme Allied Commander Europe (SACEUR), 14, 16, 21, 41

Supreme Commander Allied Expeditionary Force, 16

Supreme Commander Allied Powers Europe, 16

T

Tangen-Hansteen, Lieutenant-General Wilhelm, C-in-C Norwegian Army and Commander of Allied Army Forces in Norway, 20

Tank-firing range Castlemartin, Pembrokeshire, Wales, 24

Task Force 502 (Carrier Striking Forces), 43

Task Force 503 (Amphibious Forces), 43

Task Force 504 (Landing Forces), 43

Taylor, Major-General Robert K. (USA), Commander of Allied Air Forces Northern Europe, 20

Toledo, Alonso Alvarez de, Spanish chargé d'affaires in Washington, 28

Treaties, 10

Truman, President Harry S. (USA), 10, 16

Turkey becomes a member of NATO, 27

U

United Kingdom Air Defence Region (UKADR), 45

United Kingdom Air Forces (UKAIR), 29, 45

United Kingdom Mobile Force, part of AMF(L), 44

United States Air Forces in Europe (USAFE), 32

US Army Berlin, 32

United States Army Europe (USAREUR), 32

United States Army Southern Command Task Force, 32

United States Commander-in-Chief Europe (USCINCEUR), 29

United States European Command (USEUCOM), 29

United States Marine Amphibious Force, part of AMF(L), 44

United States Marine Corps, 32

United States Naval Forces Europe (USNAVEUR), 32

United States Sixth Fleet, 32, 41

United States Strategic Air Forces in Europe during the Second World War, 32

V

Valluy, Général (France), NATO Standing Group, 21; as Commander-in-Chief Allied Forces Central Europe, 23

Vandenberg Resolution (US Senate Resolution No. 239) of 11 June 1948, 11

W

Wagner, Konteradmiral G. (FRG), Commander Naval Forces Baltic Approaches (COMNAVBALTAP), 34

Washington, Treaty of, 10

Western Approaches, 47

Western European Planning Group, 23

Western European Union (WEU), 10

Western Mediterranean Area, 22, 42

Western Union Defence Organization, 10

Whiteley, General Sir John (UK), NATO Standing Group, 21

Wright, Admiral Jerauld (USA), Supreme Allied Commander Atlantic (SACLANT), 22

Wyman, Lieutenant-General Willard G. (USA), Commander LANDSOUTHEAST, 41

Y

Yavuztürk, Zeki, Turkish Defence Minister, 28